AdvancED ActionScript 3.0: Design Patterns

Ben Smith

friendsof ED™

DESIGNER TO DESIGNER™

an Apress company*

AdvancED ActionScript 3.0: Design Patterns

Copyright © 2011 by Ben Smith

ISBN-13 (pbk): 978-1-4302-3614-6
SBN-13 (electronic): 978-1-4302-3616-0

Distributed to the book trade worldwide by Springer Science+Business Media LLC., 233 Spring Street, 6th Floor, New York, NY 10013. Phone 1-800-SPRINGER, fax (201) 348-4505, e-mail orders-ny@springer-sbm.com, or visit www.springeronline.com.

For information on translations, please e-mail rights@apress.com or visit www.apress.com.

Apress and friends of ED books may be purchased in bulk for academic, corporate, or promotional use. eBook versions and licenses are also available for most titles. For more information, reference our Special Bulk Sales–eBook Licensing web page at www.apress.com/bulk-sales.

The source code for this book is freely available to readers at www.friendsofed.com in the Downloads section.

Credits

President and Publisher: Paul Manning	**Copy Editor:** Tiffany Taylor and Mary Behr
Lead Editor: Ben Renow-Clarke	**Compositor:** Bronkella Publishing
Technical Reviewers: Koen De Weggheleire and Peter Elst	**Indexer:** BIM Indexing & Proofreading Services
Editorial Board: Steve Anglin, Mark Beckner, Ewan Buckingham, Gary Cornell, Jonathan Gennick, Jonathan Hassell, Michelle Lowman, Matthew Moodie, Jeff Olson, Jeffrey Pepper, Frank Pohlmann, Douglas Pundick, Ben Renow-Clarke, Dominic Shakeshaft, Matt Wade, Tom Welsh	**Artist:** SPI Global **Cover Image Artist:** Corné van Dooren **Cover Designer:** Anna Ishchenko
Coordinating Editor: Anita Castro	

In loving memory of my cat Buttercup, who passed during the writing of this book.

To my wife, for her tolerance of the late evenings as well as for her constant encouragement—I thank you always.

—Ben Smith

Contents at a Glance

Contents

About the Author

Ben Smith is an accomplished Flash developer with years of experience creating advanced rich Internet applications (RIAs) for well-known digital agencies. He is an Adobe Community Professional and has contributed articles to both InsideRIA and the Adobe developer community. Ben began his career in Connecticut and spent several years working in New York and Florida. Ben is currently back in New York where he both works and resides. He is passionate about higher learning, which he believes comes from experimentation and experience. With more than 10,000 hours of experience with Flash, he does not consider himself a master of Flash, but a student of what Flash requires him to know.

About the Technical Reviewer

 **Koen De Weggheleire** is a faculty member of the Technical University of West-Flanders in Belgium (HOWEST) where he teaches multiscreen Flash Platform Solutions (Flash, Flex, AIR) with a smile. As Adobe Community Professional for the Flash Platform, Koen is heavily addicted to the community and inspires the community by his blog at www.newmovieclip.com/ and by speaking at several (inter)national industry events (Adobe MAX, FITC, 360 Flex, Flashbelt, Flash On The Beach, Flash on Tap). He coordinates the yearly Belgian multimedia conference Multi-Mania (www.multi-mania.be/) where 2,000 people from around the world come together to learn from industry experts and to share knowledge. Koen also is co-author of *Foundation Flex for Developers* (friends of Ed, 2007), *Flash CS4 AIR Development* (friends of ED, 2009) and the *Adobe AIR Cookbook* (O'Reilly, 2009).

When he's not doing any of the above activities, you can find Koen at his company HappyBanana, together with Wouter Verweirder, doing Flash Platform consultancy on advanced, award-winning, rich multiscreen applications. When Koen is not talking ActionScript, you can find him producing music, collecting goodies, eating pizza, or renovating his 100 year old house.

About the Cover Image Artist

 **Corné van Dooren** designed the front cover image for this book. After taking a brief hiatus from friends of ED to create a new design for the Foundation series, he worked at combining technological and organic forms, the results of which now appear on this and other book covers.

Corné spent his childhood drawing on everything at hand and then began exploring the infinite world of multimedia—and his journey of discovery hasn't stopped since. His mantra has always been, "The only limit to multimedia is the imagination"—a saying that keeps him constantly moving forward.

Corné works for many international clients, writes features for multimedia magazines, reviews and tests software, authors multimedia studies, and works on many other friends of ED books. You can see more of his work at and contact him through his website at www.cornevandooren.com.

Acknowledgments

I'm happy to acknowledge the work of Professor Trygve Reenskaug for his conception of the Model View Controller. A friend and pioneer of design patterns, I thank you for your wisdom.

Introduction

Design patterns are an abstract concept and a subject that involves being vague to help solve problems. This is somewhat ambiguous and makes design patterns a difficult topic. Fortunately, a difficult subject does not necessarily mean one that is complicated in its understanding. This will be evident in *AdvancED ActionScript 3.0: Design Patterns*.

This book requires prerequisite knowledge of ActionScript and Object Oriented Programming, but it demonstrates the hand-in-hand relationship of OOP and design patterns. The beginning chapters of this book discuss and detail OOP principles, and while some aspects may be review, all will be preparation for upcoming chapters. Each chapter will prepare you for the next. Until Chapter 5 (the first review quiz), you will be reinforcing your knowledge up to that point, as well as creating a foundation for your understanding of the design pattern chapters. Chapters 6-8 thoroughly cover design patterns. Each pattern discussed is demonstrated and explained with examples, real-life analogies, and answers to frequently asked questions. Chapter 9 (the second review quiz of the book) again reinforces your knowledge up to that point. Chapters 10-12 round out the book by covering the use of combining patterns and discuss how to remain object-oriented in a fast-paced industry.

Welcome to *AdvancED ActionScript 3.0: Design Patterns*.

Chapter 1

Object-Oriented Programming

Object-oriented programming (OOP) is the practice of creating a software architecture that enables flexibility through modular design. A programmer who is object-oriented isn't necessarily one who is a more advanced coder, but one who chooses to be a more strategic coder, and who adheres to the principles of OOP. OOP isn't a language; it's the practice of architecting and the thought process behind it that leads to applications and languages being object-oriented, such as ActionScript (AS) 3.0.

AS 3.0 was built as an object-oriented language to mirror the mental model of a programmer who knows the benefits of breaking code into a series of objects that can message one another. But many who choose to develop with AS 3.0 don't use OOP. This is due to the somewhat daunting nature of OOP, as well as the time required to learn it. AS 3.0 is meant to support the development of flexible architecture, and using OOP can help prevent unmanageable code. Flexible architecture is easier to modify because the objects that make up the application possess distinct boundaries, which simplifies substituting among the objects you're working with. Therefore, it's beneficial to code with an object-oriented thought process. However, that isn't saying you can't use AS 3.0 with a procedural programming mindset and be successful.

Procedural programming, which is a linear method of developing, often culminates in lines of code that have no separation of behaviors or train of thought. The language becomes nothing more than a series of routines and subroutines. Procedural programming can work well if you're the sole developer on a project, because you're familiar with your code. However, when more programmers are involved, it can be cumbersome for them to become familiar with one another's code and sift through the lines to see where a change needs to be made. With OOP, each behavior in the application is contained in a unique class, providing a more elegant way to view object collaborations. Because each unique class possesses a name, it's easy to track down; and because it should possess a single behavior, the class has only one reason to ever change.

The image in **Figure 1-1** is the result of the procedural code provided in **Listing 1-1**. The code uses an image of my cat (Buttercup), and analyzes the pixel information to generate a halftone image.

Figure 1-1. A color image of my cat Buttercup being converted to that of a halftone image

Listing 1-1. The following code converts an image into that of a halftone

```
import flash.display.BitmapData;
import flash.display.Sprite;
import flash.display.StageAlign;
import flash.geom.ColorTransform;
import flash.geom.Rectangle;

var img : BitmapData = new Buttercup( 1 , 1 );
var sampleSize : int = 4;
var brushSize : int = 4;
var pixelsTall : uint = img.height;
var pixelsWide : uint = img.width;
var rect : Rectangle = new Rectangle( 0 , 0 , sampleSize , sampleSize );
var totalBytesToScan : int = pixelsWide * pixelsTall;
var position : int = 0;
var offset : Number = sampleSize * .5;
var averageColor : uint;
var pixels : Vector.<uint > ;
var darks : Number;
var halftone : Shape = new Shape();
var scale : Number;

while ( position <= totalBytesToScan )
{
        pixels = img.getVector( rect );
```

```
        averageColor = grayScaleAverage( pixels );
        darks = brightness( averageColor );

        if ( darks > 0 )
        {
                halftone.graphics.beginFill( averageColor , 1 );
                scale = (255 - darks) / 255;
                halftone.graphics.drawCircle( rect.x + offset , rect.y + offset , ➡
                scale * brushSize );
        }

        if (rect.x >= pixelsWide)
        {
                rect.x = 0;
                rect.y += sampleSize;
        }
         else
        {
                rect.x += sampleSize;
        }
         position += sampleSize * sampleSize;
}

addChild( halftone );

function brightness( color : uint ) : int
{
        var R : uint = color >> 16 & 0xff;
        var G : uint = color >> 8 & 0xff;
        var B : uint = color & 0xff;
        return int( 0.2126 * R + 0.7152 * G + 0.0722 * B );
}

function rgbAverage( pixels : Vector.<uint> ) : uint
{
        var colors : uint;
        var pixelLength : int = pixels.length;
        var averageR : uint = 0;
        var averageG : uint = 0;
        var averageB : uint = 0;
        var localPixels : Vector.<uint > = pixels;

        while ( --pixelLength >= 0 )
        {
```

```
                color = uint( localPixels[pixelLength] );
                averageR += color >> 16 & 0xFF;
                averageG += color >> 8 & 0xFF;
                averageB += color & 0xFF;
        }

        averageR /= pixels.length;
        averageG /= pixels.length;
        averageB /= pixels.length;
        color = averageR << 16 | averageG << 8 | averageB;
        return color;
}

function grayScaleAverage( pixels : Vector.<uint> ) : uint
{
        var color : uint;
        var pixelLength : int = pixels.length;
        var averageR : uint;
        var averageG : uint;
        var averageB : uint;
        var localPixels : Vector.<uint > = pixels;

        while ( --pixelLength >= 0 )
        {
                color = uint( localPixels[pixelLength] );
                averageR += color >> 16 & 0xFF;
                averageG += color >> 8 & 0xFF;
                averageB += color & 0xFF;
        }

        averageR /= pixels.length;
        averageG /= pixels.length;
        averageB /= pixels.length;
        var luma : int = ( averageR * 0.3 + averageG * 0.59 + averageB * 0.11 );
        color = luma << 16 | luma << 8 | luma;
        return color;
}
```

This can be considered, and very well may be, a perfectly working system with only 87 lines of code. However, the code could easily begin to grow unmanageable. I even added a bit of extra code, in case I want to make a change to the system: the rgbAverage method lets me generate colored halftones if I wish.

Briefly glancing at **Listing 1-1** shows it to be cumbersome and gives you little understanding about the application and how the code functions. You would probably need to analyze the code line by line to gain true insight into how the application works. But the code can be made much more organized and flexible if it's built with the four principles of OOP in mind, *encapsulation, polymorphism, inheritance, and data hiding*.

Encapsulation

If you have to ask, "What am I looking at?" there is a good chance that what you're viewing is far from the norm. For example, you know there is an engine under the hood of a car, yet you ignore such mechanics and focus on what you're required to interact with while driving the vehicle—or so it appears. In reality, you're concerned with what it takes to get you comfortably from point A to point B. This is known as a *problem domain*: what requires the focus in this case is how to remain comfortable or navigate directions.

If you're attempting to understand engines but they don't relate to your occupation or a hobby, you've probably changed your focus to a new problem domain: your broken-down engine and how you can fix it.

What you need to know per problem domain must be properly separated from what you don't need to know, so you aren't overloaded with extraneous information. This way, you can maintain your focus.

With this in mind, let's apply this understanding to the halftone application. The goal of the application is to take an image and digitally alter its tone, revealing a halftone effect. If, much like the car example, you separate the engine from everything else to reveal what physically allows the application to move, then you focus on the code in **Listing 1-2**.

Listing 1-2. The "engine" of the application

```
import flash.display.BitmapData;
import flash.display.Sprite;
import flash.display.StageAlign;
import flash.geom.ColorTransform;
import flash.geom.Rectangle;

var img : BitmapData = new Buttercup( 1 , 1 );
var sampleSize : int = 4;
var brushSize : int = 4;
var pixelsTall : uint = img.height;
var pixelsWide : uint = img.width;
var rect : Rectangle = new Rectangle( 0 , 0 , sampleSize , sampleSize );
var totalBytesToScan : int = pixelsWide * pixelsTall;
var position : int = 0;
var offset : Number = sampleSize * .5;
var averageColor : uint;
var pixels : Vector.<uint > ;
var darks : Number;
var halftone : Shape = new Shape();
var scale : Number;

while ( position <= totalBytesToScan )
{
```

```
pixels = img.getVector( rect );
averageColor = grayScaleAverage( pixels );
darks = brightness( averageColor );
if ( darks > 0 )
{
        halftone.graphics.beginFill( averageColor , 1 );
        scale = (255 - darks) / 255;
        halftone.graphics.drawCircle( rect.x + offset , rect.y + offset , ➥
        scale * brushSize );
}

 if (rect.x >= pixelsWide)
{
        rect.x = 0;
        rect.y += sampleSize;
}
 else
{
        rect.x += sampleSize;
}
position += sampleSize * sampleSize;
}

addChild( halftone );
```

Remarkably, you've reduced 87 lines of code into 40 lines that define your system; this code is what you expect to find as the engine under the hood. The removed lines of code perform behaviors to be used by the engine and should be separated from the code in **listing 1-2** so you can begin to create distinguishable roles.

Polymorphism

Defining boundaries among your system's roles allows for interchangeability among other behaviors with similar method parameters, method name, and return type. These three components of a method are the contracts that proper messaging requires and together are referred to as a signature. As long as the signatures between varied implementations remain the same, the behaviors can be swapped to achieve various results without having to modify much code, if any.

Let's consider two behaviors extracted from **Listing 1-2**: grayscaleAverage and rgbAverage. These behaviors are responsible for determining the average brightness of the parameterized vector of pixels and returning the calculated value. Whether the value returned possesses three color channels or one is determined by the method used to perform the calculations.

Because these two behaviors possess individual method names, the invoker of the behavior must be aware of what behavior is being called, which lessens the flexibility between the messenger and receiver.

To allow the two behaviors to be interchanged indistinguishably, you must ensure that both methods expose a common interface. Because the signatures and return types of both methods are exact, you must devise a common name by which you can invoke the method. Both methods average the brightness of a given pixel sample, so you can state that average is the common link between your algorithms (see **Figure 1-2**).

```
//color halftone behavior
function rgbAverage( pixels:Vector.<uint> ):uint{
    // return RGB average
}
```

```
//grayscale halftone behavior
function grayscaleAverage( pixels:Vector.<uint> ):uint{
    // return Grayscale average
}
```

Figure 1-2. Both methods must reflect a consistent interface.

But a common interface isn't enough to enable code substitution with procedural programming. While both methods make use of the same name, they can't be added into the application and be compiled without throwing an error. What we need is a way to distinguish both implementations, while still making use of the common method name. Enter inheritance.

Inheritance

The concept of inheritance is modeled in object-oriented languages, enabling developers to write code in the form of hierarchical relationships. As facilitators of OOP, programmers can encapsulate a collection of behaviors and attributes into an isolated body known as an *object*. Such an object can then be used when you create additional objects, which you can do by deriving them from the original object. Much like children who benefit from the possessions of their mother and father, so can objects benefit through inheritance. Compartmentalized attributes and behaviors are used by *child* objects, creating a hierarchy between the two. A child object in a hierarchy of objects is referred to as a *subclass*, and its parent is referred to as its *superclass*.

Just as humans can be classified as mammals, any subclass in an object-oriented language can be generalized as a particular collection of attributes and behaviors of any of its ancestors. The referral to all encapsulated behaviors and attributes as *objects* indicates that the hierarch of all relationships is an encapsulation known as Object. Such generalization among varied implementations is required to fulfill polymorphic behavior.

To use polymorphic behaviors, your references must be typed to a generalization, thus ensuring that any and all objects to which the reference is assigned possess similar interfaces. This is so the substitution among objects doesn't break the messaging between client and receiver.

To create a generic type that ensures both grayscale and color halftone behaviors expose the average interface, you must create a hierarchical relationship. In this case, the two behaviors are siblings that inherit the average interface from a common superclass. Not only does inheritance establish a hierarchy to allow this application to use polymorphism, but it also enables code reuse, which can minimize duplicate and repetitive code.

As **Table 1-1** shows, the two implementations appear nearly identical in a side-by-side sibling comparison. The only difference between the two is the declaration of the luma variable and its calculation in the grayscale implementation.

Table 1-1. Side-by-side comparison of both halftone algorithms

```
//color halftone behavior                    //grayscale halftone behavior
function average(pixels:Vector.<uint>) ➡     function average(pixels:Vector.<uint>) ➡
: uint{                                       :uint{

var color : uint;                             var color : uint;
var pixelLength : int = pixels.length;        var pixelLength : int = pixels.length;
var averageR : uint;                          var averageR : uint;
var averageG : uint;                          var averageG : uint;
var averageB : uint;                          var averageB : uint;
var localPixels : Vector.<uint > = pixels;    var localPixels : Vector.<uint > = pixels;

while ( --pixelLength >= 0 )                   while ( --pixelLength >= 0 )
{                                             {
color = uint( localPixels[pixelLength] );     color = uint( localPixels[pixelLength] );
averageR += color >> 16 & 0xFF;               averageR += color >> 16 & 0xFF;
averageG += color >> 8 & 0xFF;                averageG += color >> 8 & 0xFF;
averageB += color & 0xFF;                      averageB += color & 0xFF;
}                                             }

averageR /= pixels.length;                    averageR /= pixels.length;
averageG /= pixels.length;                    averageG /= pixels.length;
averageB /= pixels.length;                    averageB /= pixels.length;
color= averageR << 16 | averageG << 8 | ➡     var luma : int = ( averageR * 0.3 + ➡
averageB;                                     averageG * 0.59 + averageB * 0.11 );
return color;
}                                             color = luma << 16 | luma << 8 | luma;
                                              return color;
                                              }
```

Referring back to the concept of encapsulation, you can maintain a localized area of focus and minimize additional lines of code by appropriately situating all common code in the originator of the behavior to which the code applies. You begin by extracting variables that are common to both methods and inserting them as attributes of their superclass, as shown in **Table 1-2**.

Table 1-2. Common variables are extracted from both siblings and inserted as attributes of their generic superclass.

```
                    //generic attributes
                        var color : uint;
                        var pixelLength : int = pixels.length;
                        var averageR : uint;
                        var averageG : uint;
                        var averageB : uint;
                        var localPixels : Vector.<uint > = pixels;

                    //generic operation
                    function average( pixels : Vector.<uint> ) : uint{
                        //do nothing
                }
```

<table>
<tr>
<td>

```
//color halftone behavior
function average(pixels:Vector.<uint>)➡
:uint{
pixelLength = pixels.length;
localPixels = pixels;

while ( --pixelLength >= 0 )
{
color = uint( localPixels[pixelLength] );
averageR += color >> 16 & 0xFF;
averageG += color >> 8 & 0xFF;
averageB += color & 0xFF;
}

averageR /= pixels.length;
averageG /= pixels.length;
averageB /= pixels.length;
color= averageR << 16 | averageG << 8 | ➡
averageB;

return color;
}
```

</td>
<td>

```
//grayscale halftone behavior
function average(pixels:Vector.<uint>)➡
:uint{
pixelLength = pixels.length;
localPixels = pixels;

while ( --pixelLength >= 0 )
{
color = uint( localPixels[pixelLength] );
averageR += color >> 16 & 0xFF;
averageG += color >> 8 & 0xFF;
averageB += color & 0xFF;
}

averageR /= pixels.length;
averageG /= pixels.length;
averageB /= pixels.length;
var luma : int = ( averageR * 0.3 + ➡
averageG * 0.59 + averageB * 0.11 );
color = luma << 16 | luma << 8 | luma;
return color;
}
```

</td>
</tr>
</table>

Without the excess variables, you can immediately see that minus two lines of code, both implementations are exactly the same. We can also move the averaging of all channels from both halftone algorithms into your superclass as the default implementation of the average interface; then both algorithms can use it.

Table 1-3 uses implementation inheritance, where the default implementation of the interface average in the superclass is available to both subclasses. In addition, both subclasses can redefine such inherited implementations, as shown in the table.

Table 1-3. The channel averaging among a sampled region of pixels has been localized to the superclass.

```
//ChannelAveraging algorithm
//generic attributes
            var color : uint;
            var pixelLength : int = pixels.length;
            var averageR : uint;
            var averageG : uint;
            var averageB : uint;
            var localPixels : Vector.<uint> = pixels;


//default operation
function average( pixels : Vector.<uint> ) : uint{
  while ( --pixelLength >= 0 )
  {
    color = uint( localPixels[pixelLength] );
    averageR += color >> 16 & 0xFF;
    averageG += color >> 8 & 0xFF;
    averageB += color & 0xFF;
  }

    averageR /= pixels.length;
    averageG /= pixels.length;
    averageB /= pixels.length;

    return null;
  }
```

```
//color halftone algorithm
function average(pixels:Vector.<uint>)➡
:uint{

super.average(pixels)
color= averageR << 16 | averageG << 8 | ➡
averageB;
```

```
//grayscale halftone algorithm
function average(pixels:Vector.<uint>)➡
:uint{

super.average(pixels)
var luma : int = ( averageR * 0.3 + ➡
averageG * 0.59 + averageB * 0.11 );
```

```return color; }```	```color = luma << 16 | luma << 8 | luma; return color; }```

Both subclasses inherit the `average` implementation to which they immediately refer via the keyword `super`, which refers to the superclass's implementation of the defined method name—in this case, `average`. From there, the superclass determines the averaged channels, which are used by the remaining implementation of both algorithms.

The end result is the reduction of duplicate code, the localization of logic specific to each behavior, and the increased cohesion of all three objects. We've also devised a generalized type where your reference can be strongly typed, enabling polymorphism between the two behaviors.

Data Hiding

Data hiding is the act of concealing information from a possible client of the application and a possible problem domain. In object-oriented languages, data hiding helps maintain proper encapsulation and is enforced by the use of namespaces such as the following:

- Attributes and behaviors that use the `private` declaration can be targeted/referenced only in the scope to which they're declared.
- `Protected` is a slightly less restrictive use of `private`. Behaviors and attributes declared as `protected` can only be used within the class that defined them, or by that classes subclasses.
- If a class's attribute or behavior is declared as `internal`, it can be viewed by any class in the same package. By default, behaviors and attributes are always internal unless declared otherwise.
- Any attribute or behavior declared as `public` can be viewed by any class of any package.

To illustrate why data hiding is so important in OOP, refer back to **Table 1-3**, which shows distinct behaviors encapsulated in three unique objects. The first object calculates the average color per color channel of a sampled range of pixels. The second object calculates those channels into a hexadecimal color, which is returned to the messaging object. The third object calculates the calculated channels of the first object into a grayscale tone value, which is returned to the messaging client.

Each object has an obvious role in the application, and when a change is required or a bug occurs, the object you must modify is apparent. The code is so clear because each object maintains control over the manipulation of its own attributes—for now, at least. But when another object erroneously references a variable that doesn't pertain to it, tracking down an error may become puzzling and delay immediate repair. Data hiding can help prevent such errors from taking place by ensuring proper visibility among messaging objects.

As shown in Table 1-4, the `average` interface is declared `public`. The attributes declared by the superclass of the halftone algorithms are another story: they're marked as both `private` and `protected`, thus ensuring that only appropriate objects can view/manipulate such data.

Table 1-4. Addition of namespace modifiers to enforce an object's ability to maintain its proper states

```
//ChannelAveraging algorithm
//generic attributes
        protected var color : uint;
        private var pixelLength : int = pixels.length;
        protected var averageR : uint;
        protected var averageG : uint;
        protected var averageB : uint;
        private var localPixels : Vector.<uint> = pixels;

//default operation
public function average( pixels : Vector.<uint> ) : uint{
  while ( --pixelLength >= 0 )
  {
    color = uint( localPixels[pixelLength] );
    averageR += color >> 16 & 0xFF;
    averageG += color >> 8 & 0xFF;
    averageB += color & 0xFF;
  }

  averageR /= pixels.length;
  averageG /= pixels.length;
  averageB /= pixels.length;

  return null;
}
```

//color halftone algorithm	//grayscale halftone algorithm
``public function average(pixels : Vector.<uint>) : uint{ super.average(pixels) color= averageR << 16|averageG << 8	➡ averageB; return color; }```	```public function average(pixels : Vector.<uint>) : uint{ super.average(pixels) var luma : int = (averageR * 0.3 + ➡ averageG * 0.59 + averageB * 0.11); color = luma << 16	luma << 8	luma; return color; }```

You can further ensure that the attributes of the superclass are read-only to each subclassed behavior by adding public getter methods as additional interfaces of the superclass. Doing so lets each subclass retrieve attribute values without being able to reassign a value to the reference. To enforce that each subclass uses the getter methods versus reading the properties to which they currently have access, you continue to mark all protected attributes of the superclass as `private`.

This example illustrates the potential power of an object-oriented language. Remaining object-oriented as you write code, which makes the code easier to maintain and more flexible. Now that we've covered the principles of OOP, let's focus on their implementation into an object-oriented language.

Note: It's always easier to say how to properly engineer a better structure after all is said and done. Don't be discouraged if you understood the previous example but can't yet create OOP code on your own. The goal is to understand how the building blocks add modularity and flexibility while reducing the possibility of disaster, by following the four principles of OOP.

ActionScript as an Object-Oriented Language

Working with an object-oriented mentality opens the door to a new manner of programming. ActionScript lets you flexibly develop rich Internet applications (RIAs) when you program according to the four OOP principles:

- Encapsulation: ActionScript allows for the compartmentalization of behaviors and data into a *class*.
- Polymorphism: Objects within a hierarchy can respond to the operations defined by their hierarch, when indistinguishably messaged by the client.
- Inheritance: Like every class in the API, a custom class is an extension of the most generalized class in the language. This most basic class is appropriately called `Object`. The `Object` class makes it possible to add custom classes to a system, as long as those classes use the proper language structure and syntax.
- Data hiding: A class ensures its own behavioral and data security by using namespaces. In the ActionScript language, five namespaces provide varying levels of security.
  - public: Add the keyword public in lowercase before the declaration of variables or methods. This namespace modifier provides no security. Behaviors and variables can be seen and manipulated by all classes and objects.
  - Internal: The default namespace. This is the first tier of security in that the class is public, but only to other classes in the same package.
  - private: The opposite of public, allowing no access except by the class that made the private declaration.
  - protected: Similar to private, but visibility among properties and behaviors are available to classes which subclass the class which defines any protected attribute or behavior.
  - final: Ensures that either class or method cannot be extended, and thus protects all declared behaviors or classes form being modified via inheritance.

- Custom namespace: Declaring a custom namespace for either a behavior or an attribute treats any such modified elements as being private, although it's only private to classes which have not *opened* the custom namespace (we'll learn more about this later in the chapter).

Defining an External Definition

Up to now, you've explored the principles of OOP and seen how the four principles of OOP work harmoniously to improve your code architecture. All that remains is to learn how to physically construct these objects in the AS 3.0 language.

Part of the burden of defining a custom object is that such an object isn't natively understood by the compiler. You must tell the compiler what the object does and also where to find it. Essentially, the compiler must be made aware of an external definition.

Any spoken language can have multiple definitions for a particular word, which may create confusion during a conversation. Similarly, computers require a way to tell which definition should be used; otherwise, unexpected errors may arise.

Because it's impossible to have two files with exactly the same name and extension in the same system folder, a definition can be differentiated by its location along with its file name. Therefore, each definition can be viewed as being unique to the compiler.

The location of a definition, noted by its folder structure, becomes the pointer to the appropriate definition. This is known as a Unified Resource Identifier (URI); it enables the compiler to differentiate among definitions of similar names.

The first step in creating an external definition is writing the wrapper that surrounds the body of the definition. This is demonstrated in **Table 1-5**.

Table 1-5. The skeletal structure of an external definition

```
1    package [folder[, folder... ]]{

2

3        [visible] type_of_definition DefinitionsName

4        {

5            //BODY OF THE DEFINITION;

6        }

7    }
```

As you can see, to begin a definition, you identify its location using the package directive. This represents the folder structure where the definition resides. The arrangement of folders for the project is entirely up to you, but it's beneficial to group your objects in a manner that represents the relationships between definitions. This grouping may be apparent in the physical naming of the folders as well as in their hierarchy. It not only keeps your classes organized, but also gives other developers a clear idea which definitions are being used and what other objects may be used with them.

As denoted by line 1 in **Table 1-5** the package directive is followed by the full path to where the definition resides, denoted with dot notation. If the class doesn't reside in a folder structure, then the folder arguments following the package directive may be left blank.

An example you're sure to have seen is the import code for the MovieClip class (see **Figure 1-3**).

```
import flash.display.MovieClip;
```

MovieClip.as

Figure 1-3. The MovieClip import reflects the MovieClip package.

As you can see, MovieClip is a class in a series of nested folders that reveals the nature of the class—you don't even need to see the code that MovieClip contains. The import refers to where the location of the definition used.

If you open the MovieClip.as file, the first line looks like: package flash.display{

Now that you've specified the location of your definition, ActionScript expects the type of definition and the name of the definition. The name must also be that of the saved .as file. Although the package and filename specify a particular definition, the actual definition, which varies depending on the type of definition being created, is placed in the body as shown on line 5 of **Table 1-5**.

ActionScript uses three types of definitions: class, namespace, and interface. The next section, describes the parts of each definition.

Parts of a Class

Even the most introductory ActionScript books cover the creation of custom classes (see **Table 1-5**). Often, this is to demonstrate the use of the language. It would be beyond the scope of those books to ensure that you have the proper object-oriented mindset as you construct your classes. With this in mind, don't be too anxious to skip ahead if you feel you may already be familiar with constructing classes.

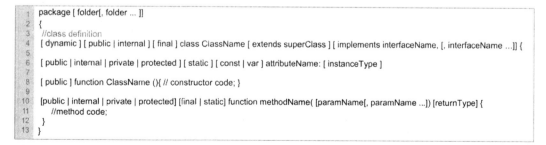

```
1   package [ folder[, folder ... ]]
2   {
3   //class definition
4   [ dynamic ] [ public | internal ] [ final ] class ClassName [ extends superClass ] [ implements interfaceName, [, interfaceName ...]] {
5
6   [ public | internal | private | protected ] [ static ] [ const | var ] attributeName: [ instanceType ]
7
8   [ public ] function ClassName (){ // constructor code; }
9
10  [public | internal | private | protected] [final | static] function methodName( [paramName[, paramName ...]) [returnType] {
11      //method code;
12  }
13  }
```

Figure 1-4. The expected syntax and structure to properly define a custom class

On line 4 in **Figure 1-4,** you used the keyword class to signify that the following definition relates to a class. The class directive can include four additional modifiers, not including its visibility. By default, you don't see any of the keywords other than class in your editor, because everything in brackets in **Figure 1-4** is optional; these elements let you make custom modifications to the class.

The first optional modifier is the keyword dynamic. Specifying that your class is dynamic lets you add properties to your class definition at runtime. Without this modifier, the class is locked: you can't add new properties or behaviors later. Dynamic can only be used to modify the definition of the class, not the properties or methods. Subclasses of a dynamic class can't inherit dynamic behavior, because it's specific to the current definition.

The next modifier specifies the visibility of the class's definition and defaults to internal, but can be specified as public to allow any classes outside the declared package view its definition. Although there are five namespaces that modify visibility, only internal and public can be used to modify the visibility of a definition.

The last optional attribute, final, specifies that the class can't be subclassed. Because inheritance is a significant part of OOP, the use of this final keyword may be confusing, but it enforces data hiding. Declaring a definition as final prohibits any classes from subclassing the definition. This ensures that the class can't be modified, short of physically changing the code in the original file.

Following the class directive, you add a name to identify the definition. To distinguish this from methods and variables that use camelCase, class names use a capital letter at the start of each word. Class names should be specific to the behavior they define. An appropriately named class can allude to the behaviors that a developer expects to find within the definition.

The remaining keywords (extends and implements), again optional, let you add your class to an existing hierarchy . By default, all classes extend the top-level Object unless specified otherwise. This is why it's said that to initialize a class is to instantiate an object. At the core of every class is an Object.

Through the principle of inheritance, your class gains all public and protected, properties and behaviors of each class in the hierarchy of the chosen superclass.

Suppose we were devising a class named Foo, and Foo requires the abilities possessed by MovieClip. Choosing to subclass MovieClip looks like the following:

```
package
{
   public class Foo extends MovieClip
   {
      public function Foo()
      {
         // constructor code
      }
   }
}
```

Because ActionScript doesn't support inheriting from multiple classes, the keyword implements allows you to add into your class the interface utilized by a specific type. By implementing an interface, in addition to adding existing public methods to your definition, you are also adding the interfaces type to the hierarchical chain of your definition as well.

Currently, our Foo class that extends MovieClip can be typed as Object, EventDispatcher, InteractiveObject, DisplayObjectContainer, Sprite, and finally MovieClip. This is because MovieClip is the subclass of another subclass, of another subclass, all the way up to the most generic class of all, Object:

MovieClip ➤ Sprite ➤ DisplayObjectContainer ➤ InteractiveObject ➤ DisplayObject ➤ EventDispatcher ➤ Object

Before you go any further, let's see what it means to extend from EventDispatcher. As you can see in **Table 1-6**, EventDispatcher is a subclass of Object and implements an interface named IEventDispatcher.

Table 1-6. The composition of EventDispatcher

Inheritance	**EventDispatcher ➤ Object**
Implements	**IEventDispatcher**

IEventDispatcher is referred to as an *interface*, which, as the word implies, declares the public methods, and only public methods, with which you can "interface" or interact. If these methods were defined as anything other than public, then technically you couldn't use them or *interface* with them—hence the term. Therefore, they must be public. An interface isn't a class, but it requires a name to which a collection of defined methods can be referred; it too can be used to add another type to your class.

The inclusion of IEventDispatcher demonstrates that the interface is what allows MovieClips and Sprites to exhibit the public methods listed in **Figure 1-5**.

Method	Defined By
addEventListener(type:String, listener:Function, useCapture:Boolean = false, priority:int = 0, useWeakReference:Boolean = false):void Registers an event listener object with an EventDispatcher object so that the listener receives notification of an event.	IEventDispatcher
dispatchEvent(event:Event):Boolean Dispatches an event into the event flow.	IEventDispatcher
hasEventListener(type:String):Boolean Checks whether the EventDispatcher object has any listeners registered for a specific type of event	IEventDispatcher
removeEventListener(type:String, listener:Function, useCapture:Boolean = false):void Removes a listener from the EventDispatcher object.	IEventDispatcher
willTrigger(type:String):Boolean Checks whether an event listener is registered with this EventDispatcher object or any of its ancestors for the specified event type.	IEventDispatcher

Figure 1-5. The IEventDispatcher interface inherited by MovieClip and Sprite

Now that you have your class's definition, you're can add the attributes and behaviors to the definition's body. You can specify their visibility as private, public, protected, internal, or using custom namespaces, and you can also declare them as being static.

Static isn't a visibility modifier, but it establishes whether the attribute or behavior is a member of the class or the instantiation itself. The difference is that if a behavior or attribute is an instance member, any assignment is localized to the individual object; but a class member signified via the keyword static is referenced by every instance (see **Listing 1-3**).

Listing 1-3. Demonstrates how class members are referenced by every instance

```
package
{
        public class StaticExample
```

```
        {
                public static var classString:String = ' I am a variable  ➡
                                                of the Class itself ';

                public var instanceString:String = ' I am a variable of the ➡
                                                instance ';

                public function changeClassMember(str:String):void
                {
                        classString = str;
                }

                public function changeInstanceMember(str:String):void
                {
                        instanceString = str;
                }

                public function traceClassString():void
                {
                        trace(classString);
                }

                public function traceinstanceString():void
                {
                        trace(instanceString);
                }

        }

}
```

Listing 1-3 defines two variables one belonging to the Class and the other to the instance. The four methods, will offer the means to trace our either of the variables, or to adjust them. **Listing 1-4**, will demonstrate how class members are referenced by any and all instances, while the object members are not.

Listing 1-4. The DocumentClass devises the behaviors of StaticExample

```
package
{
    import flash.display.Sprite

    public class DocumentClass extends Sprite
    {

        private var _staticExampleInstanceA:StaticExample;
```

```
        private var _staticExampleInstanceB:StaticExample;

        public function DocumentClass()
        {
                _staticExampleInstanceA = new StaticExample();
                _staticExampleInstanceB = new StaticExample();

                _staticExampleInstanceA.changeInstanceMember( 'an instance ➡
        member is independent' );
                _staticExampleInstanceB.changeClassMember( 'a class member is ➡
        not' );

                _staticExampleInstanceA.traceClassString(); //a class member is ➡
        not

                _staticExampleInstanceB.traceInstanceString();    //I am a ➡
        variable of the instance

                _staticExampleInstanceA.traceClassString(); //class member is ➡
        not
        }
    }
}
```

As demonstrated in **Listing 1-4**, a class member is referenced by an instance rather than copied into the instantiation itself.

The keyword variable, or var, as it's written in ActionScript, shouldn't be new to you, but the keyword const may be. Much like var, const is used to hold properties or values; but whereas values declared with var can change, values declared as const can't. The keyword const is short for constant, and as the name implies, it doesn't allow the value to change. You use const when there is a reference that isn't expected to change after a value has been decided. Some examples are values in physics, like gravity, or the days in a year. Using a constant is insurance that the value will never be modified by any oversight, unless you change it at compile-time.

Constants can prevent the need to track down literals in your code as well. This is the preferred manner of adding literals. It's also a convenient way to refer to the same literal on multiple lines, because if the value must change, it's only changed in one place. The identifier must be assigned at the moment of its declaration.

The Constructor

The constructor is your point of origin for using a class and is the only way to instantiate an object of this class into your program. To ensure that all definitions of all superclasses are linked, the constructor method initiates and invokes the constructor of its superclass, and so forth, until the Object class's constructor is initialized. This is called an *inheritance chain*, and it reflects the manner in which you create your classes onto your reference. Along with any inheritance initiations, you can use the constructors to initialize chosen variables or constants with specific assignments.

Custom Namespaces

Namespaces are nothing new to the world of OOP and determine the visibility of definitions, attributes, and methods. The predefined namespaces public, protected, private, and internal are well known, but custom namespaces are rarely used. Thus a custom namespace is the epitome of data hiding, because it's the road less traveled. The lack of familiarity makes it a great way to hide data; and the fact that you can name the definition makes it all the more unlikely that the namespace will be used without being opened specifically.

Using a custom namespace is the equivalent of hiring a bouncer to secure the door of a back-room poker game where only invited guests know the password. The only way an uninvited guest can get through the door is if the password leaks out.

Creating and using a custom namespace is as easy as this:

1. Declare the namespace identifier.

2. Prefix your definition with the custom namespace identifier.

3. Open the custom namespace to the reference that's attempting to target your customized definition.

The following sections explain these steps.

Declaring the Namespace Identifier

Because you need to define your namespace, you must define an external definition by which the namespace can be referred to and located. The type of definition is indicated via the namespace directive, along with the name by which the definition can be identified. Remember, the definition name must reflect the saved .as filename. Finally, it's optional to redefine a URI string that ensures that the namespace isn't duplicated. If you choose not to supply a URI, the package structure is inserted to prevent name conflicts when compiled:

```
package
{
        [ visible ] namespace custom_name_space = "http://namespaces/customnamespace"
        {
        }
}
```

As with all definitions, if you wish to modify the visibility of this namespace, you can. Although, public and internal are your only available options. If you fail to modify the visibility, remember that it defaults to internal at compile time. Because no body is expected or even allowed, it's common to see namespaces without the extra brackets surrounding the body, as shown here:

```
package
{
```

```
        public namespace custom_name_space = 'http://namespaces/customnamespace'
}
```

Applying a custom namespace

Once a custom namespace has been defined, you can use it by importing its definition into the class and then declaring the custom namespace as the modifier of the definition you wish to customize. Use it as the prefix for your chosen attribute or behavior definition:

```
package
{
    import custom_name_space

    public class Foo extends MovieClip
    {

        custom_name_space function aRandomFunction():void
        {
        }

    }
}
```

Opening a namespace within a class

Finally, because Flash isn't expecting to use your custom definition, you must make sure your compiler (bouncer) knows that you have the secret password by referring to it.

AS 3.0 allows for not just definitions but also statements in a body. If a statement appears in the body but not in a defined operation, it's executed once at the moment the class definition is encountered. Thus, in the class that you wish to open your custom namespace, you can apply the following statement immediately after you create your definition:

```
package
{

    import Foo;
    import custom_name_space;

    public class DocumentClass extends Sprite
    {
        use namespace customNameSpace;


        public function DocumentClass()
        {
```

```
            var foo:Foo= new Foo();
                foo.aRandomFunction();
        }
    }
}
```

Using the directive use namespace can open an individual namespace or a set of namespaces within the class. This lets you access all declared attributes and behaviors marked with the custom namespace of our referenced class Foo.

Constructing an Interface

The final type of external definition that you can define is an Interface. You do so using the interface keyword directive. **Table 1-7** shows an example.

Table 1-7. The structure of an interface definition

```
package [folder[, folder... ]]


    interface IInterfaceName [ extends InterfaceName ]

    {

        //BODY OF THE DEFINITION;

    }

}
```

In this example, the definition's name, InterfaceName appears to begin with two /s. The first I is to indicate that the name refers to an interface. Like a class definition, an interface definition can specify a superclass, but it must be that of an interface. Just as the name implies, and as you saw earlier when analyzing the IEventDispatcher Interface, all methods declared must be public.

Change

Sometimes change can be good. However, nine out of ten times, change in the world of programming is a bad thing. Simple changes on paper can turn into hours of work, depending on how the code is written. Rather than fear change, embrace it. Roll out the red carpet and let change take its place in the spotlight. Change is a diva and needs to be treated as such.

When you decide to give change center stage, you're better prepared to deal with maintenance, rather than making adjustments on demand. Rather than leave a ticking time bomb in your code, isolate it and allow it to be used in your system like any other object.

I believe that many developers have learned to rely too much on the use of subversioning systems. Subversioning is a very useful technique in which code can be saved to backups with detailed notes about what changes have been made. At the time of subversion, a version number is assigned to the file, allowing for code rollbacks to a previous version. Although I promote the use of versioning, changes to code and rollbacks should be the role of inheritance and polymorphism.

General Terms and Definitions

This list doesn't include all words that are discussed in the book, but it defines for you terms that are used frequently when dealing with OOP:

- Class: The classification of defined properties, states, and behaviors that can be shared/modified among instances.
- object: An instantiated type referred to by its inherited traits.
- Object: The top-level class.
- Unified Modeling Language (UML): The standard representation used to build models for large and small computer applications.
- Encapsulation: The principle of separating and localizing behavior into an object
- Abstraction: Being absent of details (a generalization).
- Composition: The manner in which arrangements of objects collaborate to fulfill the behaviors that make up a distinct object.
- Delegation: The process of using behaviors of another object to achieve a result communicated by the original object.
- Inheritance: The means by which subclasses inherit attributes and behaviors of a superclass.
- Interface: The exposed methods on an object, which another object can message.
- Implementation: The code used in the body of a declared method.
- Private: This modifier limits the visibility of any attributes/behaviors to the scope that declared them.
- Subclass: A class belonging to the hierarchy of a superclass.
- Superclass: The parent class of a subclass.
- Properties: The attributes that make up the states of an object.
- Behavior: The expected response of an object
- Message: The communication between objects; a request.
- Namespace: A directive, which enables the visibility of a class's properties and methods.
- `Public`: This modifier extends the visibility of a defined property or method to all scopes
- `Protected`: This modifier specifies the visibility of property or method as being visible to class, which declared them as well as that classes subclasses.
- Concrete: A class's or object's inability to be generalized due to its implemented specifics.
- Type: The category of a class, which is based on its exposed Interface.
- Polymorphism: Latin meaning *many faces*; a process that allows interchangeability among objects with the same interface.
- Spaghetti code: Unorganized code with no clear structure, intertwined with no clear beginning or ending.
- Hashtable: A data structure used to store data in key/value pairs.

- Procedural code: Code that separates data from associated behaviors.
- Loose coupling: The generalized collaboration among objects.
- Tight coupling: The act of collaboration among objects with reference to concrete objects.
- Object-oriented programming: The practice of architecting a system that adheres to four principles (*encapsulation*, *polymorphism*, *inheritance, and data hiding*), thereby promoting flexibility.
- Design pattern: A core solution to solving a particular and reoccurring problem.

Summary

OOP is a structural device, rather than the act of making objects. Having a better structure lets you compartmentalize your code by using distinctions that allow for more efficient assembling, interchangeability, and readable language. On the other hand, OOP can add complexity to a system, and it generally takes patience, forethought, and—most important—time to perfect. All in all, using classes properly and putting thought into each class reflects the flexibility you aim for, but you must understand the importance of encapsulation, polymorphism, inheritance, and data hiding.

The largest misconception about OOP is the belief that to be object-oriented, you must be working with objects. Working with objects merely for the sake of appearing object-oriented increases the likelihood of failure and negates the benefits of programming in an object-oriented manner. It's imperative that you understand the four principles to which objects are formed. A plethora of objects doesn't enhance code flexibility but instead becomes an obstacle in the way of maintenance, upkeep, and change.

This chapter has provided a lot of information and has more than likely left your brain hurting—which means your brain is working. OOP isn't something that happens immediately; it takes practice, a lot of it, to realize why it's a beneficial practice to follow.

Don't resort to mimicry or memorization. Understanding is the only key to being object-oriented. Spend some time considering how you could take already-developed code and transform it into a properly structured system, using the four OOP principles. Being able to point out behaviors that can be encapsulated, and interchanged, will help you understand the chapters to come. Knowledge is half the battle. *Go code!*

Key Points

- Code can be made much more efficient if it's built with the four principles of OOP in mind: encapsulation, data hiding, polymorphism, and inheritance.
- Generalizing common behavior allows for interchangeability.
- The goal of OOP is to build an architecture that allows flexibility and easier maintenance.
- Class names should be specific to the behavior they define and should always begin with an uppercase letter.
- The keyword `implements` lets you add into your class the methods required by other defined types.
- The point of creating a class isn't only to use it to build objects, but also to separate behaviors and/or data. Instantiating an object means you expect the behaviors and/or state to change.

- Don't resort to mimicry or memorization when practicing OOP.
- OOP is a structural device and is not the same as the act of making objects.
- OOP can add complexity to a system.
- Changes to code and rollbacks should be the role of inheritance.
- Change is a constant

Chapter 2

ActionScript 3.0: The Facts Behind the Basics

As you know, a procedure can be carried out several ways. "Hello World," for example, is often the very first application implemented when you're learning a language. If you were to write down the many unique ways to output "Hello World," I'll bet you could devise at least 10. The more you learn the API of a language, the more options available to you as a developer.

Not every object-oriented language is written similarly. Each language has its own set of nuances that developers come to love or dread. To best implement your object-oriented code, you must become familiar with such aspects of the ActionScript 3.0 language.

This chapter explores specifics of the ActionScript language. It will benefit your object-oriented implementations and further your understanding of the language.

ActionScript 3.0

ActionScript is a total rewrite of its lingual predecessors. Originally, ActionScript followed the Ecma standards and was modelled around the prototype as the means to develop classes. To add to the object hierarchy, you used the fundamental prototype object to model objects with the properties of another object. In ActionScript 2.0, the `class` directive was added, but the use of the word *class* was nothing but a superficial way to work with objects. It didn't change the fact that behind the scenes, the prototype continued to link the classes together.

It wasn't until ActionScript 3.0, which finally moved toward a class-driven, object-oriented language, that actual change took place behind the scenes of compilation. These tweaks brought both good and bad and included the following: performance, garbage collection, the event model, strong typing, the display model, and method closures.

The Traits Object

New to the ActionScript language, the `traits` object was added to provide true class inheritance. The inclusion of a traits object greatly reduces the delay caused by property lookup. In previous ActionScript languages, object properties were shared among cloned objects by what was known as the *prototype chain*. If the property targeted on an instantiated object couldn't be found, the expected property is searched for within the next object up the chain, and the search continued until the top-level object was found.

The `traits` object vastly enhances property lookup by eliminating the need for the prototype chain. Every class, when compiled, possesses a number of objects, one of which is the new `traits` object. The `traits` object is supplied with all the properties that are inherited. As long as the class is not marked as dynamic, performance is significantly improved.

Although the `traits` object is new to ActionScript 3.0, it doesn't fully replace the prototype object. To remain compatible with the Ecma specification, the prototype object remains, but the ActionScript 3.0 preferred manner of inheritance is to use the `traits` object and fixed inheritance. Only properties declared within a class can be passed, versus dynamic assignments of properties and methods at runtime. If you've ever opened a top-level class, this is the reason it contained function declarations.

Although the `traits` object remains behind the scenes and isn't accessible by code, it's the model for each object among many of the methods you'll see in this chapter.

Garbage Collection

Each object created in an object-oriented programming (OOP) language requires a particular allocation of system memory. Each object's allocation of memory varies, but the more objects created, the more memory consumed, and the fewer resources remain available. When objects are no longer used by the system, they're gathered and destroyed in order to reclaim the memory they consumed.

Compartmentalization makes a system more flexible and modular but increases the number of objects used in an application. Using design patterns to achieve a flexible and loosely coupled architecture enables code reuse and polymorphism. However, the collaborations among objects that allow for such flexibility require attention to memory management. This isn't a drawback to the patterns themselves, but it's a reality that OOP developers must consider as Garbage Collection requires the Developer to be proactive.

Memory Management

Knowing how to eliminate weeds is great, but understanding how to prevent their growth is even better. It's no surprise that the majority of Flash developers aren't computer science majors. It's also no surprise that being a Flash developer has evolved from a hobby to a profession. Therefore, you can understand why developers often fight memory management as a result of poor performance.

The transition to ActionScript 3.0 has introduced developers to memory management, which for many is an incredibly new concept. Those who migrated from previous versions of ActionScript have never concerned themselves with memory, and those who have developed solely with ActionScript 3.0 have focused on memory almost as little as those who transitioned from an earlier release.

The most difficult aspect of memory management is understanding the memory used within the application. Most of the ActionScript literatures focuses on removing events as the end of the memory consumption issue.

The tool to understanding memory consumption is the flash.sampler package, which also isn't well known among developers (see **Figure 2-1**).

Figure 2-1. The flash.sampler package and its contents

The sampler package was originally supplied with Flex and was uses by a profiler added to the compiler. The package gives you greater insight into the internal workings of the role each object plays and the resulting impact on memory resources. Even if you don't have a special editor such as FDT or Flash Builder, you can fully use the contents of this package; the only requirement is that you run the compiled code in the Flash Player Debugger version 9.0.115.0 or later.

It goes without saying that the more specialized the object hierarchy is, the more memory it probably requires. Without knowing how memory use varies among objects, you can't choose the objects that best suit the requirements of the chosen behavior. The static method getSize(obj:Object):Number in the sampler package enables you to view the amount of memory resources used by an application object.

The object passed as a parameter of the getSize method is analyzed. The return value is the number of bytes in memory the object uses. Here's an example:

```
trace( getSize( new Object() ));        //results in 40 Bytes;
```

As you see, the instantiated Object is passed into the getSize method, and its value in memory is returned (40 bytes in this case).

Figure 2-2 shows that each object has a specific value that it imposes on memory resources. A reference alone, either `Complex` or `Primitive`—excluding `Number`—reserves 4 bytes of memory. `Number`, because it's a double float precision, requires twice that amount (8 bytes). `String` is a slightly different matter. String values are calculated based on the characters used; the memory required varies depending on whether the string is static or dynamic at the time of reference creation, and whether it's a single character.

```
MAC 10,1,102,64
Primitive References          Primitive Instances
 4 var string:String           4 new String()  //""
 4 var integer:int             4 new int()      //0
 4 var uinteger:uint           4 new uint()     //0
 4 var boolean:Boolean         4 new Boolean() //false
 8 var number:Number           4 new Number()   //0

Complex References            Complex Instances
 4 var object:Object           40 new Object() or Object literal {}
 4 var dict:Dictionary         56 new Dictionary() or new Dictionary(true)
 4 var array:Array             56 new Array() or Array literal []
 4 var shape:Shape            224 shape=new Shape() or new Shape()
 4 var sbutton:SimpleButton   240 sbutton=new SimpleButton() or new SimpleButton()
 4 var sprite:Sprite          392 sprite=new Sprite() or new Sprite()
 4 var mClip:MovieClip        428 mClip=new MovieClip() or new MovieClip()
 4 var tField:TextField      1248 tField=new TextField() or new TextField()

Strings
  var sentence:String = "Lorem ipsum dolor sit amet, consectetuer adipiscing elit. Duis scelerisque facilisis tortor. Aliquam semper gravida
  ligula. Vestibulum sodales lacinia leo. In turpis justo, placerat eu, ultrices vel, auctor a, tortor. Aliquam lorem justo, tepor at, vehicula ac,
  porttitor id, felis. Ut eget orci at odio congue nonummy. Aliquam wisi. Vivamus suscipit nonummy eros. Praesent bibendum consectetuer
  neque. Donec vitae eros ut mi adipiscing mollis. Vestibulum eleifend. Maecenas ultrice. Ut vitae velit."

Static Strings
 24 '' or new String("")
 24 AB or new String("AB")
 24 Lorem ipsum dolor sit amet, consectetuer adipiscing elit. Duis scelerisque facilisis tortor. Duis scelerisque facilisis tortor....
    -or new String("Lorem ipsum dolor sit amet, consectetuer adipiscing elit. Duis scelerisque facilisis tortor. Duis scelerisque... ")
 32 a or new String("a")
Dynamic Strings
512 sentence + sentence or new String(sentence + sentence)
```

Figure 2-2. The results of a few trials of the `getSize` method

Using `getSize`, you can compile a class and calculate the number of bytes your class adds as overhead in an application. The code in **Listing 2-1** defines class `Circle`, which extends the built-in ActionScript 3.0 object `Shape`. The class has the properties such as `_color`, `_radius`, and `_object`.

Listing 2-1. The `Circle` class extends `Shape` and has three properties: `_color`, `_radius`, and `_object`.

```
package
{
    import flash.display.Shape;

    public class Circle extends Shape
    {
        private var _color : uint;
        private var _radius : Number;
        private var _object : Object;
```

```
    public function Circle( radius : Number )
    {
      _radius = radius;
      _object = new Object();
    }

    public function get color() : uint
    {
      return _color;
    }

    public function set color( color : uint ) : void
    {
      _color = color;
    }
  }
}
```

Before you instantiate the Circle class, let's predict how much memory will be used by an instance of a Circle object. You can refer to **Figure 2-2** for assistance.

The Circle class inherits its properties from Shape, which you know uses 224 bytes of memory. It has two primitive references: a Number (8 bytes) and an unsigned integer (4 bytes). It also has an Object reference, which you know requires 4 bytes. Now, if you add those values, you can predict that an instance of Circle requires approximately 240 bytes.

If you were wondering why the instantiation of Object within the constructor isn't included in the equation, the answer is simple. Although you know that an instance of Object requires 40 bytes, only primitives retain a value; complex references of objects are merely pointers (you learn more about pointers in the section "Mark and Sweep"). These pointers refer to the location in memory where these objects exist. 40 bytes are added to your application as soon as you instantiate the Circle object, but those 40 extra bytes are calculated as part of the total memory consumed, not in the Circle instance.

```
trace( getSize( new Circle( 0 ) ) )   // 240 Bytes
```

Note that the memory required is 240 bytes. Due to the many bug fixes implemented from one player to the next the memory consumption varies. The values used here are from the Flash player 10.1.102 build.

Let's look at another example. This time, we'll use MovieClip as the superclass. Let's name this class MovieClipExtension and, for demonstration purposes, supply absolutely nothing beyond a constructor:

```
package
{
   import flash.display.MovieClip;

   public class MovieClipExtension extends MovieClip
   {
```

```
        public function MovieClipExtension()
        {
        }
    }
}
```

If you estimate the file size, you assume it's that of an instantiated `MovieClip`, or 428 bytes. But here's the call to `getSize()`:

```
trace( getSize( new MovieClipExtension ( ) ) )  // 412 bytes
```

The application states that `MovieClipExtension` consumes 412 bytes of memory resources, which is not what you expected. However, recall that `MovieClip` is a dynamic class: therefore it supplies memory for a hashtable, where it stores dynamically added properties at runtime. `MovieClipExtension`, on the other hand, wasn't declared as a dynamic class and is considered a sealed class by default. The hashtable that resides in the instance of a dynamically defined `MovieClip` isn't added to the `traits` object of `MovieClipExtension`, and therefore you save a few bytes. If you were to declare your new class as dynamic, `getSize` would reveal `MovieClipExtension`'s memory consumption to be equal to that of an instantiated `MovieClip`.

The impact of 412 bytes on a system may not appear to be much; in fact, it may appear to be laughable. But in any application, bytes can add up quickly. In a system like ActionScript 3.0, where garbage collection can't be forced and is activated only when too much memory has been consumed, preserving memory resources is a vital. Choosing the appropriate objects is a must in any object-oriented language, and you must reflect this in the classes for your patterns.

Mark and Sweep

To reduce the overhead of running a tedious algorithm, which can stutter the player's performance, the garbage collector (GC) is triggered only at a specific point. The GC uses a *mark and sweep* approach, where as long as zero pointers target a location in memory, that memory is considered eligible to be emptied. As you know, in ActionScript, a primitive reference is an actual copy; therefore it isn't as much of a threat in an object's persistence as a complex reference. Complex references are physical pointers to memory locations, as a means of maintaining memory. Although pointers aid in reducing memory duplication, they also prevent the GC from dumping its target.

Let's look at an example. In **Figure 2-3**, although it appears that a variable possesses properties and methods declared by the new instance of `Object`, the properties aren't copied onto it. Rather, a location of blocks in memory is endowed with all that your template has to pass on, and then a direct connection to its location, like a bridge, is adhered to a reference.

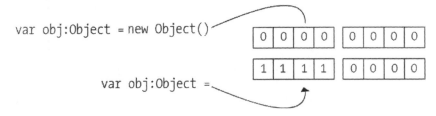
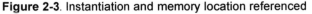

Figure 2-3. Instantiation and memory location referenced

Only by nullifying this bridge can you make the GC view the memory as no longer being referenced within the application (see **Figure 2-4**). Doing so enables the GC to dump the contents of data blocks that are no longer being used, thus freeing up memory. But while the memory address is in use, other variables can point to the same location in memory, thus preventing the release of memory from your program even when obj's bridge is nullified.

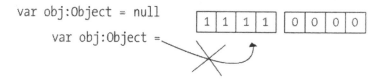

Figure 2-4. Location to memory severed

In order to efficiently free up memory, you must set to null all references to any memory location, as shown in **Figure 2-4**. Doing so marks the location as eligible to be freed. All references that are marked are added to a zero count stack, where it's determined whether they're available to be emptied.

Figure 2-5 demonstrates that while the reference 'obj' may be set to null, secondaryObj has not been, and therefore the memory consumed from the Objects instantiation cannot yet be reclaimed.

```
var obj:Object = new Object()        var secondaryObj:Object = obj
         var obj:Object = null        1 1 1 1
```

Figure 2-5 Instantiation and memory location referenced via secondaryObj;

Design patterns, whether creational, behavioral, or structural, pass references for delegation and modification. Some examples are the Observer pattern (discussed in Chapter 7) and the Command pattern (also discussed in Chapter 7), just to name two. The relationships among objects may prevent memory from being released, so you need to ensure this release when you no longer require the objects' services.

Implementing a Disposable Pattern

Hooray, your first pattern! The Disposable pattern, as it's appropriately named, is one of many behavioral patterns. The intent of this pattern is to separate the logic required among objects from the modeled behavior defined in the abstract class during the removal of composed references. As you can see in **Figure 2-6**, the collaborators in the pattern are as follows:

1. Disposable interface

2. Abstract class

3. Concrete class

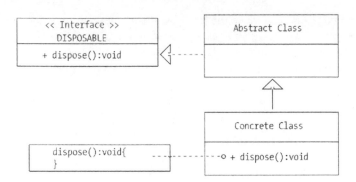

Figure 2-6. Class diagram of the Disposable pattern

Without specific lingual pattern interpretation, you can't merge such a pattern into an ActionScript system, due to the language's preexisting conditions. The reasons are as follows.

First, there are no proper directives that can absolutely enforce an abstract class, as of the current release of ActionScript 3.0. You can pretend a class is abstract, but there is no foolproof way to ensure that this class will never be used. As the definition of an abstract class specifies, it's a class that will and can never be instantiated.

The closest you can get to an abstract class is to create a class that throws an error in the constructor, preventing the compiler from continuing without this error being corrected (see **Listing 2-2**).

Listing 2-2. Faux abstract class in ActionScript 3.0, which results in an error if you try to instantiate it

```
package
{
    public class AbstractClass
    {
        public function AbstractClass()
        {
            throw new IllegalOperationError( "This class is intended as an abstract➥
class and mustn\'t be instantiated" );
        }
    }
}
```

This faux manner of devising an abstract class does the intended job of enforcing that the class can't be instantiated. However, it lacks proper ability to enforce its subclasses to override all abstract methods it contains. I've seen some clever means by which this has been made possible, but enforcement is only available at runtime, which can slow development.

> Note: Feel free to explore "Runtime Enforcement of Abstract Classes in AS3" by Josh Tynjala at http://joshblog.net/2007/08/19/enforcing-abstract-classes-at-runtime-in-actionscript-3/.

The next best option is to inject your method directly into your top-level class, thus trickling it into any subclass defined by a developer. Unfortunately, this is also impossible while adhering to fixed inheritance. In an effort to obtain optimal performance and use as few memory resources as possible, properties and methods are added to the `traits` object using fixed inheritance, as discussed earlier. Fixed inheritance also prevents you from adding methods and properties at runtime via the prototype object. To inject a `dispose` method into the language's classes, you need to physically modify the classes that came with your OOP language. This becomes an issue in itself, because each developer must have the same modified language classes, which can cause a lot of confusion with future releases and legacy code. Plus, if new developers are hired, they too need to modify their classes.

Because you can't rely on inheritance as the sole means to establish your disposable method, you're left with only one viable solution to make this pattern available: implement the interface into every custom class defined. This is an efficient approach that all developers can use. It's the ideal implementation for the Disposable pattern in the ActionScript 3.0 language.

Not every object in ActionScript requires a null value to its reference, although it's better to overdo it than not. Primitive data types do allocate memory within an application, but they do so only for the lifespan of the object in which they're declared. Complex types, on the other hand, require all pointers to be severed. The implementation of the `destroy` method is specific to the class and the references that it contains.

To properly remove all complex objects, it helps to be able to see all references within a class. This allows you to directly target the references and to set them to `null` in the disposal method. Unfortunately, when you use nested library clips, the instance names are often added to the classes at compile time. This is known as *stage instance declaration*, and each project, by default, is an automatic occurrence.

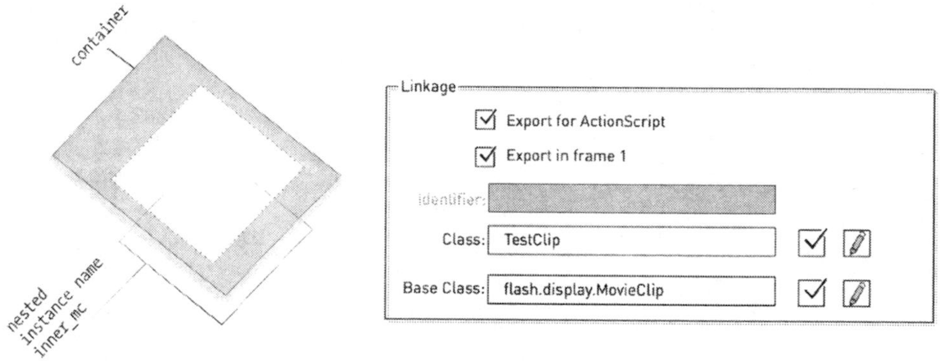

Figure 2-7. A nested clip whose instance name is that of `inner_mc` in `TestClip`

For example, using the `flash.sampler` package, let's demonstrate the compiled complex reference that is inserted into an object using the static method `getMemberNames()`. This method accepts two parameters: the object, from which it retrieves all QName members; and whether to include any instance names that may be available to the object.

QName is an ActionScript 3.0 class; it's short for *qualified name*. Chapter 1 discussed how the compiler can locate and refer to a particular definition with a URI along with the definition's name. All definitions in the language are referenced absolutely behind the scenes as qualified names, which eliminates any ambiguity about which definition is being referred to. This is referred to as being *fully qualified*.

Therefore, when an instance member is found and returned via getMemberNames, it's returned as a qualified name. Appropriately, QName provides two properties that a qualified name uses: localName and uri. localName represents the member name, and uri is the namespace in which localName remains unique. Here's an example making use of our TestClip from **Figure 2-7**:

```
var tc:MovieClip= new TestClip()
for each ( var members:QName in getMemberNames( tc , true ) )
{
    trace( members.localName )  //inner_mc, currentScene, currentFrameLabel, etc..
}
```

As you can see, inner_mc is added as an object reference in the TestClip object. What is slightly misleading is that you may think you're calling the clip through the instance name, but the compiler inserts an identifier to match that of your declared instance name.

Tip: As a best practice, you should always deselect Automatically Declare Stage Instances, to enforce your class physically declaring any necessary instances with which it associates.

To deselect this option in Flash CS5, choose File ➤ Publish Settings ➤ Flash ➤ Settings, and locate the Stage property as shown in **Figure 2-8**.

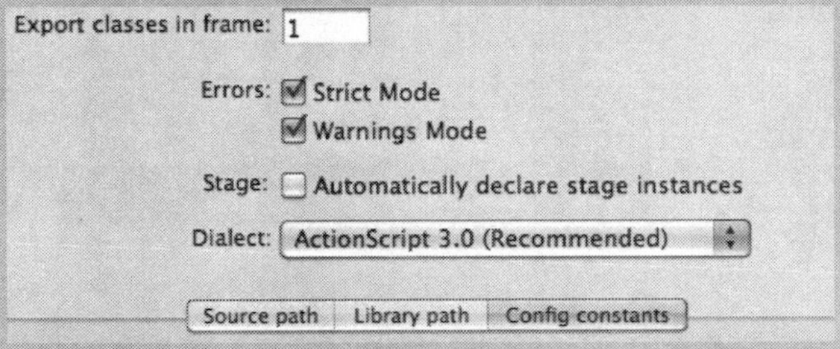

Figure 2-8. *Deselect the Automatically Declare Stage Instances option.*

Unfortunately, this option defaults to being selected on a per .fla *basis.*

If you remove ActionScript's ability to supply instances automatically to your code, you're required to manually declare any and all instances as properties among the appropriate classes.

Manually Declared Stage instances

With your handy dandy object-oriented skills, you know that it's always wise to separate the implementation from its structure, allowing for flexibility. Having disabled automatic stage instance declarations, you have to declare the reference yourself; otherwise, when you compile your code, a `ReferenceError` occurs:

```
ReferenceError: Error #1056: Cannot create property inner_mc on TestClip.
    at flash.display::Sprite/constructChildren()
    at flash.display::Sprite()
    at flash.display::MovieClip()
    at TestClip()
    at DocumentClass()
```

To add a variable representing the nested clip, open the `TestClip` class and add `private var inner_mc`. But you find that again, at compile time, you're confronted with a `ReferenceError`. Unless you specifically declare `inner_mc` as a public variable, you continue to face the same `ReferenceError`. Why? This has to do with the order in which things are compiled and the hashtable used by `MovieClips` that enabled the clips to be added. Because `MovieClips` let you add dynamic properties, its references must remain public. By extending the `MovieClip` class to allow `TestClip` to be defined, the hashtable is removed unless you specify dynamic behavior for `TestClip` as well. This allows the nested clip to be accepted after your classes are compiled. If you were to define your clip as dynamic, you could get away with defining `inner_mc` as private. Again you've broken the concept of encapsulation, because you're allowing dynamic behavior on the class. This is exactly what would occur if you declared `TestClip` as a sealed class and used it as the base class of `ContainerClip`.

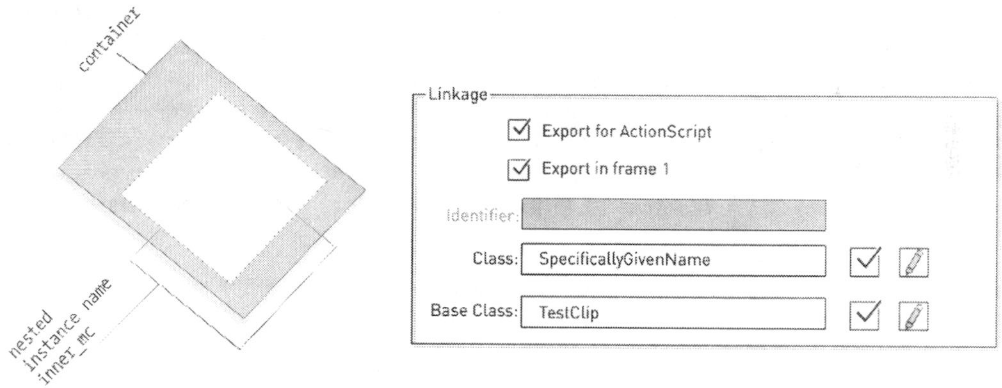

Figure 2-9. Clip using `TestClip` as its base class

Now, when you compile the clip, because you've defined `private var inner_mc` in the class `TestClip`, the compiler no longer throws a reference error. The reason is apparent when you use the `describeType` method from the `flash.utils` package. This method reveals the details of the parameterized object instance, in the form of XML:

```
trace( describeType( new SpecificallyGivenName() ) )
// <type name=" SpecificallyGivenName " base="TestClip" isDynamic="true"➥
 isFinal="false" isStatic="false"> ...
```

When the Flash compiler can't find a class labeled SpecificallyGivenName, it supplies one at the time of compilation; and to fulfill its role, SpecificallyGivenName is defined as being dynamic. This leaves you with the solution of defining your references as being public, so you can continue to seal your class to further maintain data hiding.

Application Domain

The *application domain*, not to be confused with problem domain, represents the memory location of an application's given definitions. When a .swf file is published, the compiler bundles all application definitions into that of an application domain. If a .swf is loaded into another .swf, the definitions of both .swfs remain partitioned from one another. This ensures that the definitions of one application don't interfere with the naming conventions of possibly same named definitions between the two .swf files.

You instantiate an ApplicationDomain by importing the flash.system.ApplicationDomain class. The ApplicationDomain class, when instantiated, accepts as an optional parameter a reference to a preexisting applicationDomain. Specifying a preexisting applicationDomain lets the devised partition use definitions from the passed-in applicationDomain (appDom for short).

Two important properties of the ApplicationDomain class are currentDomain and parentDomain. currentDomain is a static property that points to the applicationDomain, which holds the code currently being executed. parentDomain is a pointer to the parent's ApplicationDomain, providing one exists.

By default, when a .swf file is published, its applicationDomain doesn't have a parentDomain, and all definitions are considered to be stored in what is referred to as a systemDomain. This is where built-in definitions of the ActionScript 3.0 language are contained (MovieClip, Sprite, Loader, and so on). The packaged definitions are partitioned onto that of the systemDomain, allowing all user-defined code to refer to the built-in definitions. Only when a .swf file is loaded into another .swf is a parentDomain possibly available. *Possibly*, because a parentDomain is available only when an instantiation of an ApplicationDomain includes a reference to an existing applicationDomain, thus creating a hierarchy among the appDoms.

When you load one .swf file into another, you can modify the partitioning of the loading .swf's definitions by specifying one of the following four application domain settings:

- Child of the loader's ApplicationDomain: The default setting when loading a .swf file, applied using new ApplicationDomain(ApplicationDomain.currentDomain). This line of code creates the new application domain on the loading .swf, but with a relationship to the application domain of the parent container. Attaching the ApplicationDomain on the parent's appDom allows the loaded .swf file to use the parent's definitions by referring to them as if they were located in the loaded .swf file's ApplicationDomain.currentDomain.

- Loader's ApplicationDomain: Specified as ApplicationDomain.currentDomain. No partition is created, allowing all definitions of the child to be loaded into the loader's appDom. This is, of course, with the exception of duplicate definitions, which are disregarded.
- Child of the system ApplicationDomain: Specified as new ApplicationDomain(null). Creates a partition among the child and parent definitions. This ensures that definitions of similar names don't interfere with one another. It also ensures that the definitions of the two .swfs aren't visible to one another, thus isolating definitions between the two.
- Child of a specified ApplicationDomain: Specified as ApplicationDomain('application_domain_here'). When you specify the relationship between a loading .swf file's definitions and another, you can partition the ApplicationDomain among the child's appDom with the visibility of another appDom's definitions. You can do so via the parentDomain property or through a reference to an appDom.

You can use the specification among ApplicationDomains only when loading .swf files published for the ActionScript 3.0 language. To specify the ApplicationDomain settings, a property on the LoaderContext object must reflect such changes, as you'll see next.

The LoaderContext

LoaderContext is an object that, when instantiated, can be passed into a Loader object, allowing for the modification of additional options. One such option is the applicationDomain property, which you can set by supplying one of the four values listed in the previous section to the LoaderContext.applicationDomain, as shown in **Listing 2-3**.

Listing 2-3. Specifies the appDom of the loading definitions to be included within the applicationDomain to which the loader's definitions exist

```
var loader:Loader= new Loader();
var urlRequest:URLRequest = new URLRequest('externalSWF.swf');
var loadContext:LoaderContext= new LoaderContext();
        loader.contentLoaderInfo.addEventListener(Event.COMPLETE,onComplete);
        loadContext.applicationDomain = ApplicationDomain.currentDomain;

        loader.load(urlRequest,loadContext);
```

Currently you've set the ApplicationDomain of the loading .swf file as a child of the loader's, of the 'externalSWF.swf's; applicationDomain.

Specifying the applicationDomain among definitions enables both the compiler and you as a developer to tap into the scope of existing definitions. Specifying the applicationDomain among loaded definitions allows for definition reuse, similar to the use of runtime shared libraries.

By understanding how definitions are compiled into the appDoms, you can further your understanding of how you work with objects and their instantiations, via the use of the new operator, as discussed in the next section.

The Class Object

All definitions in ActionScript 3.0 are instances of the built-in Class object. Although the Class object is of little use to a developer, its instances are a different matter. You use these all the time when you use the new operator. Each Class object can be referenced by the name it was given when you specified its external definition. As you saw earlier in **Figure 2-3**, any reference that remains within scope can be obtained.

Fortunately, the scope of your application, and your definitions' longevity, can coincide with the applicationDomain of the particular .swf file. If you have a reference to the current appDom and want to retrieve a particular Class object with which to work, you can do so using the getDefinition and getDefinitionByName methods.

Suppose the externalSWF.swf file from **Listing 2-3** was defined by an attached class DocumentClass, shown in **Listing 2-4**.

Listing 2-4. Base class of externalSWF

```
package
{
    import flash.display.Sprite;

    public class DocumentClass extends Sprite
    {
        public function DocumentClass()
        {
            // constructor code
            trace( 'DocumentClass instantiated' );
        }
    }
}
```

The base class, DocumentClass, is converted into a Class object and appropriately partitioned in one of the four manners the applicationDomain allows.

getDefinition()

The getDefinition method retrieves a Class object from an existing applicationDomain explicit to the definition name parameterized within. This is reflected in the method signature: getDefinition(memberName:String):Class.

To demonstrate how you can use getDefinition to retrieve a Class object, specify DocumentClass as the memberName you wish to retrieve from the applicationDomain of externalSwf.swf from within the currentDomain of the parent .swf file (see **Listing 2-5**).

Listing 2-5. Retrieving the DocumentClass Class object from the currently executing appDom via getDefinition

```
var loader:Loader= new Loader();
var urlRequest:URLRequest = new URLRequest('externalSWF.swf');
var loadContext:LoaderContext= new LoaderContext();
    loadContext.applicationDomain = ApplicationDomain.currentDomain;
    loader.contentLoaderInfo.addEventListener(Event.COMPLETE,onComplete);
    loader.load(urlRequest,loadContext);


function onComplete(e:Event) :void
{
var returnedObject:Class= e.target.applicationDomain.getDefinition('DocumentClass'));
    trace(returnedObject) ;   //[class DocumentClass]
}
```

As demonstrated in the **listing 2-5**, you can retrieve the DocumentClass Class object from the appDom of the currentDomain after externalSWF.swf has been loaded. When you obtain the desired Class object, you can do with it as you see fit. You can pass the reference, retain the reference, or even instantiate it via the new operator.

The returned Class object of the getDefinition isn't limited to class definitions. The returned object can be a class, a namespace, or even an interface; all are subclasses of the Class object.

getDefinitionByName()

Much like getDefinition, getDefinitionByName also retrieves a public Class object from an ApplicationDomain explicit to the definition name parameterized within. The difference between the two is that getDefinitionByName is a global function and can only return a Class. In other words, don't expect to retrieve namespaces or interfaces via getDefinitionByName. **Listing 2-6** shows an example.

Listing 2-6. Retrieving the DocumentClass class object from the currently executing appDom via getDefinitionByName

```
var loader:Loader= new Loader();
var urlRequest:URLRequest = new URLRequest('externalSWF.swf');
var loadContext:LoaderContext= new LoaderContext();
    loadContext.applicationDomain = ApplicationDomain.currentDomain;
    loader.contentLoaderInfo.addEventListener(Event.COMPLETE,onComplete);
    loader.load(urlRequest,loadContext);


function onComplete(e:Event):void
{
        var returnedObject:Class = Class(getDefinitionByName('DocumentClass'));
        trace(returnedObject);     //[class DocumentClass]
}
```

As you can see, getDefinitionByName doesn't need to succeed the reference of an applicationDomain, because it always points to the currently executing appDom. Another noteworthy difference is that getDefinitionByName returns a Class object, but the method's signature specifies a return type of Object. To provide strong-typing to the reference, knowing the object is a Class object, you can cast the return value to be Class:

```
var returnedObject:Class= Class(getDefinitionByName('DocumentClass') );
```

The next section takes a look at what it is to Strong Type a reference.

Strong Typing

Data typing is nothing new to the ActionScript language, but the performance gained by supplying data types is. Strong typing facilitates proper use of objects in a system by associating, or *binding*, the reference to an object's intended interface. Associating a variable with a data type optimizes the bytecode and improves player performance significantly.

Although performance should be reason enough to use typing data, it also provides many benefits in terms of productivity by reducing errors.

Because ActionScript is a dynamically typed language, it provides runtime type checking. Although this makes the language incredibly versatile, it leads to slower debugging, because errors are revealed only when your code is running. Fortunately, the Flash IDE (when in strict mode) offers compile-time checking as well.

Runtime Type Checking

Dynamic languages let an application modify its behavior at runtime. When a program can constantly adapt, you can only verify mismatch errors and type coercions with runtime type checking.

Runtime type checking, as the name suggests, ensures there no improper mismatches take place while the application is running. To accomplish this, the interpreter must determine and imply data types as they're being used. Thus, although runtime type checking allows the language to remain fluid, it can slow the debugging process.

New to ActionScript 3.0 is the addition of compile-time type checking, which lets you predict and prevent any possible mismatch or type-coercion errors that may occur while your code is running.

Compile-Time Type Checking

Typing a reference preserves the contract among object messaging within the system. It there's any incorrect use of the object through an attempt to call a method or property, you're made aware of it either at the moment of compilation or even while authoring, via a type-mismatch error. The editor may determine the means by which you're informed. Compile-time type checking also ensures the proper passing of references and assists you if any improper mismatches occur during development.

Compile-time checking is optional, and its use does *not* prevent runtime type checking from occurring. Using compile-time type checking doesn't ensure that all runtime errors are eliminated.

By default, the Flash IDE settings enable compile-time checking. Deselecting the Strict-Mode option in settings defers all type checking to runtime checking.

Although strict mode provides type checking, data types among variables and/or expressions must be typed within your code.

Restricting a Dynamic Language

The benefit of typing variables, parameters, and return types is the optimization of ActionScript bytecode (ABC), which reduces the interpreter's need to imply data types at runtime. It also gives you immediate feedback from the editor in an effort to prevent type errors early on.

Practicing optimal implementation of design patterns in ActionScript 3.0 requires you to choose the most appropriate types to bind to the expressions and variables among each pattern's collaborative objects. Using types that are overly specific reduces the pattern's reusability, leading to tightly coupling. However, falling back on an overly generalized type requires careful collaboration and attention to your system and its parts. The beauty of many patterns is their ability to assist with generalizations among objects that you may not otherwise have foreseen.

Unfortunately, subclasses can't redefine types among variables or expressions defined by their superclass. This often reduces code reuse because you must write more to satisfy such needs. If code reuse appears to outweigh the optimization of typing, ActionScript offers a solution.

Although I'm not advocating the use of weakly typed data or the lack of typing, the compiler isn't as flexible the interpreter, known as AVM2. Because ActionScript is a dynamic language, runtime reflection is possible, which can make your applications more flexible.

ActionScript 3.0 lets you bypass compile-time checking by using the untyped property or wildcard annotation represented by the multiply symbol *. Assignment to an untyped property doesn't cause compile-time errors because the reference is recognized as holding any value. These assignments are, on the other hand, type-checked and properly cast at runtime.

Casting

When you pass references among objects to that of a generalized type, you often have to cast an object back into its actual data type. There are two ways to cast an object in ActionScript 3.0: the cast operation, which wraps an expression such as `Type( expression )`, and the as operator (`expression as DataType`). Both approaches have distinct advantages over the other, such as readability, conversion precedence, and casting failures.

Typically, in ActionScript 3.0, you use the as operator to properly cast an object into another data type. Why? Because, unfortunately, too many developers mimic behavior presented to they learned the language. This is due to three reasons.

First, not every cast works properly when used as a wrapped expression. The following code compares the readability of type casting using the two acceptable approaches:

```
obj as MovieClip  versus  MovieClip(obj)
```

To many developers, it's clearer that obj as MovieClip is type casted. MovieClip(obj) may be mistakenly read as a new Instantiation.

Second, the attempted casting of an array to an object and back to an array demonstrates a casting faux pas when using the wrapped cast of an expression:

```
var ar:Array = [ 'bob' , 'tom' , 'mike' ];
var obj:Object = ar;
var arTyped:Array = Array( obj );
trace( arTyped.length );  // 1
trace( arTyped[ 0 ] );  //  'bob','tom','mike'
trace( arTyped[ 0 ][ 0 ] );  //  'bob'

arTyped = obj as Array
trace( arTyped.length );  // 3
```

Unfortunately, not all casting operations work as you may expect. In this example, attempts to upcast the Array to an Object and downcast it back to an Array aren't particularly successful. You expect to end with an array that possesses an index of 3. The result is correct when you use the as operator but not otherwise. Instead, your object is downcast to an array and then wrapped in the first index of a new array.

Finally, the following attempt to cast the instance of an object into that of a MovieClip demonstrates the cast failure between both cast manners:

```
var object:Object= {}
trace( MovieClip( object ) )  // TypeError: Error #1034: Type Coercion ➥
failed: cannot convert Object@30f68f71 to flash.display.MovieClip.

trace( object as MovieClip )  // null
```

When a cast is successful, the original object is returned for continued use *without* interruption. When a cast is unsuccessful, the object isn't returned, and any reference to the expected return is set to null.

As you can see, you can use as to successfully cast an object without any unexpected side effects. Unfortunately, as you can also see, using casting via the as operator doesn't offer a type-cast error at runtime.

The truth is that the as operator is useful, but it doesn't offer much in the way of development beyond readability. Although it successfully casts an Array, it offers no assistance in the way of debugging your system. This is why you should avoid the as operator for type casting if possible and instead use a cast operation.

Configuration Constants

Every tool has a particular feature that makes it useful. A screwdriver is a simple tool, and yet it's the most commonly used. As often as you use it, you keep it tucked away, out of sight. For whatever reason, a screwdriver isn't a conversation piece. This seems to be the case with one of my favorite features of the Flash IDE: the configuration (config for short) constants.

Throughout the build process of any rich Internet application (RIA), it's uncommon to succeed without the assistance of debugging. During this process, you can end up with numerous unnecessary lines of code that wind up getting compiled into your application. These lines are not unlike those of traces, but the Flash compiler offers a means to remove such declarations from your code. It also lets you eliminate specific statements if they're based on the condition of a config constant. The Flash compiler includes a few perks; config constants are one of them. Consider the following lines of code:

```
//handle intro if the swf is not loaded into a container
                if ( this.parent != null ) {
                        force_intro()
                }
```

Often, when working in a team environment, developers toggle code on and off when attempting to test and debug code that is meant to work with a framework after it's loaded into another .swf file. Typically, in such web site development, a loaded asset doesn't perform its intro until told to do so by the container. In order to test a file properly, you must either test it within the container or remove the code that prevents the .swf file from running its intro.

The previous code demonstrates a conditional statement that runs a particular operation if the parent of the .swf file doesn't exist. Suppose this conditional statement runs in the constructor of the document class. Because the .swf file runs outside of the container, there is no parent; therefore you force the intro to occur on your application. Throughout the duration of the build, you add a slew of conditionals to ensure that things work according to your needs. The more you allow such conditionals to build up, the less likely you are to remove them later, and the more memory you use.

This is where the beauty of the config constants comes into play. If you construct your code around an intended config constant, you can easily remove those lines from the compilation of the .swf file, therefore reducing file size and enhancing performance.

To use config constants, choose File ➤ Publish Settings ➤ Flash ➤ Settings ➤ Config Constants, as shown in **Figure 2-10**.

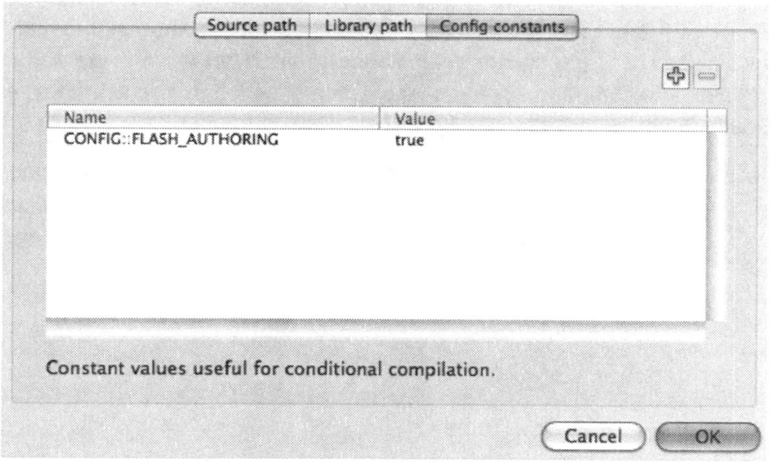

Figure 2-10. Configuration constants for conditional compiles

As you can see, FLASH_AUTHORING is supplied automatically. You can supply as many constants as you please by clicking + in the upper-right corner.

Just like any conditional used in your code, a config constant must satisfy a requirement. As long as the condition is met, the code within the conditional statement is added to your compiled .swf file; otherwise, say goodbye to the code, because it is *not* added. This is the beauty of config constants versus plain old conditional statements.

Here's an example of a config constant used around a conditional statement for conditional compiling:

```
if ( CONFIG::FLASH_AUTHORING == true){
        force_intro();
}
```

The only drawback to config constants is that they're specific to the Flash IDE. Recent releases of the FlashDevelop application include added support for config const, as well as Flash Builder.

ActionScript Editors

When you use encapsulation, the more modular your code, the more objects your system can use. Understanding their relationships is crucial in managing the objects in your application; but for ease of maintenance and development, having a good editor is very important.

Unfortunately, the Flash IDE doesn't have the proper tools to enable effective RIA construction. The power of the IDE lies in its library and the ease of using a visual editor to develop down-and-dirty assets.

Many phenomenal Flash/Flex editors are available that warrant your attention. They include Adobe Flash Builder, FlashDevelop, IntelliJ IDEA, and—my personal favorite—FDT. Each does a terrific job of providing code hints as you type; these hints visually help you recall the available interface without having to pause your thought process.

Profiling is another great bundle. Why just debug a system, when at the same time you can see all aspects of how it's functioning? FDT and Flash Builder tap into the sampler package and reveal the memory used, the instances currently used, and the cumulative instance count. Working in these editors gives you many tools for creating classes and can often save you time. Code completion, live warnings, and refactoring are some of the time-saving techniques that can help you get ahead of a deadline.

Finally, one of the most useful aspects of these editors is the visual representation of your project's packages and their contents (see **Figure 2-11**). The days of opening and closing folders are long gone, and searching for a specific class is easy as 1, 2, 3. I don't know where I'd be without my FDT editor.

Figure 2-11. The `flash.sampler` package and its contents, as viewed in FDT

These are just a few of the many features offered by ActionScript editors. Some of them have advantages over the others. With that said, it's wise to use the same editor as your team members, because each editor has particular behaviors and/or exclusive features. This doesn't mean you should merely follow your team's lead—after you research the capabilities of each editor, take the time to discuss their benefits with your team and suggest how a particular editor can improve overall development.

Summary

The idea that sometimes things don't go your way is important as a guide during development. You can strive for optimal flexibility, but you can only do so much to loosen the binds of your architecture while keeping it structurally sound. As revealed through the `Vector` class, you must make do with what your foundations allow. You must strive for loosely coupled relationships among your objects, perhaps by downcasting to `Object`. If this is the case, you need to use compile-time and runtime errors to help fix mismatches among `Object` casting. Always do what is best to keep your application on track.

Understanding the impact of an object in your language is a great strength. It enables you to realize potential weaknesses the object may have on your system. You must consider all aspects of the language you use in order to achieve the best implementation of your design patterns. By gathering information about your system and its objects, you can build efficiently.

Key Points

- Design patterns don't include language specifics.
- The preferred manner of inheritance in ActionScript 3.0 is fixed inheritance.
- Design patterns require appropriate attention with consideration to memory management.

- The `Flash.sampler` package gives you insight into each object's impact on memory resources.
- Pointers may prevent the garbage collector from dumping memory.
- Design patterns pass object references for delegation and modification.
- ActionScript 3.0 doesn't recognize abstract classes.
- Always deselect the Automatically Declare Stage Instances option.
- Strong typing facilitates the proper use of objects in a system.
- Strong typing optimizes ActionScript bytecode.
- Avoid the as operator for up/down casts if possible.
- Use config constants for conditional compilation.
- `getDefinition` and `getDefinitionByName` return `Class` object.
- Special editors provide special tools for ActionScript developers.

Chapter 3

Decision-Making and Planning

The ability to make wise decisions is important when you're doing something as demanding as building rich Internet applications (APIs). One decision you may have to make involves choosing to do what is best for your or what is best for the team. The choice may seem obvious on paper, especially if you're a team player—but late nights and frustration with a project may begin to influence your decision about what's best for you rather than the team.

Making poor decisions about object-oriented practices may result in even more late nights and greater frustration for both you and your team. You can only make a sound decision when you really understand the problem you're trying to solve. Only when you've analyzed any and all problem domains can you determine a plan of action. As Louis Pasteur said, "Chance favors the prepared mind"; and if you're prepared, then if and when change is introduced, you'll be able to address it effectively.

Object-Oriented Analysis (OOA)

Using OOP with RIAs offers a practical way to divide code into smaller and more manageable pieces. The act of OOP, as explained in Chapter 1, means strictly adhering to principles that enable your architecture to be flexible, modular, and maintainable. Your code will be properly encapsulated and separated from the inner workings of other behaviors that may require change. OOP, in short, helps you build quality objects that in turn enable flexibility, modularity, and easier maintenance.

Often, developers jump right in and implement objects at the beginning of a new project. Doing so molds rigidity into the system's foundation. This "shoot first, ask questions later" mentality is understandable when time is working against you, but it will come back to haunt you. The next time you're driving over a bridge or leaning over the balcony of a 10-story building, consider the possible result if a civil engineer had jumped right into the construction phase of the project.

In order to properly and successfully use a good structure, you must know all possible behaviors before you can devise a plan. You learn about the behaviors through an iterative process known as *object-oriented analysis (OOA)*.

OOA is a process that aims to reveal all necessary behaviors and objects related to a given problem domain. Only when you've completed an analysis can you hope to construct a design. Such a design can then be used as the blueprint from which you model the implementation of a system. This design process has come to be known as *object-oriented design* (OOD).

Utilizing a micro-site from past experience, I will demonstrate the OOA & OOD process.

Case Study

Suppose that as an RIA developer, you've been tasked to develop a microsite to promote a new line of windbreakers. The client has requested a site to demonstrate the weather conditions for which their product is the optimal apparel. They would like to focus on each product, the details of the product, and colors it comes in. In addition, the client wants to show each product being used in the specified weather conditions.

At this point, you may or may not be a part of the conception phase; it depends on a clear definition of team roles. In this case, let's assume that a creative team has already conceptualized what this site will look like, and you've just been tasked to build it.

The Kick-Off

The client request that was delivered to the designers is delivered to the developer team along with the designed compositions shown in **Figure 3-1**. Although the discussion in this section may vary based on your position and or job description, as a developer, your role is ultimately to assemble the features required by a client using the presentation shown by a designer. Although the compositions reveal the end result of the project, they don't deliver everything you need. A picture is worth a thousand words, so it's easy for a message to be improperly delivered to the viewer. The intended audience may be the developer or the client. The people who see the comps can easily have their own interpretations, which can lead to future confusion. This is why your first decision as a developer must be to properly analyze the system.

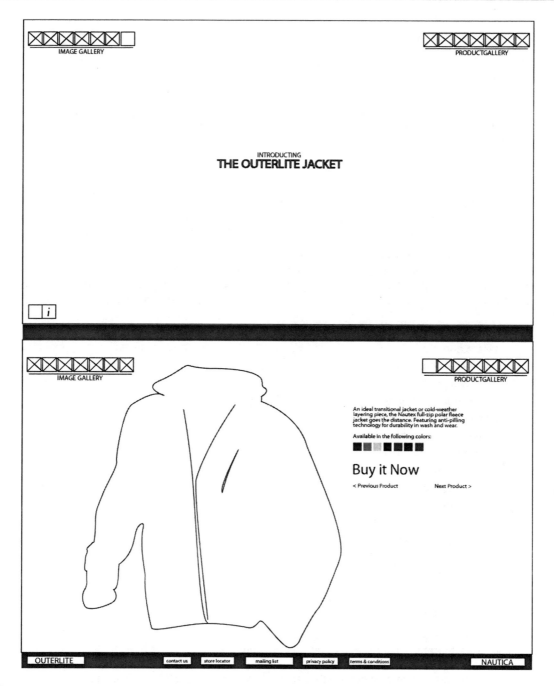

Figure 3-1. The above image is the wireframe of the comps that I received.

Turning Off the Volume

The material on the site has been designed by professionals to do exactly what it's supposed to do. It may be supposed to grab your attention or guide your eyes to follow a particular path. Much like Odysseus and his men traveling past the islands of the sirens, you mustn't allow the designer's techniques to lure you in.

Instead of focusing on what is presented, you need to focus on what is necessary to devise a quality application. To keep yourself from being swayed by the visual messaging of the comps, you can rely on use cases to demonstrate the system's goals.

Use Case Scenario

A *use case* is nothing more than sequential actions performed within the confines of a scenario. These steps move toward accomplishing a specific goal. Each scenario has a clear beginning and ending, and there is always only one goal per use case. In short, a use case is a story that explains the system.

Depending on the agency for which you work, getting your hands on the statement of work (SOW) is the optimal way to determine your use case. A SOW is a document that details the project requirements and defines the agency's work activities. If you don't have access to a SOW, ask the designer to detail the steps their comp demonstrates, as they understand them, and then walk through the comp with them.

Here's are possible case scenarios for the example site:

- User Landing
  A user comes to the site.
  The user views a blurb about the product.
  The site navigation is revealed.
- Product Gallery
  A user selects a product.
  Display product image and detailed specs.
  User purchases the product.
- Image Gallery
  A user selects a photo image.
  Display weather conditions photo.
  Present information callout.
  User browses images.
  Update information callout.

Because I didn't have a SOW available, I relied on the designer's understanding. You should build to these specifications and not to the visuals, because the visuals are more likely to change.

Your goal is to get rid of specifics in order to remain loose and general, because design assets may not be completed yet and, therefore, may change. Yet from the moment your kickoff began, so did the countdown toward your deadline. This is another reason to only concern yourself with the features requested by the client: these are the aspects of your system that are most solid and least likely to change.

Requirements from the Features

When you devise a list of features, it is possible to obtain additional requirement details from them. Keep in mind I say "possible" because many things can go hand in hand. For example, if I say "peanut butter and _____," you may reply, "jelly." This is because these two things often go together. Although your project features as stated may only include peanut butter, the clients may not realize that jelly is a key requirement for the peanut butter to be possible. Also, consider the creation of a form. While it may appear that this means a client requires a submit button and an email field, one may not consider the necessities of an error box, or the success message.

Therefore, site design takes advantage of the needs and wants of the users, and inferences are made to better support the abilities of the user.

Note: Requirements from features are susceptible to change, so it's important not to mix them with what you assume to be constants.

If you review the features from the User Landing use-case scenario, you can determine related requirements for the project build. For instance, as **Figure 3-2** shows, you can deduce that a preloader and a footer are possible development requirements, even though they aren't marked as client features.

Dev Requirements

User Landing

1. A user comes to the site ———————————— Preloader
2. The user views a blurb about the product
3. Navigation enters ———————————— Footer

Figure 3-2. Supplemental requirements of the User Landing use-case scenario

You need the preloader when the site is ready to progress to the landing page. It is a way for users to understand that a process is taking place and they should be patient.

The footer is a general feature that's part of the navigation. Specifics of what's in the footer are generally geared toward the client and therefore don't need to be added now, because they may change.

The Product Gallery use case, shown in **Figure 3-3**, illustrates that you need to write XML to contain a product and any specs the product requires. This way, you can keep specifics out of your system. And because the XML will be loaded into the application, you can adjust its language without having to republish any code. Because you don't know how many products you're showing at a given time, your system doesn't include this information and only knows to iterate over the number of children in the XML.

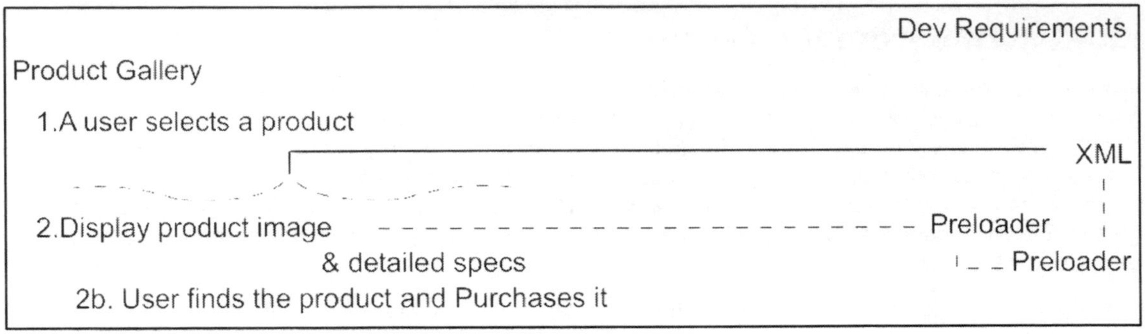

Dev Requirements

Product Gallery

1. A user selects a product

XML

2. Display product image — — — — — — — — — — — — — — — — Preloader

& detailed specs

Preloader

2b. User finds the product and Purchases it

Figure 3-3. Supplemental requirements of the Product Gallery use-case scenario

This raises the fact that the XML needs to be loaded. At this moment you're uncertain whether it will be loaded before or after the landing page. And you know that if a product image needs to be displayed, you must load it as well. Again, when will it be loaded? For now it's irrelevant, because all you're doing is fulfilling supplemental requirements.

According to the client, each client has some form of navigation to go along with it. This is marked in **Figure 3-3**.

Finally, as shown in **Figure 3-4**, another preloader is required to help load the scenic photos.

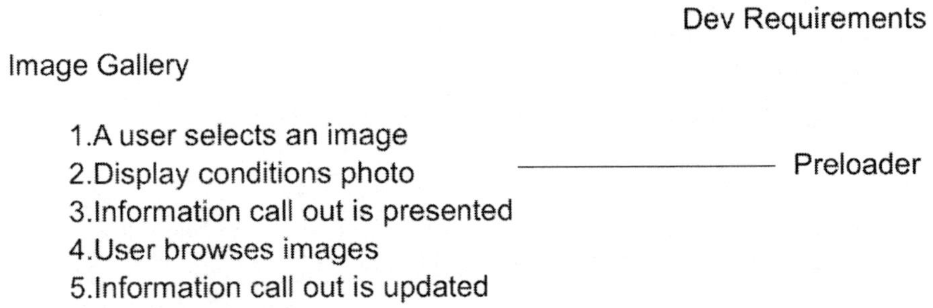

Dev Requirements

Image Gallery

1. A user selects an image
2. Display conditions photo ——————————— Preloader
3. Information call out is presented
4. User browses images
5. Information call out is updated

Figure 3-4. Supplemental requirements of the Photo Gallery use-case scenario

Flow Chart

Flow charts are another tool that can prevent dilemmas. A flow chart maps out the possible sequence of steps the user may take when navigating through a system. It's beneficial because it helps to point out essential concepts that may not have been designed or considered. For example, if the user is asked to submit a form, what happens if an error occurs? How is the user redirected back into the system? What paths can they take from that point?

Figure 3-5 shows the different scenarios a user may face, based on their decisions. The user may directly or indirectly take the actions on the system.

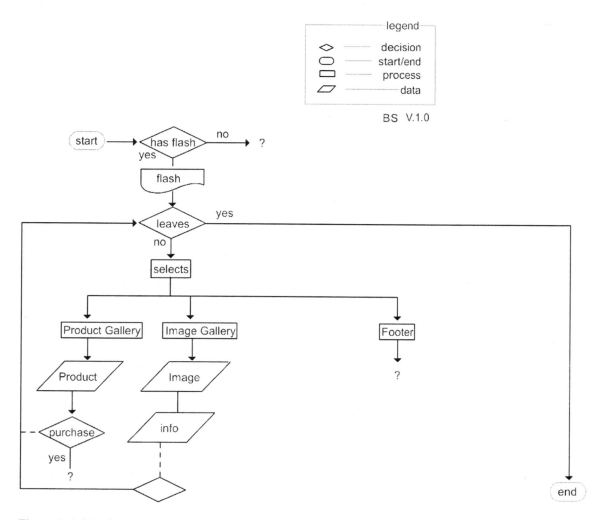

Figure 3-5. The flow chart of your current user experience

Many software applications create flow charts, but the simplest approach is always to use paper. It's not necessary to add a legend or note about who generated the flow chart, although doing so can help someone who hasn't viewed the chart before—everyone has their own style in producing a flow chart, and you want to ensure that the viewer clearly understands the flow. What *is* required is the flow chart's version number. This helps viewers to understand the model's progression, lets you track changes, and indicates the version in which a change took place.

As indicated by the question marks in **Figure 3-5**, some paths require more clarification. What happens if a user decides to purchase a product? Are they redirected? Do you need to devise a new section? What if a user doesn't have Flash—does the site have an HTML page? And what if the user clicks within the footer? Do they go to an external page, or do you display new content in the current page? The answers to these questions should be as generic as possible so they don't interfere with your current process.

Performance

The next step in being preemptive toward problems requires both generic and specific information about your current system. You need to ensure that the site will work optimally before you back yourself into a corner with the implementation. Before you get into the next round of analysis, you should make sure you consider the limitations of ActionScript 3.0. Such limitations include the frame rate and its dependence on the browser's redraw speed, which depends on the user's processor and connection (such as wireless or high-speed Ethernet). You also need to be aware of the number of server requests, the amount of time it takes to parse an XML file, and, always, how much memory your application requires. The Flash player is a browser plug-in, and this is also performance related. If a user doesn't have the player installed, how will your application perform?

The type of RIA you're building also helps determine the performance issues you need to consider. For instance, if you're building a desktop application, you don't need to be concerned with the browser's connection to your application's frame rate. Of course, there may be other performance issues you need to be concerned about.

Your first pass through the analysis doesn't reveal any cause for poor performance. But having done your due diligence, you know to be careful about a few particulars. As you continue to analyze your system, be aware of how you store and load data. During every iteration of the analysis, new issues may arise that you can't see at this stage.

Layering

You've gathered a satisfying amount of information from your initial analysis of the system. To recap what you have thus far, you've devised a use-case scenario to explain the features expected by the client, and you've determined what requirements accompany those features. From there, you determined whether additional requirements are necessary to ensure a smooth user experience. Finally, using the knowledge you've accumulated, you've noted any areas of performance concern that should be corrected before they cause issues in your system.

Layering is an iterative process that attempts to increase the amount of specifics to a structure in order to best combat unforeseen change. Of course, because change is a constant, anything may change at any time; but your work hasn't been fruitless. The immediate goal is to remain ahead of the changes by separating the generic from the specific and remaining flexible. While you gather information, remain aware of potential concerns for the application.

Your initial analysis of the system revealed a great deal of information you can use. But as you saw in the flow chart in **Figure 3-5**, a few questions need to be answered in order for the application to run smoothly. Eventually, all generics must become specifics, or you'll end up with an application that does nothing. You can consider each analytical pass to be another layer that tries to fill the gaps revealed by the layers below. Each pass grows more specific and reveals the modifications of behaviors that were once generic. The number of passes you make depends on the size of your application, the aspects of the application, and your desired level of magnification (that is, how closely you want to analyze each object).

Although each iterative pass may seem to analyze the same system, your analysis is applied to a new problem domain each time you add a layer of specifics. The repetition reveals the union (overlap) of objects in the system. This repetition makes you better acquainted with the system's requirements and objects, which lets you handle change efficiently.

The beauty of layering is that each layer represents additional system behaviors you've added. It also magnifies your bird's-eye view so you can zoom in on the system.

Analysis Continued

Having completed your first analytical pass, you must repeat the cycle to fill in the missing pieces. Currently you have three open-ended paths, as revealed in the flow chart in **Figure 3-5**. As long as paths remain open-ended, the system will include generalized behaviors as well as specialized behaviors. You need to concern yourself with the complete flow of the system.

Currently, you don't know what happens if the user doesn't have the Flash player plug-in, if the user clicks a footer link, or when a user purchases a product. We're informed that the site should prompt the user via an HTML document that that they need Flash to view the site. The other two questions can only be answered by the project manager and the designer, and the answers may or may not be simple. Therefore, you'll leave those questions unanswered until the answers are necessary.

Figure 3-6 reflects these changes, updates the legend to reveal a new symbol, and states the current version of the flow chart.

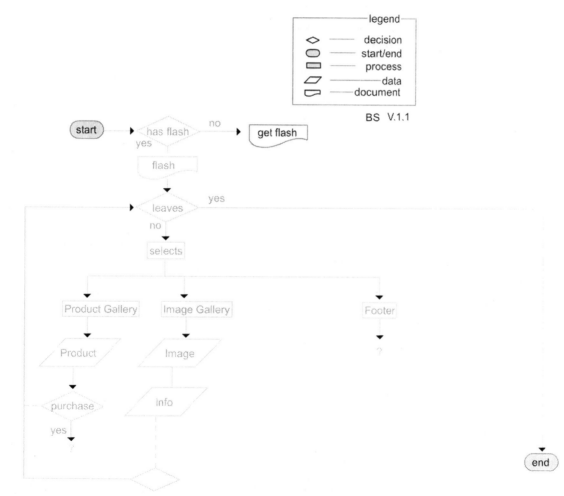

Figure 3-6. User flow chart reflecting the latest revisions

The Breakup

You're said to be working at a low level when you look at your system as a whole. This is because to view a system in its entirety, you must back up to a specific distance to be able to see everything. Much as in real life, you often have to increase your distance from multiple objects to see them in the same frame. As you back up or zoom out, you also minimize the details of the items you're trying to view. The loss of details lets you keep your focus on the system as a whole. When you manage to assess the big picture, you can begin to increase the magnification and look at details. The easiest way to do that is to break the whole into the sum of its parts.

Product Gallery

You've already seen the features necessary to the client. Now you need to consider the specifics that the designer has added to achieve those features. By viewing the comps and speaking with the designer, you can understand their vision of how the product gallery will be presented.

According to the designer, the steps involved in a user selecting a product in the product gallery are as shown in the following use-case scenario:

- Product Gallery
    - Product Selected
        1. Display product image and detailed specs.
            a. The user views the product image.
            b. The user views the description.
            c. The user views all available colors.
            d. The user views all available sizes.
            e. The user views interior navigation.
                i. The user can purchase the current product.
                ii. The user can navigate between products.

The new details added to the product-selection use-case scenario may also reveal developmental requirements that need to be added, as **Figure 3-7** shows.

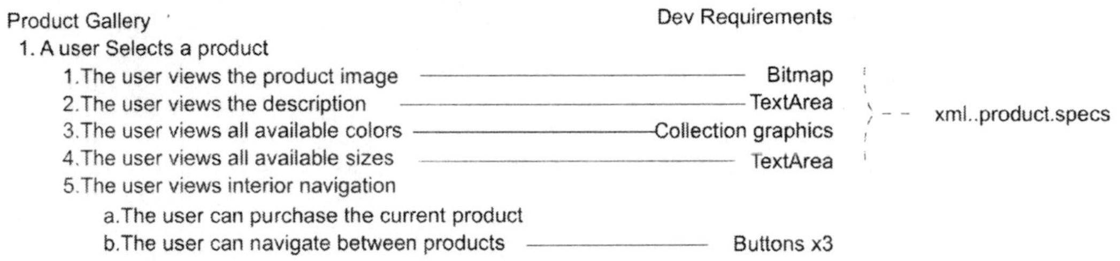

Product Gallery   Dev Requirements
   1. A user Selects a product
      1. The user views the product image ——————————— Bitmap
      2. The user views the description ——————————— TextArea   ⎫
      3. The user views all available colors ———————Collection graphics   ⎬ ─ ─ xml..product.specs
      4. The user views all available sizes ——————— TextArea   ⎭
      5. The user views interior navigation
         a. The user can purchase the current product
         b. The user can navigate between products ——————— Buttons x3

Figure 3-7. Updated requirements for the Product Gallery use case

You know you're using XML; and if multiple parts will be pulled in, you can separate them into different nodes of the XML. Given what the designer has in mind for the page that shows the product and its description, you know what type of elements to use. As shown in **Figure 3-7**, you can add references to specific objects in ActionScript 3.0. Where the page has text, you know you use a text field. Where the page uses images, you require bitmaps. Because there are two display colors, you need a collection of the graphics object. There is an in-page navigation where the designer lets the user purchase a product and enhances the user experience by supplying Previous and Back buttons. And on the topic of the buttons, this is a good opportunity to find out what occurs if the user clicks Buy It Now.

A quick conversation with the designer and the project manager reveals that you aren't responsible for the e-commerce section of the site. When a user clicks the Buy It Now button, they go to an external web page. You can reflect this in the flow chart, as shown in **Figure 3-8**.

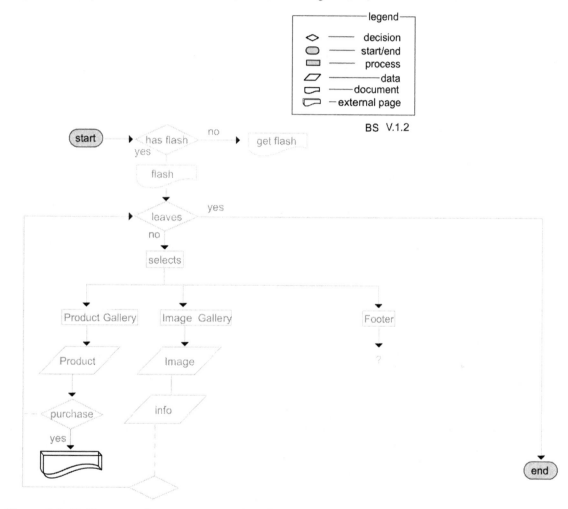

Figure 3-8. Making a purchase opens an external page.

Performance

Again you've reviewed and added to your system. Now you need to work on preventing performance problems: repeat the earlier performance analysis to see if you recognize any other potential issues due to your recent changes.

Nothing causes any concerns at the moment; but a problem could occur that's so small, it can't be foreseen. For example, an external link could hinder performance later, depending on what that page holds. Suppose you're using a sound analyzer. If a second page from another domain opens and plays sounds, your analyzer will fail due to a security error. Because the sound analyzer is global to all players, it reads bytes from every player. When bytes are served from a server other than yours, if you can't find a policy file with the proper permissions, the sound player will be prevented from reading those bytes.

Scenic Gallery

In discussing the designer's vision for the Image gallery, the designer reveals the approach used to lay out the design. Using this information, you can sprinkle another layer of specifics onto the original Image Gallery use-case scenario:

- Image Gallery

    1. An image is chosen displaying an outdoorsman wearing the product.

        f. The user views the image.
        g. The user views the image Information callout.
            i. The user clicks the information to read about the image.
            ii. The user can download the current image in one of three resolutions.

Again, you attempt to gather any supplemental requirements from the use case. **Figure 3-9** shows the necessary developmental requirements. Much as with the Product Gallery use case, you use XML to hold the information about the image.

Dev Requirements

Image Gallery
1. A scene is chosen displaying an outdoorsman wearing the product.
   1. The user views the image ———————————————————————— Bitmap
   2. The user views the Scene information callout ——————————————— Container – – xml..scenary.details
    2b. The user selects the Scene information callout ————————— TextArea
     a. The user clicks on the information to read about the scene
     b. The user can download the current scene in one of three chosen resolutions. — Buttons x3 ——— Progress bar

Figure 3-9. Developmental requirements for the Image Gallery

With the new information provided by the detailed use-case scenario, you again come across a possible break in the flow of the user experience. If a user decides to download the current image in one of three possible resolutions, you have to account for any issues that may arise. You need to be aware of the File Reference object that ActionScript 3.0 uses to download a file. File Reference lets you listen in on specific events, but it doesn't natively display any visual indication to the user about whether their download is complete or unsuccessful; it also doesn't display a progress bar during the download. You need to add information that the designer didn't think of. The updates shown in **Figure 3-10** reflect the latest revisions.

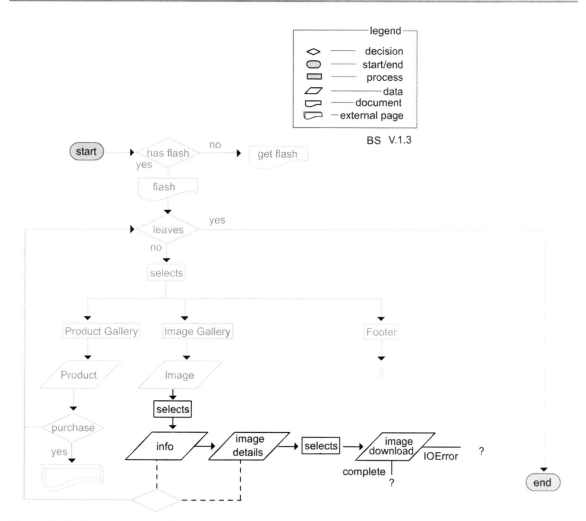

Figure 3-10. The sequence reflecting the download of an image

The downloaded image may or may not require an error box or a success box that informs the user the status of the image they selected.

Footer

Because the footer is part of the site's navigation, you need to refine what links a user will find there and the way you present them (see **Figure 3-11**):

1. The user views the footer navigation.

   The user clicks Contact Us.

   The user clicks Store Locator.

   The user clicks Mailing List.

The user clicks Privacy Policy.

The user clicks Terms & Conditions.

Product Gallery

   Dev Requirements

1.User views Footer Navigation enters ————————————————— Buttons x5

     1b.User clicks on Contact Us

     2b.User clicks on Store Locator

     3b.User clicks on Mailing List

     4b.User clicks on Privacy Policy

     5b.User clicks on Terms of Conditions

Figure 3-11. The footer has five buttons.

Again, we need to see if the footer links add to your system by talking to the designer and project manager to ensure these additional comps aren't overlooked. We're informed that we aren't expected to add functionality to the system to reflect the footer links; they will take the user to eternal pages. **Figure 3-12** shows the revised flow chart.

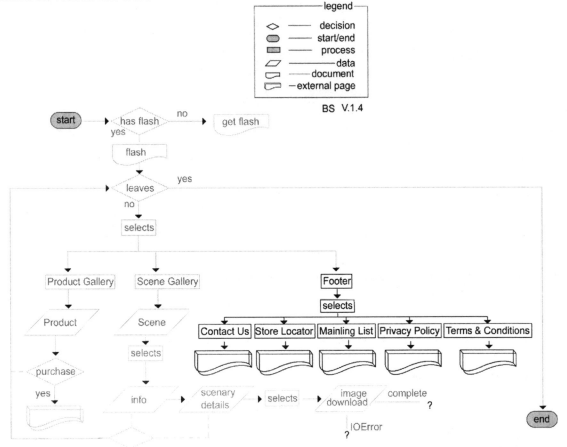

Figure 3-12. Each link in the footer opens an external page.

Because the footer doesn't add complexity, it shouldn't cause any performance issues.

Wrapping Up the Analysis

When you've explored all possible user paths, you can be confident that you've analyzed all client features, designer features, and developmental features for the system. Having an overview of the system along with each subsystem's parts gives you a starting point when determining objects and their associations during the design phase. Again, because change is a constant, you should have a documented list of all possible objects from your complete analysis before you make any further modifications.

In this case, the identified objects are as follows:

- Shell
  - Site-loader
- Site
  - Blurb
  - Navigation
    - Product
    - Image
    - Footer
  - Scenic Image XML
  - Image Gallery
    - Image XML
    - Image Preloader
    - Photo
    - Information Callout
      - Info photo
        - Information XML
        - Progress bar
        - Image description
  - Product image XML
  - Product Gallery
    - Product XML
    - Interior navigation
      - Buy It Now
      - Previous
      - Next
    - Image Preloader
    - Product image
    - Specs
      - Description

- Available colors
- Available sizes
- Buttons
- Footer
  - Contact Us
  - Store Locator
  - Mailing List
  - Privacy Policy
  - Terms & Conditions
  - Buttons

This list contains what you believe to be all objects required for the application; you can only confirm this by making proper object associations. You can identify how the objects work together to fulfill the requirements. Much like a brand-new jigsaw puzzle spread on a table, you must assemble the pieces you currently have in order to identify any missing pieces or revealing pieces you no longer need.

Object Oriented Design (OOD)

Now that you've completed the analysis phase, you can begin to think about the objects and their relationships. At this stage, you evaluate each object's necessity and continue to look for other objects that are required for the intended behaviors between associations. Being able to orchestrate the objects before you attempt to implement them gives you a greater ability to adapt their behaviors.

The following steps are required before you implement objects:

1. Review the current objects, and remove any duplicates or extraneous objects you've documented.

2. Document appropriate names and behaviors for the remaining objects. Each object should have only one defined behavior, which means it has only one reason to ever need to change.

3. Based on the behaviors, separate generalized objects from any behaviors that may require change. If behaviors don't vary, there is no need for an abstract class.

4. Make associations, and create new objects if needed to achieve specific behaviors.

Unfortunately, to develop optimal associations and reuse elements, you must be aware of the many ways to do so. Even with years of experience, your object associations may prevent you from architecting a framework that enables your object-oriented goals. For now, you must stop here, to avoid making improper decisions about your objects until you know more about design patterns. You continue the OOD phase of this case study in Chapter 11.

Summary

OOP, meaning working with objects, doesn't help you discover all the objects required for a system. But OOA does.

As you've seen in this chapter's case study, iterative sweeps and incremental additions to the system help you develop the requirements to complete the system's user flow. By remaining distant from the specifics, you can view the entire system. And by slowly layering on the specifics, you're better able to see how they may affect the behavior or performance of the application, as well as recognize potential pitfalls before the build begins. The analysis phase, as repetitive and arduous as it is, is a must to achieve maximum flexibility in a system.

The case study illustrates why change is a constant. First and foremost when developing an application, you must pay strict attention to capturing all of the client's desired features. The designer may attempt to enhance these features through presentation and/or user experiences, and may inadvertently make client-requested features less prominent or inject a feature that increases your workload. For example, if the designer added thumbnails for Facebook and Twitter icons, your workload could potentially increase by two days or more, depending on the additional screens, behaviors, or technology required.

Proper incremental analysis enables you to anticipate areas of concern during review and design, rather than during implementation.

OOD, on the other hand, uses conceptualized objects from the analysis and devises flexible and loosely coupled associations between them. OOD lets you realize class behaviors, establish elements for reuse, and reduce the dependencies among them.

Key Points

- Building a perfect system is an iterative process.
- You should do most work on paper because you won't try to salvage it and it's faster.
- When you write code, you instinctually try to fix existing code.
- OOA and OOD make up 80% of project development.
- Ideas are often compounded.
- A flow chart's version becomes a log of the analysis performed on the system.
- Use-case scenarios demonstrate the steps taken toward accomplishing a goal.
- OOA uses iterative passes to reveal all behaviors in the project.
- OOD models the associations of realized requirements.

Chapter 4

Intro to Design Patterns

Although many developers were slow to adopt object-oriented programming (OOP), in the 1990s a handful of computer scientists at IBM were making strides in devising structures based on object-oriented principles. They addressed solutions to reoccurring programmatic issues that decreased the scalability and maintainability of their applications. In their debut book, *Design Patterns: Elements of Reusable Object-Oriented Software* (Erich Gamma, Richard Helm, Ralph Johnson, and John M. Vlissides; Addison-Wesley, 1994), the so-called Gang of Four demonstrated the practicality of using OOP.

As you saw in Chapter 3, you can determine a list of objects that you may be able to implement into your application. Although analysis reveals such objects, it doesn't reveal the means by which these objects can collaborate with and message one another in a flexible structure. The many variations among object-oriented languages helps as well as hinders our efforts to architect a flexible structure. You also need a clear understanding of the benefits an object-oriented language provides; hence the inclusion of Chapter 2 in this book.

Without adequate OO knowledge, developers can still use object collaborations, but at the cost of efficiency, possible structural flexibility, and with the potential for personal frustrations.

Not all developers fall victim to such dilemmas. Experienced developers over time have learned numerous techniques they use to combat flexibility issues. As each project changes, such solutions are modified and tweaked to suit the new variations.

At the suggestion of OOP pioneers (James Coplien, for example), many developers have documented the implementations they use to overcome particular problems. This documentation provides a catalog of solutions that overcome the lack of flexibility in the design of collaborative objects.

Design Patterns Catalog

Before ActionScript was a language, the answers to many programmatic challenges had already been tested, refined, solved, and documented. Many of these are probably obstacles you have, at some point, struggled to work around. These issues existed long before you or me and will always remain in this field. This is because change is a constant.

What began as theories and hacks came to be time-tested solutions to reoccurring problems that developers face. These patterns provide solutions to the need for flexibility of behaviors, structure, and creation of collaborative objects in an application.

In most cases, these patterns target the objects themselves, using dynamic binding and polymorphism; others deal with the code that is fixed in classes and their subclasses. Design patterns introduce solutions you may not have previously seen or known about.

In addition to providing solutions, design patterns serve as a language developers can use to describe an arrangement of code. The more familiar you become with specific patterns, the easier it will be to realize how they can help you loosen the couplings between objects and achieve a more reusable, scalable, maintainable system.

Selecting Patterns

Over time, developers are drawn to certain patterns and eventually become so familiar with those patterns that they use them almost without thinking. More important than your affinity for specific patterns is choosing a pattern based on the circumstances, or what the problem dictates. By analyzing the problem at hand, you can arrive at the necessary pattern.

Many patterns have been cataloged according to their purpose, the category to which they pertain, and their name. This book focuses on three categories: creational, behavioral, and structural. The following definitions are from *Design Patterns: Elements of Reusable Object-Oriented Software*:

> *Creational patterns abstract the instantiation process. They help make a system independent of how its object are created, composed, and represented.*

> *Behavioral patterns are concerned with algorithms and the assignment of responsibilities between objects. They describe not just patterns of objects or classes but also the patterns of communication between them.*

> *Structural patterns are concerned with how classes and objects are composed to form larger structures.*

Pattern Identification

Every pattern has a specific name. This name is the identifier by which a solution is known and referred to by programmers. In the case of a design pattern, the name symbolizes the objects used, the collaboration in which they work, and the behaviors they possess.

Reading a Design Pattern

The football players in **Figure 4-1** may be in the right positions, but you can't tell how they work together to achieve their goal. The simple use of lines and arrows brings the strategy to life, indicating the relationships of the players as shown in **Figure 4-2**.

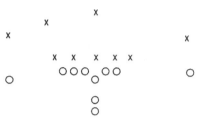

Figure 4-1. Representation of a team formation

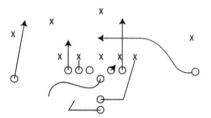

Figure 4-2. Representation of a team's strategic game play

A professional developer's design-pattern books are much like the playbook of a professional team, showing the actions of every athlete on the field. But in the developer's case, the star athletes are objects.

Why do you need to be able to read a design pattern? Simple. Design patterns aren't lines of code that can be easily copied and pasted into your application. Instead, they illustrate the means to conquer a specific problem via diagrams like the one in **Figure 4-2**. As you've seen, no two object-oriented languages are the same; and therefore not all implementations are the same, even if the difference is a mere matter of syntax. What does remain the same is the mental model the language mirrors. Think of a design pattern as a seed waiting to blossom with your help.

In order to achieve maximum flexibility, patterns often use added levels of indirection, which can complicate object-oriented designs. Being able to understand the ways in which a pattern is presented can make all the difference in your ability to understand it. They will illustrate the object distinctions and the relationships they possess.

UML

As you may know, Unified Modeling Language (UML) is the tool used to lay out all object-oriented designs. It's the language spoken between an architect and a developer, and it's the standard used to represent model-driven architecture.

Having a standard ensures that models can be understood by developers using varying software languages. This is an advantage, because to be adopted by the widest possible audience, patterns should avoid language specifics. To read a design pattern, you need to be able to properly interpret its UML class diagram.

The Class Diagram

The class diagram is the most common form of modeling you'll see in design patterns. These diagrams, as the name suggests, expose the classes used in a system/subsystem and the relationships among them. Class diagrams don't show the steps an object takes to message another; sequential diagrams and interaction diagrams illustrate that behavior, which is beyond the scope of this book.

Classes

The classes in a class diagram represent specific elements of the system or subsystem used in the pattern. Classes in a design pattern diagram typically expose only the public methods to which another object can message. This is because the diagram is only concerned with exposing aspects that reflect the relationships among the objects, not implementations. However, some attributes are often included to further illustrate object behaviors.

Class Name
+ public property   : type - private property   : type # protected property : type
+ public signature - private signature # protected signature

Figure 4-3. A typical Class Diagram

As illustrated in **Figure 4-3** attributes and behaviors can be seen following symbols that denote the appropriate visibility of the member.

Relationships

The objects in each system serve special roles, and their relationships help reveal how they're used. Some relationships indicate collaborations, some compositions, and some indicate subclasses. The relationships among system classes are represented using association and generalization.

Association

Associations among objects are illustrated by the way objects in a class diagram are connected to each another. The simplest way to indicate a relationship is to draw a line connecting two classes (see **Figure 4-4)**. This is referred to as a *common association*.

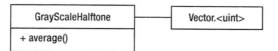

Figure 4-4. Illustrates a common association between `Vector.<uint>` and `GrayScaleHalftone`

Although the line signifies the connection between the two classes, the diagram doesn't specify ownership or the flow of communication between the objects. Some diagrams remedy this lack of specifics by using association roles; to do so, you add text above the association, explaining the relationship. In **Figure 4-4**, you could identify the objects' roles by adding uses > above the association, indicating that `GrayScaleHalftone` uses the vector, and not the other way around.

Often, the line between objects in a diagram is dashed or dotted, representing an object or behavioral implementation:

- Object implementation: A dashed line from one class to another represents the instantiation of an object. The dashed line begins at the object initiator and points to the class that will be instantiated.

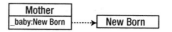

- Behavioral implementation: When a behavior supplies a specific implementation, a dashed line flows from the method to a callout that shows the specific behavior.

Aggregation

An aggregated relationship is one in which multiple parts are combined to produce a distinct object. You can think of an aggregation as a "has-a" relationship: the whole is produced by the sum of its parts. The behaviors of the parts aren't limited to benefitting the whole they help create. An unfilled diamond connecting the whole to a part defines the relationship as an aggregation; it signifies the object's ability to exist independently of the whole.

An example of aggregation is the relationship of an RSS feed to a blog, where the feed is created from the combination of many articles. Without the articles, the RSS feed can't exist; but the articles exist independently of the RSS on the blog (see **Figure 4-7**).

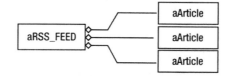

Figure 4-7. An illustration of 3 Generic Articles as an aggregate to some RSS feed.

Composition

Composition is a type of association in which one or more objects together produce a whole, and exist only to perform behaviors on that whole. Due to this dependence, the parts are meaningless as individual objects outside their roles within the whole. The UML representation of a composition relationship is a solid diamond connecting the part to the whole (see **Figure 4-8**).

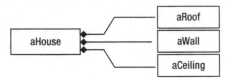

Figure 4-8. House requires a roof, walls, and a ceiling to fulfil the role of a house

Generalization

The last type of association is generalization, which you can think of as inheritance. The hierarchy among objects is identified by a common association from the subclass to its superclass. An unfilled arrowhead appears at the superclass end of the connecting line (see **Figure 4-9**).

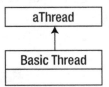

Figure 4-9. Using a generalized association to an abstract class aThread

Interfaces

Much like a class, an interface's name appears in the first segment of the UML diagram; its public method is shown in the second segment (see **Figure 4-10**). The fact that this is an interface is indicated by the interface declaration above the name, prefixed by two left arrows (<<) and suffixed by two right arrows (>>).

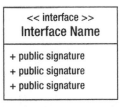

Figure 4-10. A defined interface in a class diagram

Many object-oriented languages, including ActionScript 3.0, don't support abstract classes. For this reason many class diagrams display an association from an implementation of an object to an interface.

Chapter Summary

This chapter explained how to approach design patterns as they are documented, and intended for use. We learned that a design pattern is the core of a solution.

No matter what Object-Oriented Language a programmer may use, a solution should be readily available to them by understanding the core of such a solution. A design pattern's documentation addresses the necessary objects and their associations in a manner that is unspecific to a programming language. Each documentation is noted with the use of the Unified Modeling Language, and, therefore, a programmer should be familiar with UML in order to understand how to read a design pattern, as well as architect his or her own Object-Oriented Designs.

Chapter 4 concludes the discussion of the necessary aspects of Object Oriented Programming and the pre-requisites of the upcoming chapters.

Key Points

- Design patterns are solutions to common object-oriented design dilemmas.

- Design patterns are divided into three categories: creational, behavioral, and structural.

- Creational patterns abstract the instantiation process.

- Behavioral patterns are concerned with algorithms and the assignment of responsibilities between objects.

- Structural patterns are concerned with how classes and objects are combined to form larger structures.

- A common association is illustrated by connecting objects with a thin line.

- Composition is a relationship among objects that share a similar lifeline.

- Aggregation is a whole made up of independent parts.

- Class diagrams, sequential diagrams, and interaction diagrams can be used to design collaborations.

- UML stands for Unified Modeling Language.

- Inheritance can be signified using an interface.

- Design patterns don't reflect a specific object-oriented language.

Upcoming Chapters

Chapter 4 is only an introduction to design patterns. The information here is supported, and reinforced in the chapters thoroughly discussing design patterns, Chapters 6-8. After this chapter, you will be able to test your knowledge from the first four chapters before proceeding to Chapters 6-8.

I encourage you to read these chapters in order, because the discussion of one pattern may reference a previous pattern. All the examples have been written to best illustrate how a design pattern appears in an actual application. As you read the code for each example, remember that patterns shouldn't be taken at face value; the code that illustrates each pattern is intended to solve an issue particular to the example. Remember, a design pattern suggests how to solve a common dilemma; it doesn't show you specifically how it should be implemented in every scenario.

Chapter 5

Q&A

It's no surprise that everyone has their own style of learning new material. Some learn material from hearing it, some from reading it, and some by trial and error. Object-oriented programming covers a vast amount of material, and books often fail to offer a means of validation about how well you've learned the information. I have always found this to be frustrating, because I prefer to have immediate feedback about how well I've understood what I read.

This chapter provides two quizzes consisting of 50 questions each, to provide you with immediate feedback about how well you know the material covered in Chapters 1-4. The questions pertain to OOP and its use with the ActionScript 3.0 object-oriented language. Due to the advanced nature of the material, some questions may be answered with previous understandings before this book. Because some people learn best from explanations provided after a test, the quizzes include detailed explanations. You won't be scored or judged on your answers, so you can use this chapter as a way to further your understanding of object-oriented thought processes in ActionScript 3.0.

Quiz 1

Understanding object-oriented programming is easy.   True   ⟨ False ⟩

1. Circle the best answer.

Learning object-oriented programming is a(n) _____ process.

      Slow   Iterative   Cumbersome   Arduous

2. Fill in the blank.

There are _____ principles of object-oriented programming.

3. What are the principles of object-oriented programming?

_____   _____

_____   _____

_____   _____

4. Match each OOP principle to the correct definition.

__ ensures properties can't be changed without your permission.

__ should possess only one behavior.

__ works well with dynamic binding.

__ allows behaviors to change.

A. Encapsulation   B. Inheritance   C. Polymorphism   D. Data hiding

5. External definitions can have custom name spaces. True   False

6. Fill in the blanks.

Object-oriented programming is the practice of creating a software architecture that enables _____ through _____ design.

7. Circle the best answer.

An object-oriented programmer is _____.

more advanced in coding   more strategic in developing

8. Match the characteristics with the programming practices.

Procedural programming   Faster performance

                                          Slower performance

Object-oriented programming   Routines

                                          Subroutines

                                          Methods

                                          Behaviors

9. Complete the sentence.

The nature of a subclass is to _____

_____.

10. List the three directives that are understood as external definitions.

_____

_____

_____

11. Fill in the blank.

_____ classes have an internal hashtable.

12. In the following code, is ClassB sealed or dynamic?

```
package
{
    import flash.display.Sprite;

    dynamic public class ClassA extends Sprite
    {
    }
}


package
{
    public class ClassB extends ClassA
    {
    }
}
```

13. How can you modify a behavior of a class that is marked final?

_____

_____

_____

_____

14. What are the uses of packages and the names of external definitions?

_____

_____

_____

_____

15. Why should you use function casting such as TYPE(expression) in AS 3.0?

_____

_____

_____

_____

16. What is an example of a wrong time to use function casting such as
TYPE(expression) in AS 3.0?

_____

_____

_____

_____

17. Circle the answer that best completes the sentence.

An interface can include _____.

    Getters and setters

    Visibility modifiers

    Attributes

    Algorithms

18. Static is a visibility modifier.   True   False

19. Given the following code, which answer is correct?

```
package
{
    public interface ISpeak
    {
```

```
        function speak() : void
    }
}


package
{
    public class Human
    {
        public function speak() : void
        {
            trace( 'hello' );
        }
    }
}




package
{
    public class Cat implements ISpeak
    {
        public function speak() : void
        {
            trace( 'meow' );
        }
    }
}
```

A.   `var itSpeaks :ISpeak= ISpeak( new Human() ) ;`

B.   `var itSpeaks :ISpeak= new Cat() ;`

C.   `var itSpeaks :ISpeak= new Human() ;`

D.   Both A and B

20. Why would you instantiate a class?

_____

_____

_____

_____

21. Fill in the blank.

Inheritance is said to have a _____ coupled relationship.

22. How does the `MovieClip` from the library break encapsulation?

_____

_____

_____

_____

23. Circle the answer that best completes the sentence.

Object-oriented programming is _____.

     a structural device

     the act of making objects

24. OOP has a few downsides. List as many as you can.

_____

_____

_____

_____

_____

25. How do design patterns help developers?

_____

_____

_____

_____

26. List the three categories of design patterns.

_____

_____

_____

27. Fill in the blank.

A good rule of thumb is to never exceed more than ___ levels of inheritance.

28. What is the difference between interface inheritance and class inheritance?

_____

_____

_____

_____

29. Fill in the blanks.

One design principle is to favor _____ over _____.

30. Circle the answer that best completes the sentence.

Composition relies on _____.

     delegation

     tight coupling

     objects

     IS-A relationships

31. Fill in the blank.

The relationship shown is _____.

Mother
_baby:New Born

- - ► | New Born |

32. Match the items in the two columns.

This type checking hates poor code.	Compile-time type checking
This type checking doesn't like mismatches.	Runtime type checking

33. Explain when you would use an abstract class instead of an interface in AS 3.0.

_____

_____

_____

_____

34. List the differences between an abstract class and an interface in AS 3.0.

_____

_____

_____

_____

_____

_____

35. Circle the answer that best completes the sentence.

Object-oriented programming begins with _____.

    objects

    implementation

    collaboration

    factoring

36. Given the following classes, circle the term that best describes its encapsulation.

```
package
{
   public class CrestTartarAndCavityProtection extends ToothPaste
   {
      public function CrestTartarAndCavityProtection() : void
      {
      }

      public function fightTartar() : void
      {
      }

      public override function fightCavities() : void
      {
      }

      public function whitenTeeth() : void
      {
      }
   }
```

```
}
```

Cohesive   Incohesive

37. When do you *not* need to perform an analysis of a system?

_____

_____

_____

_____

38. Performance can change requirements.   True   False

39. Consider the following code:

```
package
{
   //Felidae is the Heirarchy of the cat family
   internal class Felidae
   {
      protected var _canPurr : Boolean;
      protected var _region : String;
      protected var _speed : int;

      public function run() : void
      {
      }

      public function sleep() : void
      {
      }

      public function eat() : void
      {
      }
   }
}


package
{
```

```
public final class Cougar extends Felidae
{
    public function Cougar()
    {
        _canPurr = true;
        _region = "South America";
        _speed = 40; // mph
    }
}
```

What conclusions can you draw about the application from the use of the `final` keyword?

_____

_____

_____

_____

40. Why is having a broad understanding of an object-oriented language important when dealing with design patterns?

_____

_____

_____

_____

41. Assign the appropriate access modifiers to achieve the following: the classes within `utils.color.type` should never be set by anything other than `ColorConverter`, but their `get` values can be read outside their package.

```
package utils.color{
  import utils.color.type.*


        static public  toLAB():LAB
        static public  toRGB():RGB
        static public  toXYZ():XYZ
    }
  }
```

```
package com.mosaic {
   static public  class ColorConverter{
      protected analyzeColor()
      protected colorDifference()
    }
  }
```

```
package utils.color.type {

  public class LabColor extends Object {
    _____ getL():uint
    _____ getA():uint
    _____ getB():uint
    _____ setL(val:uint):void
    _____ setA(val:uint):void
    _____ setB(val:uint):void
    }
  }
```

```
package utils.color.type {

  public class RGBColor extends Object {
    _____ getR():uint
    _____ getG():uint
    _____ getB():uint
    _____ setR(val:uint):void
    _____ setG(val:uint):void
    _____ setB(val:uint):void
    }
  }
```

If you need to add any definitions, do so here

```
package utils.color.type {
  import utils.color.mixer;
  public class XYZColor extends Object {
    _____ getX():uint
    _____ getY():uint
    _____ getZ():uint
    _____ setX(val:uint):void
    _____ setY(val:uint):void
    _____ setZ(val:uint):void
    }
  }
```

42. Fill in what is needed to ensure that someObject doesn't linger with the garbage collector when remove() is called.

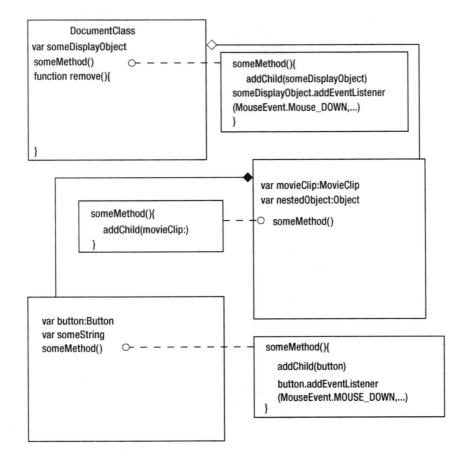

43. Explain what the top-level function getDefinitionByName is used for.

_____

_____

_____

44. Rank the likelihood of change among the following, where 1 means least likely to change and 5 means most likely to change.

__ Client requirements

__ Design layout

__ Transitions/Motion

__ User flow

__ Creative assets

45. Using the following table, which displays the bytes per object, how many bytes will SomeClass occupy?

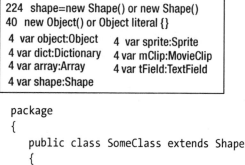

```
224  shape=new Shape() or new Shape()
40   new Object() or Object literal {}
4  var object:Object      4  var sprite:Sprite
4 var dict:Dictionary     4 var mClip:MovieClip
4 var array:Array         4 var tField:TextField
4 var shape:Shape
```

```
package
{
    public class SomeClass extends Shape
    {
        private var _tField : TextField;
        private var _obj : Object;

        public function SomeClass()
        {
            _obj = {};
        }
    }
}
```

SomeClass takes up _____ bytes.

46. On deployment, all documents used during analysis can be tossed out in celebration.
True   False

47. Why is it best to implement the disposable pattern as nothing more than a class interface?

_____

_____

_____

_____

_____

_____

_____

48. The time used during the build process is best spent in implementation.   True   False

49. All classes are expected to have their behaviors changed.   True   False

50. All classes created during a project are best left in the project's general source folders.
True   False

Answers to Quiz 1

Understanding object-oriented programming is easy   True   (False)

Explanation: Object-oriented programming is a very advanced concept, and is often misunderstood by some advanced programmers. Despite what some may say, understanding OOP isn't easy. Remember this through your frustrations.

1. Circle the best answer.

   Learning object-oriented programming is a(n) _____ process.

   Slow   (Iterative)   Cumbersome   Arduous

   Explanation: Although learning OOP is slow, cumbersome, and arduous, only *iterative* truly describes the process required to understand all OOP concepts. Much of OOP is a thought process that isn't often learned in a linear fashion.

2. Fill in the blank.

   There are <u>4</u> principles of object-oriented programming.

3. What are the principles of object-oriented programming?

Encapsulation	Inheritance
Polymorphism	Data hiding

4. Match each OOP principle to the correct definition.

   <u>D</u> ensures properties can't be changed without your permission.

   <u>A</u> should possess only one behavior.

   <u>C</u> works well with dynamic binding.

   <u>B</u> allows behaviors to change.

   A. Encapsulation   B. Inheritance   C. Polymorphism   D. Data hiding

5. External definitions can have custom name spaces. True   (False)

   Explanation: The `Dynamic`, `Final`, `Public`, and `internal` keywords are the only modifiers of a directive. Custom namespaces are allowed within external definitions as access modifiers of a property and/or behavior.

6. Fill in the blanks.

Object-oriented programming is the practice of creating a software architecture that enables <u>flexibility</u> through <u>modular</u> design.

Explanation: Through the use of objects, you can compartmentalize code, which lets you introduce polymorphism into your code more easily. The greater the separation between the system and the code that creates it, the more flexibility developers are granted.

7. Circle the best answer.

An object-oriented programmer is _____.

more advanced in coding   ⟨more strategic in developing⟩

Explanation: It's a misconception that if you do something on a daily basis, you must get to be amazing at it by the time you reach a certain age. There are plenty of cases that prove this is far from the truth. Most college basketball players, although great, don't make it to the NBA despite having played all their lives. Being an object-oriented programmer doesn't mean you're more advanced because you understand OOP; rather, you've embraced OOP for the structure it enables.

8. Match the characteristics with the programming practices.

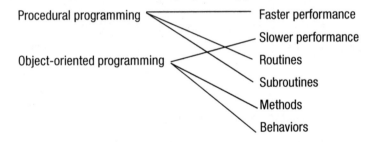

Procedural programming   Faster performance

                               Slower performance

Object-oriented programming   Routines

                               Subroutines

                               Methods

                               Behaviors

9. Complete the sentence.

The nature of a subclass is to <u>supply the behavior of an abstract method, or add a more specialized behavior to an existing behavior.</u>

10. List the three directives that are understood as external definitions.

> Interface

> Namespace

> Class

11. Fill in the blank.

<u>Dynamic</u> classes have an internal hashtable.

12. In the following code, is ClassB sealed or dynamic?

```
package
{
    import flash.display.Sprite

    dynamic public class ClassA extends Sprite
    {
    }
}
```

```
package
{
    public class ClassB extends ClassA
    {
    }
}
```

<u>Sealed</u>

Explanation: Remember from Chapter 2 that classes remain sealed unless specified as dynamic.

13. How can you modify a behavior of a class that is marked final?

<u>When a class itself is marked final, the only way to modify any behavior of the class is to open the file and modify it. But don't do so at any cost. That would break an OOP design principle: a class should be open for extension and closed for modification.</u>

Explanation: The final keyword ensures protection from modification by any means, short of overwriting the file's contents. This protection may not always be for the class's best interest but for yours. Consider a class that is broken but that will serve a key role in later development. By marking the class final, you can ensure that no team members will have any behaviors that are affected by future class modifications.

14. What are the uses of package structures and the names of external definitions?

The name of an external definition should precisely define the intended behavior the definition provides to an application. The defining package in which it resides elaborates on the associations it uses and provides additional context for the named behavior. Finally, package structures guarantee uniqueness among definitions.

15. Why should you use function casting such as TYPE(expression) in AS 3.0?

Function casting operations are best used to acquire thrown errors when a cast is unsuccessful. This aids in debugging, which is always a good thing.

16. What is an example of a wrong time to use function casting such as TYPE(expression) in AS 3.0?

Type(expression) is the equivalent syntax to instantiating a new object, if the constructing arguments are manipulated by the class. Because of the operation, an unexpected error may occur.

17. Circle the answer that best completes the sentence.

An interface can include _____.

Getters and setters

Visibility modifiers

Attributes

Algorithms

18. Static is a visibility modifier.   True   False

Explanation: The internal, public, private, protected, and custom namespaces are the only access modifiers, or visibility modifiers. Using the static keyword declares an attribute or behavior that is owned by the class itself, not the instance of the class.

19. Given the following code, which answer works best?

```
package
{
    public interface ISpeak
```

```
    {
        function speak() : void
        {
        }
    }
}


package
{
    public class Human
    {
        public function speak() : void
        {
            trace( 'hello' );
        }
    }
}


package
{
    public class Cat implements ISpeak
    {
        public function speak() : void
        {
            trace( 'meow' );
        }
    }
}
```

A.   var itSpeaks :ISpeak= ISpeak(new Human()) ;

B.   var itSpeaks :ISpeak= new Cat() ;

C.   var itSpeaks :ISpeak= new Human() ;

D.   Both A and B

Explanation: Although it may appear that answer D is correct, the proper answer is in fact B. The interfaces are exact, but to enable typecasting, the object must have the expected type in its `traits` object. `Cat` is the only class to use the `ISpeak` interface, which is why only an instance of `Cat` can fulfill the binding of an `ISpeak` variable.

20. Why would you instantiate a class?

By copying a predefined template, objects can modify their attributes and/or states independently of one another, allowing for a reduction in the collective number of static classes used to achieve the same goals.

21. Fill in the blank.

Inheritance is said to have a <u>tightly</u> coupled relationship.

Explanation: Because a subclass inherits class attributes and behaviors, any change to the superclass directly affects the subclass. Thus a subclass, although able to inject its own specifics, is at the mercy of any errors caused by the classes from which it derives its behaviors.

22. Why does the `MovieClip` from the library break encapsulation?

When you use a `MovieClip` from the library, nested clips must be defined as `public`, which doesn't allow the class to monitor all modifications made to it.

23. Circle the answer that best completes the sentence.

Object-oriented programming is _____.

(a structural device)

the act of making objects

24. OOP has a few downsides. List as many as you can.

Object-oriented programming can add more complexity to a system.

Object-oriented programming requires memory management.

Instantiating objects takes time, which makes OOP slower than procedural programming.

OOP requires a lot of planning and strategy.

If you use OOP improperly, your code will be harder to maintain.

Learning OOP != understanding OOP.

25. How do design patterns help developers?

Design patterns introduce solutions you may not have previously seen or known existed. Beyond their generalized solutions, design patterns are like a language, because they're a road map to your code.

26. List the three categories of design patterns.

Creational

Behavioral

Structural

27. Fill in the blank.

A good rule of thumb is to never exceed more than 3 levels of inheritance.

Explanation: The further you are from the origin of the inherited behaviors and/or attributes, the more errors can occur among the subclasses due to the slightest modification of any of the superclasses. The greater the number of levels of inheritance, the greater the impact the error may cause.

28. What is the difference between interface inheritance and class inheritance?

Interface inheritance enables an object to be bound to a reference in lieu of another object, whereas class inheritance defines an object's behavior in terms of a superior's implementation.

29. Fill in the blanks.

One design principle is to favor composition over inheritance.

Explanation: Whereas inheritance fails to offer a loosely coupled relationship to behavioral modification, composition promotes it. Composition is the preferred solution, but you end up with more classes if not more objects.

30. Circle the answer that best completes the sentence.

Composition relies on _____.

(delegation)

tight coupling

objects

IS-A relationships

31. Fill in the blank.

The relationship shown is <u>instantiation</u>.

Mother
_baby:New Born

- - ▶ | New Born |

32. Match the items in the two columns.

This type checking hates poor code. ───────── Compile-time type checking

This type checking doesn't like mismatches. ──────── Runtime type checking

33. Explain when you would use an abstract class instead of an interface in AS 3.0.

<u>When you're dealing with inheritance, or IS-A scenarios, it's best to use an abstract class so</u>
<u>that defined methods and/or variables can be inherited by the subclass, reducing duplicate</u>
<u>code. Although an interface can provide a type for an object, it doesn't localize the</u>
<u>commonalities that objects share, because it only concerns itself with public methods. An</u>
<u>abstract class, on the other hand, is an object; and an object is a group of code encapsulated</u>
<u>within a definition. This localizes states and behaviors so they can be used by multiple objects</u>
<u>known as subclasses. Using an abstract class also ensures that minor fixes are reflected in all</u>
<u>subclasses. And finally, it separates the specifics of behaviors from the interface, enabling a</u>
<u>more flexible means of extension.</u>

34. List the differences between an abstract class and an interface in AS 3.0.

<u>An abstract class can contain code but is never instantiated.</u>

<u>An interface can't contain code.</u>

<u>An abstract class's attributes can include visible modifiers.</u>

<u>An interface can only declare public methods.</u>

<u>You can use multiple interfaces, but you can extend only one class.</u>

35. Circle the answer that best completes the sentence.

Object-oriented programming begins with _____.

objects

implementation

collaboration

factoring

36. Given the following classes, circle the term that best describes its encapsulation.

```
package
{
    public class CrestTartarAndCavityProtection extends ToothPaste
    {
        public function CrestTartarAndCavityProtection() : void
        {
        }

        public function fightTartar() : void
        {
        }

        public override function fightCavities() : void
        {
        }

        public function whitenTeeth() : void
        {
        }
    }
}
```

Cohesive   Incohesive

Explanation: Unless you're a dental junkie and have witnessed that CrestTartar&Cavity protection does in fact whiten teeth, the proper answer is incohesive. The chosen class name alludes to a behavior that prevents tartar and cavities but offers an additional behavior: whitening. A cohesive class provides one and only one behavior that is relevant to the expected task of the class. Because this class includes more than one behavior, it isn't cohesive.

37. When do you *not* need to perform an analysis of a system?

Proper analysis is always required, and therefore the only time it doesn't need to be performed is when it has already been done.

38. Performance can change requirements.   (True)   False

Explanation: Performance is a reason to change a design and/or technical requirements, but never client requirements. Only technical limitations should modify what a client wants.

39. Consider the following code:

```
package
{
    internal class Felidae
    {
        protected var _canPurr : Boolean;
        protected var _region : String;
        protected var _speed : int;

        public function run()
        {
        }

        public function sleep()
        {
        }

        public function eat()
        {
        }
    }
}


package
{
    final public class Cougar extends Felidae
    {
        public function Cougar()
        {
            _canPurr = true;
            _region = "South America";
            _speed = 40;
            // mph
```

```
        }
      }
    }
```

What conclusions can you draw about the application from the use of the `final` keyword?

The application doesn't care about subcategories of `Cougar`. Also, because `Cougar` doesn't modify behaviors of the `Felidae` class, any subclass that intends to modify `Felidae` should be done by subclassing `Felidae` directly.

40. Why is having a vast understanding of an object-oriented language important when dealing with design patterns?

design patterns are absent of any language specifics in efforts for developers to apply them to any object-oriented Lanaguage. Having a vast knowledge of both the classes, and syntax used by the OOL, you can be best assured to implement a pattern in the most efficient manner possible.

41. Assign the appropriate access modifiers to achieve the following: the classes within `utils.color.type` should never be set by anything other than `ColorConverter`, but their get values can be read outside their package.

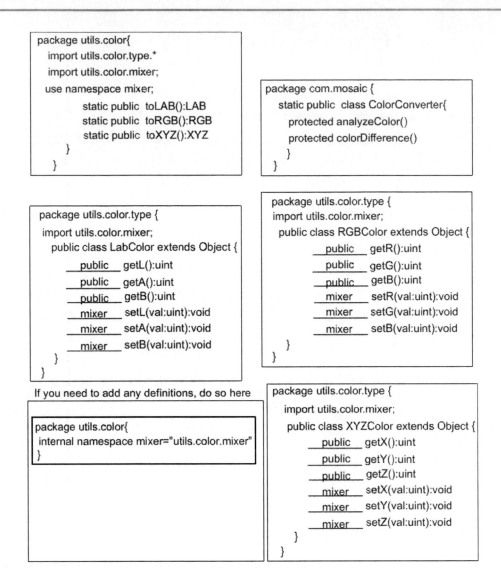

```
package utils.color{
    import utils.color.type.*
    import utils.color.mixer;
    use namespace mixer;
            static public  toLAB():LAB
            static public  toRGB():RGB
            static public  toXYZ():XYZ
        }
    }
```

```
package com.mosaic {
    static public  class ColorConverter{
        protected analyzeColor()
        protected colorDifference()
    }
}
```

```
package utils.color.type {
    import utils.color.mixer;
    public class LabColor extends Object {
        __public__  getL():uint
        __public__  getA():uint
        __public__  getB():uint
        __mixer__   setL(val:uint):void
        __mixer__   setA(val:uint):void
        __mixer__   setB(val:uint):void
    }
}
```

```
package utils.color.type {
    import utils.color.mixer;
    public class RGBColor extends Object {
        __public__   getR():uint
        __public__   getG():uint
        __public__   getB():uint
        __mixer__    setR(val:uint):void
        __mixer__    setG(val:uint):void
        __mixer__    setB(val:uint):void
    }
}
```

If you need to add any definitions, do so here

```
package utils.color{
    internal namespace mixer="utils.color.mixer"
}
```

```
package utils.color.type {
    import utils.color.mixer;
    public class XYZColor extends Object {
        __public__   getX():uint
        __public__   getY():uint
        __public__   getZ():uint
        __mixer__    setX(val:uint):void
        __mixer__    setY(val:uint):void
        __mixer__    setZ(val:uint):void
    }
}
```

42. Fill in what is needed to ensure that `someObject` doesn't linger with the garbage collector when `remove()` is called.

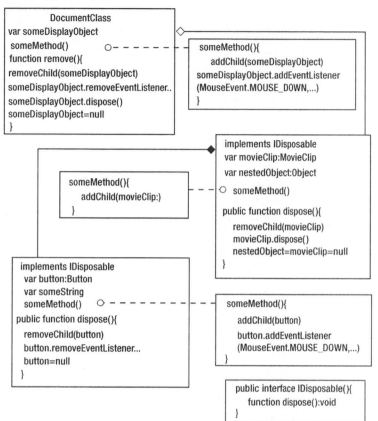

43. Explain what the top-level function `getDefinitionByName` is used for.

getDefinitionByName is a means to retrieve a `Class` object belonging to a fully qualified class name from the application's current domain. The returned object can create new instances or be used to view its class members.

44. Rank the likelihood of change among the following, where 1 means least likely to change and 5 means most likely to change.

0 Client requirements

1 Design layout

3 Transitions/Motion

2 User flow

4 Creative assets

Explanation: The least likely to change is always the client's requirements because clients know what they want—that's why they approached your company. Before moving into the development phase, the requirements need to be approved, most often by the client: that's the design layout. A user flow is the backbone representing the path the user takes to fulfill client requirements as expressed by the designer's layout. A user flow is more likely to be enhanced than changed significantly. Transitions, behaviors, and creative assets are very specific, and specifics are always likely to change. Transitions and behaviors are concepts that designers already have in mind, whereas assets tend to get worked out along the way.

45. Using the following table, how many bytes will `SomeClass` occupy?

224 shape=new Shape() or new Shape()	
40 new Object() or Object literal {}	
4 var objectObject	4 var sprite:Sprite
4 var dict:Dictionary	4 var mClip:MovieClip
4 var array:Array	4 var tField:TextField
4 var shape:Shape	

```
package
{
   public class SomeClass extends Shape
   {
      private var _tField : TextField;
      private var _obj : Object;

      public function SomeClass()
      {
         _obj = {};
      }
   }
}
```

`SomeClass` takes up <u>232</u> bytes.

46. On deployment, all documents used during analysis can be tossed out in celebration.

True (**False**)

Explanation: Similar to the way City Hall keep building blueprints on file, all forms of analysis should be stored to serve as the blueprints for any remodeling in the future.

47. Why is it best to implement the disposable pattern as nothing more than a class interface? For memory management purposes, almost every class requires the `dispose` method. You can't inject the method into top-level classes, so you must develop a new subtype for every class you need to extend. This can be problematic if you forget to use your new subtypes and may lead to new issues later when you try to correct any mistakes. By adding the behavior as an interface, you add a protocol to upcast to `IDisposable` and bypass any issues that may arise when you try to add a subclass.

48. The time used during the build process is best spent in implementation.
True   False

Explanation: Implementation should occupy the least amount of time during development. You should spend the most time performing object-oriented analysis and design.

49. All classes are expected to have their behaviors changed.   True   False

Explanation: This isn't true and shouldn't be in your mind during class development, because it would lead to using many `public` and `protected` modifiers and potentially breaking the rule of data-hiding. During OOA and OOD, class hierarchies present themselves, and should be separated from specific behaviors rather than those that are generalized. These relationships determine which classes are expected to have their behaviors changed, and you can design those classes accordingly.

50. All classes created during a project are best left in the project's general source folders.
True   False

Explanation: Although it's wise to ensure that you download all appropriate classes from a repository, doing so doesn't enable one of the most powerful features of the object-oriented process: reuse. During the course of your build, you develop classes with specific behaviors and classes that use those behaviors to achieve specific goals within your application. Many of these behaviors may be used outside this application, and thus should be stored in their own team library.

Quiz 2

Understanding object-oriented programming is easy.   True   ~~False~~

1. Why is inheritance the cornerstone of OOP?

   _____

   _____

   _____

   _____

2. Consider the following figure:

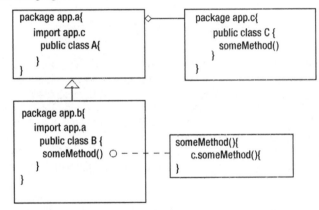

   If class B inherits class A, which already imported the definition of class C, why does class B require the definition of class C as well?

   _____

   _____

   _____

   _____

3. Composition builds systems by combining less complex parts.   True   False

4. Fill in the blank.
   A class that doesn't define an interface for subclasses is known as a(n)
   _____ class.

5. Circle the best answer.

someMethod(obj:Object):void is known as a _____.

      function   method   signature   receiver

6. Complete this design principle: Program to a(n) _____, not to a(n) _____.

7. Circle the best answer.

An object's type refers to its _____.

      superclass   behaviors   interface   signatures

8. Explain how EventDispatcher can enable flexible architecture.

_____

_____

_____

_____

9. Explain how inheritance breaks encapsulation.

_____

_____

_____

_____

10. Why is it best to add an interface to a concrete class versus adding a method?

_____

_____

_____

_____

11. Consider the following figure:

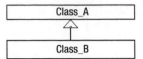

```
var cb:Class_B = new Class_B()
```

Explain why this is poor OOP.

_____

_____

_____

_____

12. Given the following class, which term best describes its encapsulation?

```
package
{
    public class WhiteningTartarCavityProtection extends ToothPaste
    {
        public function WhiteningTartarCavityProtection() : void
        {
        }

        public function fightTartar() : void
        {
        }

        public override function fightCavities() : void
        {
        }

        public function freshenBreath() : void
        {
        }
    }
}
        Cohesive          Incohesive
```

13. Circle the answer that best completes the sentence.

Object-oriented programming ends with _____.

     objects

     implementation

     collaboration

     factoring

14. Memory management is necessary in Flash.   True   False

15. Break this object into smaller components and define their collaborations via simple associations.

16. Generalize the following objects, and create a class diagram displaying their associations.

Piano		Saxaphone		A Chord		B Chord		Note

17. Return types should be specific.   True   False

18. Show the appropriate associations.

19. Explain why stage instances must be turned off.

_____

_____

_____

_____

20. Static code can be polymorphic.   True   False

21. Circle the best answer *based on your opinion*.

Learning object-oriented programming is a(n) _____ process.

        slow   Iterative   involved   complicated

22. You don't need to supply the `import` directive if you refer to an external definition via the fully qualified name.   True   False

23. Interfaces can use interface inheritance.   True   False

24. Show the appropriate association.

25. Protected constants can be overwritten by subclasses.   True   False

26. Match the items in the two columns.

internal   I'm seen.

private   You have to be aware of me to see me.

protected   I'm seen by those around me.

custom   I can't be seen by those like me.

public   I'm seen by those like me.

27. Fill in the blank.

_____ is a lesser benefit of OOP due to the lifespan of an RIA.

     Modularity   Flexibility   Scalability   Maintainability

28. Complete this design principle: Closed for _____, open for
_____.

29. Circle the answer that best completes the sentence.

A team build should only divide and conquer after _____.

          kick-Off

          it has determined the requirements

          design patterns have been applied

          a system flow chart has been crafted

30. Class variables can't be changed.   True   False

31. Explain the importance of understanding that designer and client requirements are more
often than not compound requirements.

32. Consider the following code:

```
package color.utils
{
    public class ColorConverter
    {
        public static function toARGB() : uint
        {
            // 32 bit unsigned integer AARRGGBB
        }
    }
}
```

Using the static class `ColorConverter` and its static method `toARGB`, you can convert any colorspace value to a 32-bit unsigned value. This is a perfect class to introduce into the color-picker API for the client. Unfortunately, the client's application can't use 32-bit unsigned integers—only 24-bit.

Devise a means to modify this behavior.

33. Uh oh: there's an object-oriented mistake in Listing 5-1. Correctly instantiate the appropriate `Sprite`s in Listing 5-2.

Listing 5-1

```
package
{
    import flash.display.Sprite;

    import com.utils.bitmapdata.Sprite;

    var topLevelSprite : Sprite = new Sprite();
    var bitmapDataSprite : Sprite = new Sprite();
}
```

Listing 5-2

```
Package
{
        import flash.display.Sprite;
        import com.utils.bitmapdata.Sprite;

        var topLevelSprite:Sprite=_____
        var bitmapDataSprite:Sprite =_____
}
```

34. Using nothing but the following image, explain the benefits of the symbols with the properties.

#protected   __private $static   public

_____

_____

_____

_____

35. Using the method `describeType(obj:Object):xml` from the `flash.utils` package, you get the following results from a `Vector.<int>` instance:

```
<type name="__AS3__.vec::Vector.&lt;int>" base="Object" ➥
isDynamic="true" isFinal="true" isStatic="false">
<extendsClass type="Object"/>
<constructor>
<parameter index="1" type="uint" optional="true"/>
<parameter index="2" type="Boolean" optional="true"/>
</constructor>
</type>
```

List all possible upcasts from the XML output.

_____

_____

_____

_____

36. A package for a definition is the definition's URI.   True   False

37. Given that `Circle` is defined in your SWF library,

```
ApplicationDomain.currentDomain.getDefinition('Circle') ➥
==getDefinitionByName('Circle')
```

True   False

38. Fill in the blank.

_____ is a container of class definitions in your RIA.

39. Explain why you should avoid *, .rest, and arguments.

_____

_____

_____

_____

40. Fill in the blank.

Using the _____ keyword lets you call a method of a superclass.

41. Getters and setters should always be public.   True   False

42. Explicit getters and setters can be used in lieu of implicit getters and setters.

```
Explicit: public function getText():String
Implicit: public function get text():String
```

Explain from an OO standpoint why one may be better than the other.

_____

_____

_____

_____

43. Class A declares a property _date as being a `protected` variable. Class B extends class A and modifies _date through the variable. This manner of modification is acceptable practice.   True   False

44. What is the purpose of the top-level class named `Class`?

_____

_____

_____

_____

45. AS 3.0 supports method overloading.　　　　　True　　　False

46. Class methods, or static methods, can access both instance and class variables.
　　　　True　　　False

47. When would you use `getDefinition` instead of `getDefinitionByName`?

_____

_____

_____

_____

48. How can runtime shared libraries work with an `ApplicationDomain`?

_____

_____

_____

_____

49. You can specify an `ApplicationDomain` in the `LoaderContext` of a `Loader`.　　　True　　　False

50. How do the return types differ between `getDefinition` and `getDefinitionByName`?

_____

_____

_____

_____

Answers to Quiz 2

Understanding object-oriented programming is easy.   True   (False)

Explanation: Object-oriented programming is a very advanced concept and is often misunderstood by experienced programmers. Despite what some may say, understanding OOP isn't easy. Remember this when you're frustrated.

1. Why is inheritance the cornerstone of OOP?

Inheritance enables polymorphism, which is the main reason object-oriented languages exist.

2. Consider the following figure:

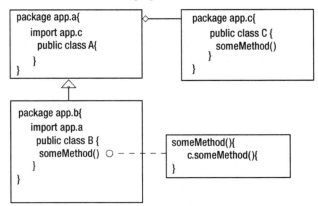

If class B inherits class A, which already imported the definition of class C, why does class B require it as well?

Unlike previous versions of the language, in ActionScript 3.0 every definition must be imported if any reference is used in the class. After the `import` directive, you can use classes by specifying either the fully qualified identifier or the class name.

3. Composition builds systems by combining less complex parts.   (True)False

4. Fill in the blank.

A class that doesn't define an interface for subclasses is known as a(n) concrete class.

5. Circle the best answer.

`someMethod( obj:Object ):void` is known as a _____.

function   method   (signature)   receiver

6. Complete this design principle: Program to a(n) <u>interface</u>, not to a(n) <u>implementation</u>.

7. Circle the best answer.

An object's type refers to its _____.

superclass   behaviors   (interface)   signatures

Explanation: Because a type defines an object's `public` methods, the only possible answer is interface. Signatures and behaviors don't specify their visibilities; you can't presume that they're `public`.

8. Explain how `EventDispatcher` can enable flexible architecture.

The events dispatched can bubble, allowing objects to know the event they're listening for and not specifically who it's coming from. This enables a very loose coupling between the dispatcher of the event and the listening object.

9. Explain how inheritance breaks encapsulation.

Encapsulation facilitates groupings among related attributes and behaviors. Although a superclass may adhere to this idea of encapsulation, subclasses merely change the behaviors of the superclass. Removing the behavior from the attributes that are related can potentially cause errors, if any changes are made to the contents of the superclass. More important, the subclass can decisions for the superclass via the protected attributes, which breaks the idea of the superclass governing its modifications.

10. Why is it best to add an interface to a concrete class versus adding a method?

Adding a method to a class doesn't offer the availability to upcast the concrete class to the interface it possesses. Thus, you'd be programming to an implementation rather than an interface. Generalizing code is always preferred.

11. Consider the following figure:

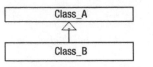

```
var cb:Class_B = new Class_B()
```

Explain why this is poor OOP.

<u>By typing cb to Class_B instead of Class_A, you're programming to a concrete, which is the same as programming to an implementation and not an interface. By classifying cb as type Class_A, you can substitute other objects, if required, in place of Class_B.</u>

12. Given the following class, which term best describes its encapsulation?

```
package
{
    public class WhiteningTartarCavityProtection extends ToothPaste
    {
        public function WhiteningTartarCavityProtection() : void
        {
        }

        public function fightTartar() : void
        {
        }

        public override function fightCavities() : void
        {
        }

        public function freshenBreath() : void
        {
        }
    }
}
```

Cohesive   (Incohesive)

Explanation: The inclusion of the FreshenBreath as a behavior continues to decrease the level of cohesion. A class should have only one reason to change, thus possessing only 1 behavior.

13. Circle the answer that best completes the sentence.

Object-oriented programming ends with _____.

objects

implementation

collaboration

(factoring)

14. Memory management is necessary in Flash.　　　(True)　False

15. Break this object into smaller components and define their collaborations via simple associations.

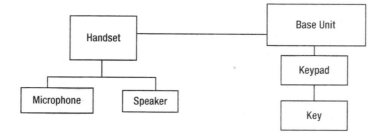

16. Generalize the following objects, and create a class diagram displaying their associations.

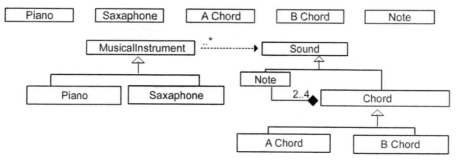

17. Return types should be specific.

Explanation: Return types should be specific only if necessary. It's best to generalize return types because doing so facilitates reuse. This doesn't mean everything should return `Objects`. The generalization should remain to the task at hand, to first and foremost ensure a working application. Return types should be those of interfaces and common types.

18. Show the appropriate associations.

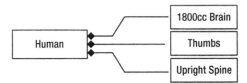

Explanation: The associations are compositions. To be considered human, you must have a brain volume of 1800 cubic centimeters, opposable thumbs, and an upright spine.

19. Explain why stage instances must be turned off.

To ensure that all complex assets are visible in the class so that you can nullify them for garbage collection, stage instances must be turned off.

20. Static code can be polymorphic. True   ~~False~~

Explanation: Fixed code can be polymorphic. For example, `var mc:Sprite = new MovieClip()` demonstrates polymorphic behavior, because MovieClip satisfies the interface of `Sprite`.

21. Circle the best answer *based on your opinion*.

Learning object-oriented programming is a(n) _____ process.

Slow   Iteritive   (involved)   complicated

Explanation: In my opinion, OOP is involved. You have to be patient and dedicated. This question is in the quiz to help you understand your own issues with OOP. Be aware of them and find a way to get past them. You've gotten this far.

22. You don't need to supply the `import` directive if you refer to an external definition via the fully qualified name.   True

23. Interfaces can use interface inheritance. True   ~~False~~

24. Show the appropriate associations.

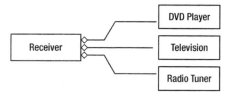

Explanation: A receiver behavior isn't defined by the DVD player, television, or radio. Therefore the relationships are aggregates.

25. Protected constants can be overwritten by subclasses.   True   (False)

Explanation: Once a constant has been declared, it can't be reassigned.

26. Match the items in the two columns.

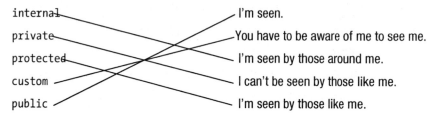

internal   I'm seen.

private   You have to be aware of me to see me.

protected   I'm seen by those around me.

custom   I can't be seen by those like me.

public   I'm seen by those like me.

27. Fill in the blank.

_____ is a lesser benefit of OOP due to the life span of an RIA.

Modularity   Flexibility   (Scalability)   Maintainability

Explanation: Although OOP provides all of these benefits, many RIAs have a short life span, and thus scalability often isn't necessary. Modularity, flexibility, and maintainability, on the other hand, offer many more opportunities during the building process and enable you to reuse code.

28. Complete this design principle: Closed for <u>modification,</u> open for <u>extension</u>.

29. Circle the answer that best completes the sentence.

A team build should only divide and conquer after _____.

kick-Off

it has determined the requirements

(design patterns have been applied)

a system flow chart has been crafted

Explanation: Without knowing all the tools in your toolbox, you can't possibly choose the most appropriate device for the job. Without knowing how to diminish tightly coupled relationships and ensure proper data-hiding, a team of developers has a higher likelihood of stepping on one another's toes.

30. Class variables can't be changed.   True   (False)

Explanation: Class variables are nothing more than variables that are global to the many instances of the class. Only constants are unable to change after they've been declared.

31. Explain the importance of understanding that designer and client requirements are more often than not compound requirements.

Designers are often influenced by external factors when they conceive a design or a behavior that something exhibits. Very rarely are a designer's thoughts so unique that this statement isn't true. The same can be said of clients and their requirements. They're easily swayed to need and want functionality based on what they've seen or have come to view as standard in the RIA realm. Because these requirements are based on past experience, every line of code you write is bound to be included in your next project. Not using proper OOP principles to devise code reuse will lead to compounded efforts on your part.

32. Consider the following code:

```
package color.utils{
        public class ColorConverter{
                static public function toARGB():uint
                //32 bit unsigned integer AARRGGBB
        }
}
```

Using the static class `ColorConverter` and its static method `toARGB`, you can convert any colorspace value to a 32-bit unsigned value. This is a perfect class to introduce into the color-picker API for the client. Unfortunately, the client's application can't use 32-bit unsigned integers—only 24-bit.

Devise a means to modify this behavior.

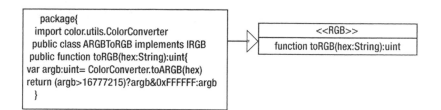

```
package{
import color.utils.ColorConverter
public class ARGBToRGB implements IRGB
public function toRGB(hex:String):uint{
var argb:uint= ColorConverter.toARGB(hex)
return (argb>16777215)?argb&0xFFFFFF:argb
  }
```

```
<<RGB>>
function toRGB(hex:String):uint
```

Explanation: By wrapping ColorConverter with your new object, ARGBToRGB, you can intercept the returned calculation and remove the Alpha value, essentially changing the object's behavior. With the RGB interface, via interface inheritance, the client doesn't need to program to the concrete creation but to an IRGB type.

33. Uh oh: there's an object-oriented mistake in Listing 5-1. Correctly instantiate the appropriate Sprites in Listing 5-2.

Listing 5-1

```
package
{
    import flash.display.Sprite;

    import com.utils.bitmapdata.Sprite;

    var topLevelSprite : Sprite = new Sprite();
    var bitmapDataSprite : Sprite = new Sprite();
}
```

Listing 5-2

```
Package
{
        import flash.display.Sprite;
        import com.utils.bitmapdata.Sprite;

        var topLevelSprite:Sprite= new flash.display.Sprite();
        var bitmapDataSprite:com.utils.bitmapdata.Sprite= ➥
                            new com.utils.bitmapdata.Sprite();
}
```

Explanation: By referring to the fully qualified path and/or supplying the Uniform Resource Identifier and Uniform Resource Name, you can prevent naming conflicts.

34. Using nothing but the following image, explain the benefits of the symbols with the properties.

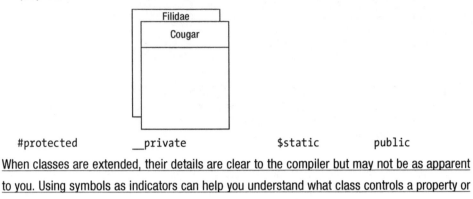

#protected   _private $static   public

When classes are extended, their details are clear to the compiler but may not be as apparent to you. Using symbols as indicators can help you understand what class controls a property or behavior. Essentially, it's a reference to scope.

35. Using the method describeType(obj:Object):xml from the flash.utils package, you get the following results from a Vector.<int> instance:

```
</type><type name="__AS3__.vec::Vector.&lt;int>" base="Object" ➡
isDynamic="true" isFinal="true" isStatic="false">
<extendsClass type="Object"/>
<constructor>
<parameter index="1" type="uint" optional="true"/>
<parameter index="2" type="Boolean" optional="true"/>
</constructor>
</type>
```

List all possible upcasts from XML output.

Object

Explanation: As you can see, the XML output states the extendsClass to that of type Object solely. Because Object is the only protocol of Vector.<int>, it can only be upcast to Object.

36. A package for a definition is the definition's URI.   (True)   False

Explanation: Via the import directive, you can open a namespace referring to a location, to which a className can be referred. Ultimately the package becomes a namespace.

37. Given that `Circle` is a Circular shape in your SWF library,

```
ApplicationDomain.currentDomain.getDefinition('Circle') ➥
==getDefinitionByName('Circle')
```

(True)　False

Explanation: Because you're trying to find `Circle` in the current domain of the static class `ApplicationDomain`, you target the same domain that would be used if we called the global function `getDefinitionByName`.

38. Fill in the blank.

`ApplicationDomain` is a container of class definitions in your RIA.

Explanation: `ApplicationDomain` is the partition of definitions within the current SWF.

39. Explain why you should avoid *, .rest, and arguments.

Using these declarations passes references blindly, which isn't object-oriented behavior. Knowing which object types to work with is object-oriented. The statements listed offer no generalizations and deter proper OO coding.

40. Fill in the blank.

Use of the <u>super</u> keyword lets you call a method of a superclass.

Explanation: Although a subclass has access to all `protected` and `public` methods/properties in its superclasses, you can only reach the method of a superclass if you haven't already specified the same method in your class. This method always takes precedence. To target the superclass's method, you can use the `super` keyword followed by the method to message: `super.superMethod();`.

41. Getters and setters should always be public.　(True)　False

42. Explicit getters and setters can be used in lieu of implicit getters and setters.

```
Explicit: public function getText():String
Implicit: public function get text():String
```

Explain from an OO standpoint why one may be better than the other.

Implicit getters/setters are very convenient and are often generated automatically by third-party editors, which makes them prevalent. The downside is that using them is like working with the physical properties of the object. Also, implicit getters and setters are always expected to be public, and that may lead to clumsy data-hiding. Explicit getters and setters, on the other hand, demonstrate physical methods being targeted and can be as visible as necessary to hide data.

43. Class A declares a property _date as being a protected variable. Class B extends class A and modifies _date through the variable. This manner of modification is acceptable practice.   True   (False)

Explanation: Data-hiding ensures that a class has full control over modifying its own attributes to prevent error. Although a `protected` attribute is visible to all subclasses, it should remain in control over its own modifications. This ensures that the anticipated behavior remains among the methods in the superclass and is visible to the superclass for use.

44. What is the purpose of the top-level class named `Class`?

Much like the `traits` object associated with a class, a `Class` object is created for each class definition in an application. Using `Class` objects lets you acquire definitions from libraries and instantiate instances of those definitions.

45. AS 3.0 supports method overloading.   True   (False)

46. Class methods, or static methods, can access both instance and class variables.   True   (False)

Explanation: Static methods can only reference static variables. Instance methods, on the other hand, can reference both instance and class variables.

47. When would you use `getDefinition` instead of `getDefinitionByName`?

`getDefinition` can return an `Object`, whereas `getDefinitionByName` returns only a `Class` object. The difference is that a `Class` is only one of the three external definitions in the AS 3.0 language. If you require a defined namespace or interface, you can get it via the `getDefinition` method. Another thing that distinguishes when to use one versus the other is when you're attempting to reach a definition outside the `currentDomain`. `getDefinitionByName` is a global function that reaches only to the `currentDomain`, whereas `getDefinition` lets you supply the memory to target.

48. How can runtime shared libraries work with an `ApplicationDomain`?

When a SWF is loaded into an application, the definitions that accompany the SWF are partitioned from current definitions. RSL works in the same manner. Each partition has exclusive access to the definitions, unless the pointer of the `currentDomain` is targeted. By loading a SWF containing definitions that can be used throughout a large RIA, you can store and retrieve those definitions

49. An `ApplicationDomain` can be specified in the `LoaderContext` of a `Loader`.
True   ~~False~~

50. How do the return types differ between `getDefinition` and `getDefinitionByName`?

`getDefinition` returns an `Object` that can be a namespace, an interface, or even a class, whereas `getDefinitionByName` can only return a class definition.

Chapter 6

Creational Patterns

Creational patterns let you separate the details required to instantiate an object from the architecture. Thus far, a common theme in this book has been how to architect a system that adheres to the four principles of OOP, thereby promoting flexibility. You achieve this flexibility by wrapping code in an object that provides a common interface, shared among other objects. This way, your system can include interchangeable behaviors.

The code is modeled around these interfaces, and the objects' behaviors are usable once they're instantiated. However, as simple as this appears on paper, many conditions in reality can render your flexible/reusable code, inflexible/un-reusable.

Listing 6-1 shows how using a concrete instantiation in code limits the method's flexibility and reuse. Although returnByteArray explicitly references the instantiation of GrayscaleImage, all values returned are always the same—not to mention that you can't get the ByteArray from another existing image. This one reference limits the remaining code's reusability, without added modification.

Listing 6-1. BitmapDataByteArray returns the ByteArray of GrayscaleImage to a client.

```
public class BitmapDataByteArray
{
     public function returnByteArray() : ByteArray
     {
        var img : BitmapData = new GrayscaleImage( 1 , 1 );
        var byteArray : ByteArray = img.getPixels( img.rect )
        img.dispose()
        img = null
        byteArray.position = 0;
        return byteArray
     }
}
```

That Which Must Not Be Named

The conundrum you're faced with is how to create an instance of an object that requires particular details, without injecting any algorithms or information unnecessarily into the body of the class. The simplest approach uses parameterization.

When you pass a reference of an object into the welcoming arms of some code, a method, a class, and so on, the code can remain ignorant of the details that created the parameterized object and still use its referenced behaviors.

Unfortunately, parameterization perpetuates the burden of creation. It removes the role of creator from one class and places it into another. In other words, something still has to create the object.

Listing 6-2 shows how the removal of the concrete reference, from the code that uses it, gives the code flexibility for reuse with different instances of the similar BitmapData type. Although returnByteArray doesn't contain any concrete references, you can see that another body of code is facing the burden of creating the instance.

Listing 6-2. A client instantiates BitmapDataByteArray and passes in a GrayscaleImage.

```
var bitmapDataByteArray:BitmapDataByteArray= new BitmapDataByteArray();
var grayscaleByteArray : ByteArray = bitmapDataByteArray.returnByteArray( new
                  ➥ GrayscaleImage(1,1) );


public class BitmapDataByteArray
{
    public function returnByteArray( bmpD : BitmapData ) : ByteArray
    {
      var img : BitmapData = bmpD
       var byteArray : ByteArray = img.getPixels( img.rect );
      img.dispose();
      img = null;
      return byteArray;
    }
}
```

Creational patterns aren't intended to replace every occurrence of the new operator, but rather offer a way to conceal concrete implementations from the code that uses the instance. In a nutshell, creational patterns provide solutions to isolate the manufacturing process of concrete instances from the code that uses their interfaces.

The patterns covered in this chapter are as follows: the Factory Method pattern, the Abstract Factory pattern, the Builder pattern, and the Singleton pattern. The discussion of each pattern includes a technical overview, a vignette, an AS 3.0 example, and frequently asked questions.

The technical overview defines the technical specifics of each patterns, its parts, a class diagram, and the pattern's purpose. The vignette is a real-world example that demonstrates and/or represents each pattern.

All the vignettes in this chapter revolve around the fast-food industry, because it provides many parallels to simplification and abstraction. Then, the example reveals the pattern as it would be used in ActionScript

3.0 code. Finally, the FAQ section discusses the answers to questions that may arise as you study design patterns.

The Simple Factory

A Simple Factory encapsulates the conditional logic used to create a product. Figure 6-1 shows the class diagram.

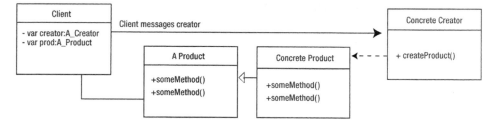

Figure 6-1. Simple Factory class diagram

A Simple Factory has the following parts:

- Abstract product
- Concrete product
- Concrete creator
- Client

Its benefits are as follows:

- Conceals the logic of product creation
- Only deals with the product interfaces

It also has this drawback:

- Lacks the flexibility to change (change is a constant)

A Comprehensive Look

Simple Factory isn't a design pattern, but it needs to be included in this chapter because the Factory Method design pattern uses what resembles a simple factory. Often, developers new to design patterns mistakenly think the Factory Method pattern is meant to create objects, giving rise to what has become referred to as the Simple Factory.

The following example doesn't show how to use the Simple Factory but demonstrates its inflexibility and why you shouldn't confuse this and the Factory Method pattern.

Example

The creational logic in **Listing 6-3** amounts to 46 lines in Shell. Although debugging 46 lines of code isn't a burden, making changes to 500 lines can be. Each time you make a change to Shell, you risk adding errors. This is never good, especially in an application framework.

Listing 6-3. An excerpt of the 500-lined logic from an application's framework, labelled Shell.

```
private function createOverlay( overlayType : String , dataObject : * = null ) : void
    {
        header.disableNavigation();
        currentSection.pause();
        if (currentOverlay)
        {
            destroyCurrentOverlay();
        }

        switch(overlayType)
        {
            case SectionEvent.VIDEO_OVERLAY:
                currentOverlay = new VideoOverlay();
                break;
            case SectionEvent.PHOTO_OVERLAY:
                currentOverlay = new PhotoViewer();
                break;
            case SectionEvent.AUDIO_OVERLAY:
                currentOverlay = new AudioOverlay();
                break;
            case SectionEvent.TWITTER_OVERLAY:
                currentOverlay = new TwitterOverlay();
                break;
            case OverlayEvent.TWITTER_SUBMIT_OVERLAY:
                currentOverlay = new AddTweetOverlay();
                break;
        }

        currentOverlay.y = SiteConfig.HEADER_HEIGHT;
        currentOverlay.addEventListener( OverlayEvent.CLOSE_OVERLAY , handleEvent );
        currentOverlay.addEventListener( OverlayEvent.INTRO_COMPLETE , handleEvent );
        currentOverlay.addEventListener( OverlayEvent.OUTRO_COMPLETE , handleEvent );
        currentOverlay.addEventListener( OverlayEvent.PLAY , handleEvent );
        currentOverlay.addEventListener( OverlayEvent.SUBMIT_TWEET , handleEvent );

        currentOverlay.addEventListener( OverlayEvent.TWITTER_SUBMIT_OVERLAY ,
        ➥ handleEvent );
```

```
      addChild( currentOverlay );

      currentOverlay.updateLayout( stage.stageWidth , (stage.stageHeight -
   ➥ SiteConfig.FOOTER_HEIGHT - SiteConfig.HEADER_HEIGHT) );

      currentOverlay.intro();
   }

   private function destroyCurrentOverlay() : void
   {
   }
```

... // truncated code

As shown in **Listing 6-4**, extracting the creational logic in Shell to a new object lets you modify the same lines of code without having to open Shell. This reduces the threat of introducing disaster into a potentially working system.

Listing 6-4. OverlayFactory was created solely to manufacture the appropriate overlay for the system.

```
package
{
   public class OverlayFactory
   {
      public function OverlayFactory()
      {
      }

      public function createOverlay( overlayType : String ) : Overlay
      {
         var currentOverlay : Overlay

         switch(overlayType)
         {
            case SectionEvent.VIDEO_OVERLAY:
               currentOverlay = new VideoOverlay();
               break;
            case SectionEvent.PHOTO_OVERLAY:
               currentOverlay = new PhotoViewer();
               break;
            case SectionEvent.AUDIO_OVERLAY:
               currentOverlay = new AudioOverlay();
               break;
            case SectionEvent.TWITTER_OVERLAY:
               currentOverlay = new TwitterOverlay();
```

```
                break;
            case OverlayEvent.TWITTER_SUBMIT_OVERLAY:
                currentOverlay = new AddTweetOverlay();
                break;
        }

        return currentOverlay;
    }
  }
}
```

Extracting the manufacturing of overlays from Shell into the new `OverlayFactory` object makes change a less disruptive force. You only need to ensure that `OverlayFactory` is kept as a reference in Shell. This lets Shell continue using instances of overlays but relieves Shell of the burden of creating them.

Listing 6-5. Updated excerpt from Shell demonstrating the reference to `OverlayFactory`

```
...
var factory : OverlayFactory = new OverlayFactory();
... cont

header.disableNavigation();
currentSection.pause();

        if (currentOverlay)
        {
            destroyCurrentOverlay();
        }

        var currentOverlay : Overlay = factory.createOverlay( overlayString );

        currentOverlay.y = SiteConfig.HEADER_HEIGHT;
        currentOverlay.addEventListener( OverlayEvent.CLOSE_OVERLAY , handleEvent );
        currentOverlay.addEventListener( OverlayEvent.INTRO_COMPLETE , handleEvent );
        currentOverlay.addEventListener( OverlayEvent.OUTRO_COMPLETE , handleEvent );
        currentOverlay.addEventListener( OverlayEvent.PLAY , handleEvent );
        currentOverlay.addEventListener( OverlayEvent.SUBMIT_TWEET , handleEvent );

        currentOverlay.addEventListener( OverlayEvent.TWITTER_SUBMIT_OVERLAY ,
        ➥ handleEvent );

        addChild( currentOverlay );

        currentOverlay.updateLayout( stage.stageWidth , (stage.stageHeight -
        ➥ SiteConfig.FOOTER_HEIGHT - SiteConfig.HEADER_HEIGHT) );
```

```
    currentOverlay.intro();
}

private function destroyCurrentOverlay() : void
{
... //truncated code
```

So far, you've removed the logic used to create the overlay from the framework that supports the application. You've not only reduced the number of lines but also managed to increase the shell's cohesiveness, by extracting unrelated functions. The point of the framework is to ensure communication among objects, not to develop the necessary logic to create objects. The more cohesive you can make your framework, the fewer reasons you have to keep opening the file to perform frivolous maintenance.

Knowing the importance of the framework, if you need to make any changes to the instantiation logic, you no longer have to concern yourself with Shell. This is beneficial, especially when you're dealing with multiple developers who are all working toward the same goal. If changes are made to the Shell, developers that may be working on Shell dependant code may also become impeded as well.

Extracting code that manufactures objects adheres to the four principles of OOP, because doing so provides the appropriate boundaries around object creation. This localization of code helps to partition or encapsulate the possibility of variation in your application. In this case, you're separating the various overlays that may be used in the application.

Although the Simple Factory works at the moment, if you need to add another overlay to the application, you'll have to edit the Simple Factory. This is the case because you haven't used an abstract class. To arrive at one of the most important features of OOP—polymorphism—you must use a hierarchy. With a hierarchy, you can make changes while using common code provided by the superclass. Additionally, including a superclass lets you program to an interface, so your factory can exhibit polymorphic capabilities.

The Simple Factory isn't a design pattern because it doesn't account for change. Classes should be open to extension but closed to modification.

FAQ

- If you used an abstract class that declares the method createOverlay, subclassed it, and overrode the method, would the Simple Factory then be considered a design pattern?

    Yes. It would then be considered a design pattern named Factory Method.

The Factory Method Pattern

The Factory Method pattern encapsulates creational logic in subclasses, allowing them to infer their own implementations. Figure 6-2 shows the class diagram.

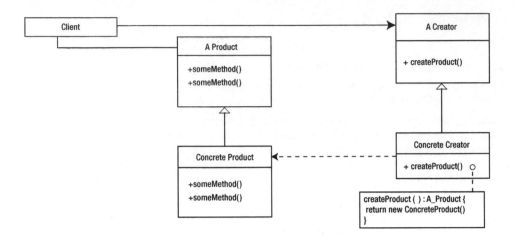

Figure 6-2. Factory Method pattern class diagram

This pattern has the following parts:

- Abstract product
- Concrete product
- Abstract creator
- Concrete creator
- Client

The pattern's benefits are as follows:

- Factory methods eliminate the need to bind application-specific classes into your code.
- The code only deals with the product interfaces.

It also has this drawback:

- Sometimes subclasses can't be created.

A Comprehensive Look

The Factory Method pattern lets you separate the instantiation and the utilization of a product using inheritance. You do so via a method in the creator class, which is the interface a subclass must override and provide an appropriate implementation for. Whereas the superclass is responsible for this abstract method and its signatures, the subclass is privy to the objects that can be instantiated and returned. The subclass uses logic or conditional statements that determine the appropriate object to manufacture.

This approach provides flexibility among possible revisions of the product(s) used, because you can create different implementations by making new subclasses of the abstraction.

The most important aspect of the Factory Method pattern is that product creation is always deferred to a subclass. The reason is the hierarchical relationship that makes polymorphism possible among different implementations.

The method in the factory gives this particular pattern its name; this method's name reflects the product and the way to achieve the product. The name should make the method easily identifiable as a factory method. Often, the `create`, `get`, and `make` prefixes are used for these method names, to help developers who are familiar with this particular pattern identify its existence in the code.

The superclass is an abstract class that acts as the base class of the manufacturer. As a template for manufacturing, it provides the necessary default behaviors that ensure proper assembly of the object type returned, as well as exposes a factory method that is used by the subclass to define the particular object(s) for creation.

The factory's subclass has a different role to accompany the superclass. The subclass's role is to hold the logic necessary in order to choose the object to instantiate for the superclass. This is performed by overriding the exposed factory method and implementing the given logic.

By separating the logic of object creation from the manner in which the object is assembled, you can more easily substitute the logic of the subclass for that of another in the system. By hiding the assembly from the subclass, you also maintain a strict means of assembly without the subclass meddling and trying to assemble the object a particular way. In other words, the abstraction ensures that products are initialized uniformly. It also localizes the particulars between the two classes: the subclass possesses the logic to instantiate a particular product, and the superclass assembles the object because it needs to use that object.

Vignette

MikeDonalds is a franchise restaurant chain. Anyone with the desire to do so can open a franchise as long as they adhere to MikeDonalds' strict policies; it isn't Joe Schmo whose name is on the line, but rather MikeDonalds and the company's continued reputation.

Now Joe Schmo wants to purchase into the McDonalds franchise because he feels it will be a huge success in his country where there currently are no MikeDonalds restaurants. The only issue is that Joe Schmo and his fellow countrymen have slightly different tastes than those served by the original MikeDonalds. Bratwurst is a cornerstone of any meal in Joe's country. Joe convinces MikeDonalds to put a bratwurst sandwich on his restaurant's menu; but because the MikeDonalds name is at stake, the company takes total ownership of the sandwich's preparation, cooking, flavor, packaging, and pricing. Joe's only say in the matter is his suggestion of a product the locals enjoy. To MikeDonalds, the bratwurst as nothing more than a new type of burger to sell.

Meanwhile, another franchise owner has a suggestion for a new product in her Chile location. Because empanadas are common to the area, she suggests empanadas with queso, and MikeDonalds approves the suggestion. To MikeDonalds, it's just another food item that requires appropriate preparation and packaging.

MikeDonalds views each specific item as a form of a generic product. If it became aware of the empanadas or the bratwurst, the product wouldn't be reusable when a new, similar product type is offered.

Each franchise owner is a representative (factory subclass) of the MikeDonalds Company as well as the provider of logic regarding which product to create for the customer (client). MikeDonalds is the company (factory) that sets the rules and tone for every product it sells; it can't afford to have the products prepped any other way, because business might decline. The most freedom the company gives those who purchase into the franchise is the chance to express their understanding about appropriate products to create.

The AS 3.0 Cast

In AS 3.0, the Factory Method pattern's parts are as follows:

- Abstract creator: The manufacturer that defines the type used in its particular factory. A factory can perform nearly any creational operation needed for a class:
    - Initialize
    - Pull in data
    - Configure
    - Set states
- Concrete creator: The factory subclass containing the logic necessary to instantiate the appropriate object in a genus of products expected by the superclass.
- Abstract product: The product genus, which exposes the interface that all concrete products of the given genus inherit.
- Concrete product: The physical object that can be instantiated and that extends the abstract product to express itself as a member of the type used in the creator's logic.
- Client: The abstract creator is, more often than not, the client of the factory method. Although, depending on the scenario, the client may be external to the creator, and may have knowledge among the product's interface. You'll see an example of this with the Memento pattern in Chapter 7.

When It's Useful

The Factory Method pattern is useful in these situations:

- When you don't know the objects that will be used at runtime, but you're aware of the common interface
- When you require uniformity/localization among product creation and product assembly
- Any time you use new in a line of code

Example

Revisiting the Shell code from **Listing 6-3**, you still need to extract the creational logic that returns the appropriate instantiation of an overlay to use.

You know that including an abstraction could have assisted you in the Simple Factory. You can also use the abstraction to separate the logic and the preparation of the product returned. Doing so provides uniformity and flexibility, and saves you from having to add the assembly to each different logic implementation. You want to ensure that the logic can be easily extended, as well as modified.

You extract the Shell logic that created the overlays (see **Listing 6-6**) and place it for the time being in a class called OverlayFactory, as shown in **Listing 6-7**. In **Listing 6-8**, you also remove the preparation of the returned product of the factory to a class called OverlayPreparation.

Listing 6-6. Revisiting the 500-line excerpt of creational logic in Shell

```
private function createOverlay( overlayType : String , dataObject : * = null ) : void
{
        header.disableNavigation();
        currentSection.pause();
        if (currentOverlay)
        {
            destroyCurrentOverlay();
        }

        switch(overlayType)
        {
            case SectionEvent.VIDEO_OVERLAY:
                currentOverlay = new VideoOverlay();
                break;
            case SectionEvent.PHOTO_OVERLAY:
                currentOverlay = new PhotoViewer();
                break;
            case SectionEvent.AUDIO_OVERLAY:
                currentOverlay = new AudioOverlay();
                break;
            case SectionEvent.TWITTER_OVERLAY:
                currentOverlay = new TwitterOverlay();
                break;
            case OverlayEvent.TWITTER_SUBMIT_OVERLAY:
                currentOverlay = new AddTweetOverlay();
                break;
        }

        currentOverlay.y = SiteConfig.HEADER_HEIGHT;
        currentOverlay.addEventListener( OverlayEvent.CLOSE_OVERLAY , handleEvent );
        currentOverlay.addEventListener( OverlayEvent.INTRO_COMPLETE , handleEvent );
        currentOverlay.addEventListener( OverlayEvent.OUTRO_COMPLETE , handleEvent );
        currentOverlay.addEventListener( OverlayEvent.PLAY , handleEvent );
        currentOverlay.addEventListener( OverlayEvent.SUBMIT_TWEET , handleEvent );
        currentOverlay.addEventListener( OverlayEvent.TWITTER_SUBMIT_OVERLAY ,
➥ handleEvent );

        addChild( currentOverlay );

        currentOverlay.updateLayout( stage.stageWidth , (stage.stageHeight –
➥ SiteConfig.FOOTER_HEIGHT - SiteConfig.HEADER_HEIGHT) );
```

```
            currentOverlay.intro();
}

private function destroyCurrentOverlay() : void
{
        ... implementation not shown
}
... truncated code
```

Listing 6-7. OverlayFactory encapsulates the logic required to instantiate the appropriate overlay.

```
package
{
   public class OverlayFactory
   {
      public function OverlayFactory()
      {
      }

      public function createOverlay( overlayType : String ) : Overlay
      {
         var currentOverlay : Overlay

         switch(overlayType)
         {
            case SectionEvent.VIDEO_OVERLAY:
               currentOverlay = new VideoOverlay();
               break;
            case SectionEvent.PHOTO_OVERLAY:
               currentOverlay = new PhotoViewer();
               break;
            case SectionEvent.AUDIO_OVERLAY:
               currentOverlay = new AudioOverlay();
               break;
            case SectionEvent.TWITTER_OVERLAY:
               currentOverlay = new TwitterOverlay();
               break;
            case OverlayEvent.TWITTER_SUBMIT_OVERLAY:
               currentOverlay = new AddTweetOverlay();
               break;
         }

         return currentOverlay;
      }
```

```
        }
}
```

Listing 6-8. OverlayPreparation

```
package
{
    public class OverlayPreparation
    {
        private var factory : OverlayFactory = new OverlayFactory()
        private var currentOverlay : Overlay

        public function OverlayPreparation()
        {
        }

        public function createOverlay( overlayType : String ) : Overlay
        {
            currentOverlay = factory.createOverlay( str )

            currentOverlay.y = SiteConfig.HEADER_HEIGHT;
            currentOverlay.addEventListener( OverlayEvent.CLOSE_OVERLAY , handleEvent );

            currentOverlay.addEventListener( OverlayEvent.INTRO_COMPLETE , handleEvent );

            currentOverlay.addEventListener( OverlayEvent.OUTRO_COMPLETE , handleEvent );
            currentOverlay.addEventListener( OverlayEvent.PLAY , handleEvent );
            currentOverlay.addEventListener( OverlayEvent.SUBMIT_TWEET , handleEvent );

            currentOverlay.addEventListener( OverlayEvent.TWITTER_SUBMIT_OVERLAY ,
            ➥ handleEvent );

            currentOverlay.updateLayout( stage.stageWidth , (stage.stageHeight -
            ➥ SiteConfig.FOOTER_HEIGHT - SiteConfig.HEADER_HEIGHT) );
            return currentOverlay;
        }
    }
}
```

The first step in devising a common link is to note the commonalities that these two objects share. The two are, in a way, related in trying to achieve the same goals, and both depend on the product type. This dependency helps to ensure that both the assembler and the factory work toward a final product that doesn't break the contract between the two classes.

Considering the contract between the two objects, it's clear that you can use this method to join the two existing classes using inheritance. The common method can be refactored into an abstract class that your subclass can override (see **Listing 6-9** and **Listing 6-10**).

Listing 6-9. `AbstractOverlayFactory` is the abstract class and declares the `createOverlay` method.

```
package
{
   public class AbstractOverlayFactory
   {
      public function createOverlay( overlayType : String ) : Overlay
      {
         throw new IllegalOperationError( 'createOverlay must be overridden' )
         return null
      };
   }
}
```

Listing 6-10. `OverlayFactory` subclasses `AbstractOverlayFactory` in order to implement logic.

```
package
{
   public class OverlayFactory extends AbstractOverlayFactory
   {
      override public function createOverlay( overlayType : String ) : Overlay
      {
         var currentOverlay : Overlay

         switch(overlayType)
         {
            case SectionEvent.VIDEO_OVERLAY:
               currentOverlay = new VideoOverlay();
               break;
            case SectionEvent.PHOTO_OVERLAY:
               currentOverlay = new PhotoViewer();
               break;
            case SectionEvent.AUDIO_OVERLAY:
               currentOverlay = new AudioOverlay();
               break;
            case SectionEvent.TWITTER_OVERLAY:
               currentOverlay = new TwitterOverlay();
               break;
            case OverlayEvent.TWITTER_SUBMIT_OVERLAY:
               currentOverlay = new AddTweetOverlay();
               break;
         }
```

```
            }
        }
}
```

Currently you generate an abstraction that enables many subclasses to be created by extending AbstractOverlayFactory and overriding createOverlay to implement its logic in determining the appropriate product to return. What you've yet to create is the means by which object preparation occurs.

The logic should have zero knowledge of how the object is prepared. Similarly, the preparation shouldn't know how an overlay is chosen. Both of the two classes should focus on is the product's type, because this is what maintains compatibility between the classes.

By adding the preparation to the factory abstraction, you get all the benefits without any additional issues. You can also create new subclasses with different logic implementations, and not have to recode their assembly, because only the objects—not their type—change.

Listing 6-11. AbstractOverlayFactory includes the assembly process for the returned object.

```
package
{
    public class AbstractOverlayFactory
    {
        public function makeOverlay() : Overlay
        {
            var currentOverlay : Overlay = createOverlay( str );

            currentOverlay.y = SiteConfig.HEADER_HEIGHT;
            currentOverlay.addEventListener( OverlayEvent.CLOSE_OVERLAY , handleEvent );
            currentOverlay.addEventListener( OverlayEvent.INTRO_COMPLETE , handleEvent );
            currentOverlay.addEventListener( OverlayEvent.OUTRO_COMPLETE , handleEvent );
            currentOverlay.addEventListener( OverlayEvent.PLAY , handleEvent );
            currentOverlay.addEventListener( OverlayEvent.SUBMIT_TWEET , handleEvent );
            currentOverlay.addEventListener( OverlayEvent.TWITTER_SUBMIT_OVERLAY ,
    ➥ handleEvent )

            return currentOverlay
        }

        protected function createOverlay( overlayType : String ) : Overlay
        {
            throw new IllegalOperationError( 'createOverlay must be overridden' )
            return null
        };
    }
}
```

To ensure that preparation is used and not bypassed, `AbstractOverlayFactory` removes `createOverlay` as part of its interface so that only the superclass can call it. As a protected method, each subclass overrides `createOverlay` with its chosen implementation; and preparation is ensured because that process is in the additional method `makeOverlay`. The `makeOverlay` method has become the factory method that any client may message; in return, the client gets a product. Although this example returns the assembled product to an external client, this isn't always the case. Even the abstraction can be the client of the product, as well as the invoker of the factory method.

`makeOverlay` delegates the responsibility of creating an overlay to the logic in an encapsulated creator. Because the subclass and the abstract class both rely on the product type, the union between product preparation and creation is localized into one object, while maintaining great cohesion for maintenance.

What results from the factory method is a cohesive set of classes that localize common behavior in a product to be used in a system. By using inheritance, you can partition preparation from instantiation while abstracting the product from the client.

Localization and the union between preparation and creation are so well contained that it appears as if all you're instantiating is a class that implements the logic for object instantiation.

FAQ

- If the subclass and the superclass form the factory, and both know about the abstract product, why separate the logic from the assembly?

   You should keep the code localized for ease of maintenance. However, by injecting the means to package and prepare a product into the logic, you remove the flexibility to add or remove new products without physical maintenance of the object. The separation offers flexibility through its use of inheritance.

- If each product differs in the way it needs to be assembled or prepared, should a subclass have more control than the abstract over the means of preparing each object?

   The factory method focuses on one abstract type to return. If the assembly of a particular object varies from other objects of its type, it may be unabstracted. If this isn't the case, you can use the Builder pattern with the factory method. However, a subclass shouldn't have any knowledge about the preparation.

- If the subclass is a smarter and more specialized form of the superclass, shouldn't you be able to modify the methods declared in the abstract if they need to be more specific?

   As stated in the previous answer, a subclass shouldn't have any knowledge about the preparation of the product. If each concrete class could modify the logic and the preparation, the hierarchy could have infinite levels. This would be poor practice, because if any change occurred in the lower levels of a subclass, an error could present itself in any subclass.

- Can a factory build more than one product?

   Yes, a factory can return more than one product. Ensure that each factory method is named appropriately for the product being returned. If the products need to reside together as a set, consider the next pattern: Abstract Factory.

Related Patterns

The following patterns are related to the Factory Method pattern:

- Abstract Factory
- Builder
- State
- Template Method

The Abstract Factory Pattern

The Abstract Factory pattern provides an interface for creating families of related products while concealing the object-instantiation process. Figure 6-3 shows the class diagram.

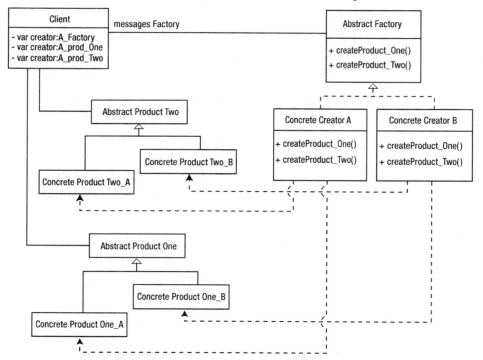

Figure 6-3. Abstract Factory pattern class diagram

This pattern has the following parts:

- Abstract product
- Concrete product
- Abstract creator
- Concrete creator
- Client

The pattern's benefits are as follows:

- Uses abstracts factories of like interfaces
- Enables the interchanging of product families

It also has this drawback:

- Introducing a new product is difficult.

A Comprehensive Look

The Abstract Factory pattern is an extension of the Factory Method pattern in that it uses many factory methods to create a subset, or related grouping of products. These product sets can then become interchangeable with other sets. This is due to the factory's polymorphism, established by the abstraction to the factory. The purpose of the Abstract Factory pattern is to group products, often of varying types. In a nutshell, an abstract factory is a collection of factory methods whose collective products work together.

The abstract factory conceals the concrete objects it instantiates by concerning itself with the product interfaces. For extensibility, the Abstract Factory pattern defers the manufacturing of objects to subclasses. This lets the caller of the request remain unfamiliar with particulars beyond those of the abstractions in use: the abstraction of the factory and the abstractions of any products the factory returns.

The factory's abstraction declares the interface that subclasses must implement. As the base class for all like-minded factories, the interfaces of all products used are exposed via the appropriate factory methods. As the Factory Method pattern states, the name of each method should describe the creation of the product. Often, the `create`, `get`, and `make` prefixes are used to help developers who are familiar with this pattern identify its existence in the code.

The factory's subclass has a different role to accompany the superclass. The subclass knows which concrete products are created and conceals this knowledge from the system, including its own abstraction. With the Abstract Factory pattern, each product is realized at author time; therefore, the methods don't require conditional logic. Rather than use a conditional statement to determine a product, a conditional statement determines the factory to use.

The client—the factory's messenger—uses each set of products via the appropriate factories as needed.

Vignette

A fast-food restaurant decided to increase its sales by adding a new breakfast sandwich to its menu. The sandwich contained eggs, cheese, bacon, and sausage. When a customer ordered, they had the option of choosing a specific type for each of the ingredients offered. The choices were as follows:

- Egg: Free-range, egg substitute, egg whites, or regular
- Cheese: Cheddar, Swiss, asiago, or muenster
- Bacon: Veggie, regular, Canadian, or turkey
- Sausage: Country, original, English, or vegetarian

Unfortunately, the fast-food restaurant wasn't delivering quick service. People liked the food—but the number of options slowed the ordering process as well as preparation time, and instead of increasing sales, caused customers to leave due to the long wait. Rather than continue to allow the delay between when the customer ordered and when they received their food, the franchise decided to narrow the options available. To do this, it picked the four most popular combinations of ingredients and offered four different breakfast sandwich options. The new selections were as follows:

- Product A: Egg whites, asiago cheese, turkey bacon, English sausage
- Product B: Egg substitute, muenster cheese, veggie bacon, vegetarian sausage
- Product C: Egg, cheddar cheese, regular bacon, original sausage
- Product D: Free-range egg, Swiss cheese, Canadian Bacon, country sausage

After the four new items were introduced to the public, wait times decreased due to more rapid ordering. However, the restaurant's wait times were still significantly longer than those of fast-food competitors. This was due to the new routine in the kitchen. Preparing items that had previously been on the menu had become second nature to the employees. But the staff were unfamiliar with the new sandwiches and had to put more thought and time into their preparation. Even though each refrigerator drawer was labeled with an ingredient—cheese, sausage, bacon, and so on—employees had to recall and differentiate options every time they made a sandwich.

The company created a new solution to quickly decrease preparation time and improve sales. Modifying the kitchen organization, the restaurant designated a drawer for each specific sandwich:

- Drawer 1: Product A
- Drawer 2: Product B
- Drawer 3: Product C
- Drawer 4: Product D

By organizing a set of ingredients per product, all the employees needed to know was which drawer to use.

The AS 3.0 Cast

In AS 3.0, the Abstract Factory pattern's parts are as follows:

- Abstract creator: The exposed interface, as well as the base factory. Defines the interface that an interchangeable set of factories can message, and defines the abstract products to be used in the factory. A factory can perform nearly any creational operation needed for a class:
  - Initialize
  - Pull in data
  - Configure
  - Set states
- Concrete creator: A factory subclass that contains the logic necessary to instantiate the appropriate object in a genus of products expected by the superclass for each factory method declared in the superclass.
- Abstract product: A product genus that exposes the interface that all concrete products of the given genus inherit.
- Concrete product: The physical object that can be instantiated. Extends the abstract product to express itself as a member of the type to be used in the logic of the creator.
- Client: The messenger of the abstract factory. Can be any aspect of the application or system that has prior knowledge of the abstract products as well as the abstract factory that is in use.

When It's Useful

The Abstract Factory pattern is useful in the following situations:

- When similar items have a reason to vary
- When you need to localize appropriate objects into a set
- When you need to add a layer of abstraction among products

Example

The Abstract Factory pattern relies on a uniform abstraction among different factories. This allows a factory to be parameterized and remain abstract to the code that uses it. The uniformity ensures that although each factory's implementation may vary, the product returned is that of a specific type.

You can see the benefit of using an abstraction with multiple factories in the overlay example. Suppose you're informed that the overlays you created are suitable only if the user comes from a particular coast. Because the United States has two coasts, you need another set of overlays that reflect the opposite coast. This value is passed in as a variable from PHP at load time.

Listing 6-12 revisits the code used in the Simple Factory example that showed the logic to create an overlay. The problem you now face is the need to create an appropriate set of products that can be interchanged depending on which coast a user comes from.

Listing 6-12. Simple Factory demonstrating the encapsulation of creational logic

```
public function createOverlay( overlayType : String ) : Overlay
{
    var currentOverlay : Overlay

    switch(overlayType)
    {
      case SectionEvent.VIDEO_OVERLAY:
        currentOverlay = new VideoOverlay();
        break;
      case SectionEvent.PHOTO_OVERLAY:
        currentOverlay = new PhotoViewer();
        break;
      case SectionEvent.AUDIO_OVERLAY:
        currentOverlay = new AudioOverlay();
        break;
      case SectionEvent.TWITTER_OVERLAY:
        currentOverlay = new TwitterOverlay();
        break;
      case OverlayEvent.TWITTER_SUBMIT_OVERLAY:
        currentOverlay = new AddTweetOverlay();
        break;
      case OverlayEvent.NEW_FORM_OVERLAY:
```

```
            currentOverlay = new NewFormOverlay();
            break;
        }
}
```

The code in **Listing 6-12** uses conditional logic to determine which overlay is necessary at runtime by using string parameterization. This determination is due to the unknown object that is required at runtime.

The Abstract Factory pattern, on the other hand, uses any number of factory methods to create a complete set of products. For this reason, conditionals are often unnecessary. Additionally, because the Abstract Factory pattern uses product sets, products can vary in type in the factory abstraction. In other words, two factory methods of different types can be used in an abstract factory.

Listing 6-13 shows an abstract class that acts as a template for every subclass. Note how the overlays, which previously were called in one operation, have been refactored into their own factory methods.

Listing 6-13. An abstract class ensures uniformity among subclassed factories.

```
package
{
    public class AbstractFactoryCoastOverlaySets
    {
        public function createPhotoViewerOverlay() : APhotoOverlay
        {
            var photoViewer : APhotoOverlay = makePhotoOverlay()
            return photoViewer
        }

        public function createVideoOverlay() : AVideoOverlay
        {
            var video : AVideoOverlay = makeVideoOverlay()
            return video
        }

        public function createAudioOverlay() : AAudioOverlay
        {
            var audio : AAudioOverlay = makeAudioOverlay()
            return audio
        }

        public function createTwitterOverlay() : ATwitterOverlay
        {
            var tweet : ATwitterOverlay = makeTwitterOverlay()
            return tweet
        }

        public function createFormOverlay() : AFormOverlay
```

```
    {
       var form : AFormOverlay = makeFormOverlay()
       return form
    }

    private function commonDisplayObjectPrep( dO : DisplayObject ) : DisplayObject
    {
       var currentOverlay : DisplayObject = dO as DisplayObject;

       currentOverlay.y = SiteConfig.HEADER_HEIGHT;
       currentOverlay.addEventListener( OverlayEvent.CLOSE_OVERLAY , handleEvent );
       currentOverlay.addEventListener( OverlayEvent.INTRO_COMPLETE , handleEvent );
       currentOverlay.addEventListener( OverlayEvent.OUTRO_COMPLETE , handleEvent );
       currentOverlay.addEventListener( OverlayEvent.PLAY , handleEvent );
       currentOverlay.addEventListener( OverlayEvent.SUBMIT_TWEET , handleEvent );

       currentOverlay.addEventListener( OverlayEvent.TWITTER_SUBMIT_OVERLAY ,
    ➥ handleEvent );

       return currentOverlay
    }

    protected function makePhotoOverlay() : APhotoOverlay
    {
    };

    protected function createVideoOverlay() : AVideoOverlay
    {
    };

    protected function createAudioOverlay() : AAudioOverlay
    {
    };

    protected function makeTwitterOverlay() : ATwitterOverlay
    {
    };

    protected function makeFormOverlay() : AFormOverlay
    {
    };
   }
}
```

Now each coast has its own factory. You do this by subclassing the abstract class `AbstractFactoryCoastOverlaySets` and applying the appropriate implementations per coast. This allows each factory to specify how each product is returned and localizes the code related to each coast.

Note the inclusion of the private method `commonDisplayObjectPrep`. This example shows that you can maintain a common preparation if all returned products require similar preparations. Otherwise, each product can also have its own prep work before it's returned to the client. This is acceptable because types are often different in an abstract factory.

Listing 6-14. West-coast overlays

```
package
{
    public class WestCoastOverlaySet extends AbstractFactoryCoastOverlaySets
    {
        override protected function makePhotoOverlay() : APhotoOverlay
        {
            return new WestCoastPhotoOverlay()
        };

        protected override  function makeVideoOverlay() : AVideoOverlay
        {
            return new WestCoastVideoOverlay()
        };

        protected override  function makeAudioOverlay() : AAudioOverlay
        {
            return new WestCoastAudioOverlay()
        };

        protected override  function makeTwitterOverlay() : ATwitterOverlay
        {
            return new WestCoastTwitterOverlay()
        };

        protected override  function makeFormOverlay() : AFormOverlay
        {
            return new WestCoastFormOverlay()
        };
    }
}
```

Listing 6-15. East-coast overlays

```
package
{
    public class EastCoastOverlaySet extends AbstractFactoryCoastOverlaySets
```

```
{
    override protected function makePhotoOverlay() : APhotoOverlay
    {
        return new EastCoastPhotoOverlay()
    };

    protected override  function makeVideoOverlay() : AVideoOverlay
    {
        return new EastCoastVideoOverlay()
    };

    protected override  function makeAudioOverlay() : AAudioOverlay
    {
        return new EastCoastAudioOverlay()
    };

    protected override  function makeTwitterOverlay() : ATwitterOverlay
    {
        return new EastCoastTwitterOverlay()
    };

    protected override  function makeFormOverlay() : AFormOverlay
    {
        return new EastCoastFormOverlay()
    };
}
}
```

By decoupling the return types from Overlay to that which each overlay generalizes, you give the compiler more control over your author-time bindings. Now all you need are abstract classes for each of product.

With two factories in your system, you need to know which factory to instantiate. **Listing 6-16** uses a simple factory to determine which factory should be used in the application. You use a simple factory rather than an abstract factory because there are only two coasts, and I don't foresee any change occurring here.

Listing 6-16. CoastOverlayLogic is a simple factory that determines the appropriate coast factory.

```
package
{
    public class CoastOverlayLogic
    {
        private const WEST_COAST:String='west_coast'
        public function CoastOverlayLogic()
        {
        }
```

```
    public function createOverlayPreparation( coast : String ) :
        ➡ AbstractFactoryCoastOverlaySets
    {
        switch(coast)
        {
            case WEST_COAST:
                return new WestCoastOverlaySet();
                break;
            default:
                return new EastCoastOverlaySet();
                break;
                return null
        }
    }
    }
}
```

To illustrate how you can add another factory, let's suppose you also need a factory for Canada. You can create another subclass as shown in **Listing 6-17** and **Listing 6-18**.

Listing 6-17. Canadian overlays

```
package
{
    public class CanadaOverlaySet extends AbstractFactoryCoastOverlaySets
    {
        override protected function makePhotoOverlay() : APhotoOverlay
        {
            return new CanadaPhotoOverlay();
        }

        protected override  function makeVideoOverlay() : AVideoOverlay
        {
            return new CanadaVideoOverlay();
        }

        protected override  function makeAudioOverlay() : AAudioOverlay
        {
            return new CanadaAudioOverlay();
        }

        protected override  function makeTwitterOverlay() : ATwitterOverlay
        {
            return new CanadaTwitterOverlay();
        }
```

```
    protected override  function makeFormOverlay() : AFormOverlay
    {
       return new CanadaFormOverlay();
    }
  }
}
```

Listing 6-18. CoastOverlayLogic reflects the addition of Canada.

```
package
{
   public class CoastOverlayLogic
   {
      private const WEST_COAST : String = "west_coast";
      private const EAST_COAST : String = "east_coast";
      private const CANADA     : String = "canada"

      public function CoastOverlayLogic()
      {
      }

      public function createOverlayPreparation( coast : String ) :
            ➥ AbstractFactoryCoastOverlaySets
      {
         switch(coast)
         {
            case WEST_COAST:
               return new WestCoastOverlaySet();
               break;
            case EAST_COAST:
               return new EastCoastOverlaySet();
               break;
            case CANADA:
               return new CanadaOverlaySet();
               break;
               return null;
            default:
               break;
         }
      }
   }
}
```

FAQ

- What distinguishes this from the Factory Method pattern?

  The Abstract Factory pattern differs from the Factory Method pattern in that it offers a set of products to be manufactured. The Factory Method pattern returns only one product.

- This pattern sounds awfully like the Factory Method pattern with extra products.

  The diagram does look a lot like the Factory Method pattern. The difference is that a factory method uses an abstraction with no need for *interchangeability in the system*, but rather for extensibility. This lets you add a new product to a subclass and use it in your application by overriding a hook.

  Because the factory method returns a product of the same type, the logic of the factory can use a conditional statement to return the instance that is required to meet the goals of the system.

  In the Abstract Factory pattern, the factory object can be made up of numerous factory methods, but this isn't the important aspect. This pattern focuses on the parameterization of a series of sets. Factories can be swapped out with other factories of product sets to meet given criteria.

- It appears that product preparation can extensively elongate the abstract class.

  This is true and worth keeping in mind. The preparations should remain small enough to work with; otherwise, they may be difficult to maintain and likely to change. As you know, everything can change, so you should be proactive about keeping this code manageable. But if it begins to become unmanageable, it's all right—the next pattern can work with the Abstract Factory pattern for this reason.

Related Patterns

The following patterns are related to the Abstract Method pattern:

- Builder
- Factory
- Template Method

The Builder Pattern

The Builder pattern separates the construction steps from the product to offer flexibility among product representations. Figure 6-4 shows the class diagram.

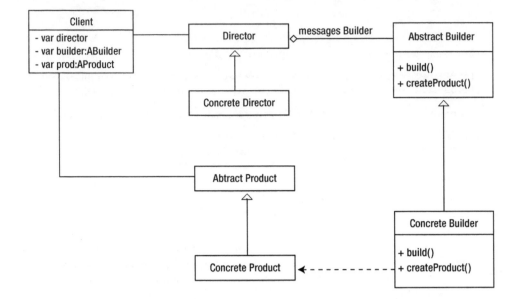

Figure 6-4. Builder pattern class diagram

This pattern has the following parts:

- Abstract product
- Concrete product
- Abstract builder
- Concrete builder
- Abstract director
- Concrete director
- Client

The pattern's benefits are as follows:

- Very high level of control over object creation
- Enables varying products from the same algorithms
- Conceals the construction process from the client

A Comprehensive Look

The Builder pattern is concerned with building objects in a manner that promotes interchangeability in the way a product is represented. Through composition and delegation, a client messages the builder with the instructions to build or return the product it requires.

The Builder pattern conceals several operations that may be involved in achieving the final representation of a product expected by the client. This makes the Builder pattern more intricate than its similar Factory colleagues. A builder can create complex objects that require more than a simple initialization, configuration, or assembly. Because a concrete builder focuses on the creation of a final product, it offers a higher level of attention to the assembly of its creation.

A concrete builder has the methods needed to create such a complex product but uses them only when messaged. This lets you manipulate the inner workings that may affect the appearance of the product.

The director takes a request from the client and uses it in a sequence of actions between the builder and itself in an effort to arrive at a final product.

Because the details of the construction are hidden from the client, the final representation of the product may remain abstract to the system. The implementation of the builder that constructs the product is flexible because its implementations are separate from that of its superclass.

Because a concrete builder subclasses an abstraction, an additional layer of abstraction can be introduced into the client, much like in the Abstract Factory pattern. Due to the advanced construction the Builder pattern offers, many of the products returned are *composites*: objects composed of one or more like objects.

Vignette

Burger Kind's has used the slogan "Your Way Right Away" for years. When you walk up to the counter, you ask for a cheeseburger, expecting the cook to ask, "How would you like the meat cooked?" Unfortunately, that doesn't happen; and before you realize that you have to ask up front for your desired preparation, the employee behind the counter hands you a packaged meal. Opening it, you find a charred patty dressed with mayonnaise and mustard. Yuck. These are things you would have asked not to have, had you known they were standard.

Disgusted with your lunch, you walk over to SubWeight. An employee greets you, much like at Burger Kind, and asks if they may take your order. Realizing your earlier mistake of keeping silent, you tell them everything you want up front. "I would like a tuna sandwich toasted on wheat with olives, onions, lettuce, black pepper, salt, jalapenos, and Swiss cheese," followed by a "please" to be courteous. The employee stares at you as if you're doing something improper. This is your first time at SubWeight, so you're unaware of their process.

The workstation shows everything available so that as your sandwich is prepared, you can oversee the process during which your sandwich is crafted. Genius: they're sandwich artists—or rather, you are.

It all begins with bread. They have a decent selection to choose from: wraps, wheat, Italian, and more. All you have to do is say "Foot-long wheat." Having the base on which to add your ingredient objects, the employee asks, "What kind of cheese?" And you answer, "Swiss." This process continues step by step, allowing you to specify the preparation to your liking. Because SubWeight offers you a say in the assembly of your sandwich, you can ask three times for more lettuce, before moving on to the next ingredient.

Finally, the employee asks if there will be anything else, signifying the end of your product's creation. Via a "No" command, you can have your sandwich returned. Then you turn over delivery to the client: your stomach.

The AS 3.0 Cast

In AS 3.0, the Builder pattern's parts are as follows:

- Abstract builder: Defines an interface that lets the director have a contract between itself and the builder. Because the builder object doesn't assemble itself, the abstract builder shouldn't have any implementations declared. And because the abstract builder doesn't have any default implementations, it's also safe to use an interface for the concrete builder. However, if you have concrete builders that share similar data, an abstract builder is a good idea.
- Concrete builder: Contains the implementations of its defined interface. Although it contains the implementations to make a product, the builder doesn't try to build the product itself. Instead, it takes directions from the named object: the director.
- Abstract director: Contains the instructions to create the final product using the builder object's interface. Because this vision may vary among products, the abstract director provides the flexibility that lets similar directors remain uniform.
- Concrete director: Encapsulates the logic to conceal the steps of product creation from the client. This separation of details from interface lets you introduce interchangeable logic, from which new representations of a product may result.
- Abstract product: Exposes the interface that all concrete products of the given genus inherit. In a few textbooks the abstract product is lacking, because, many times, the product returned is so specific and unlike other products that the builders create. Your goal isn't to program to concretes, but to an interface, and therefore you need either an abstract class or an interface for the product.
- Concrete product: Extends the abstract product to express itself as a member of the type to be used by the client. Often this product is a composite that requires many steps to construct.
- Client: The messenger of the builder. It can be any aspect of the application or system that has prior knowledge of the abstract products, as well as the abstract factory being used.

When It's Useful

The Builder pattern is useful in the following situations:

- When you're using third-party APIs
- With factories, to help with complicated preparations
- When you're constructing composites

Example

The best thing about the Builder pattern is its ability to create numerous representations from a given pool of resources. This is an amazing behavior to have in RIA development. Imagine purchasing Lego blocks in bulk on eBay. Depending on how many Legos you have, you may be able to make several different structures from only six basic shapes.

You can create so many different formations thanks to your imagination. The pieces don't change, but your ideas do, and because of this you can vary your representations even though you're using the same blocks.

This pattern is very common in AS 3.0, especially as applications have grown larger and more complex. Display objects and display object containers become composites and vary from scene to scene. But a builder isn't just for composites, and that too makes it special.

The following example uses a recognizable game to simulate the advantage of the Builder design pattern. The image in Figure 6-5 is the final product created by the collaboration between a director and builder. **Listing 6-19** through **Listing 6-24** show the code used. It all begins with an interface.

Figure 6-5. Stage 1-0 of a game

Listing 6-19. `AbstractMarioEsqueLevelEditor` defines the interface of the builder.

```
package
{
   public class AbstractMarioEsqueLevelEditor
   {
      private var _bitmap : BitmapData
      private var _backgroundColor : uint
      private var _width : int
      private var _height : int
      private var _pt : Point
      private var _tile : Shape

      public function AbstractMarioEsqueLevelEditor()
      {
         _tile = new Shape()
         _pt = new Point( 0 , 0 )
      }

      final public function createMap() : void
```

```
{
   bitmap = doCreateMap()
}

final public function getLevel() : BitmapData
{
   return _bitmap
}

final public function createStone( rect : Rectangle ) : void
{
   addTile( doCreateStone() , rect )
}

final public function createSolidBrick( rect : Rectangle ) : void
{
   addTile( doCreateSolidBrick() , rect )
}

final public function createBreakableBrick( rect : Rectangle ) : void
{
   addTile( doCreateBreakableBrick() , rect )
}

final public function createMoneyBox( rect : Rectangle ) : void
{
   addTile( doCreateMoneyBox() , rect )
}

final public function createCloud( rect : Rectangle ) : void
{
   addTile( doCreateCloud() , rect )
}

final public function createHill( rect : Rectangle ) : void
{
   addTile( doCreateHill() , rect )
}

final public function createBush( rect : Rectangle ) : void
{
   addTile( doCreateBush() , rect )
}
```

```
final public function createCastle( rect : Rectangle ) : void
{
   addTile( doCreateCastle() , rect )
}

final public function createPipe( rect : Rectangle ) : void
{
   addTile( doCreatePipe() , rect )
}

final public function get width() : int
{
   return _width;
}

final public function set width( width : int ) : void
{
   _width = width;
}

final public function get height() : int
{
   return _height;
}

final public function set height( height : int ) : void
{
   _height = height;
}

final public function get backgroundColor() : uint
{
   return _backgroundColor;
}

final public function set backgroundColor( backgroundColor : uint ) : void
{
   _backgroundColor = backgroundColor;
}

final public function get bitmap() : BitmapData
{
   return _bitmap;
}
```

```
final public function set bitmap( bitmap : BitmapData ) : void
{
   _bitmap = bitmap;
}

protected function doCreateMap() : BitmapData
{
   return new BitmapData( width , height , false , backgroundColor );
}

protected function doCreateStone() : DisplayObject
{
   throw new IllegalOperationError( 'doCreateStone must be overridden' );
   return null;
}

protected function doCreateSolidBrick() : DisplayObject
{
   throw new IllegalOperationError( 'doCreateSolidBrick must be  overridden' );
   return null;
}

protected function doCreateBreakableBrick() : DisplayObject
{
   throw new IllegalOperationError('doCreateBreakableBrick must be overridden');
   return null;
}

protected function doCreateMoneyBox() : DisplayObject
{
   throw new IllegalOperationError( 'doCreateMoneyBox must be overridden' );
   return null;
}

protected function doCreateCloud() : DisplayObject
{
   throw new IllegalOperationError( 'doCreateCloud must be overridden' );
   return null;
}

protected function doCreateHill() : DisplayObject
{
   throw new IllegalOperationError( 'doCreateHill must be overridden' );
```

```
      return null;
   }

   protected function doCreateBush() : DisplayObject
   {
      throw new IllegalOperationError( 'doCreateBush must be overridden' );
      return null;
   }

   protected function doCreateCastle() : DisplayObject
   {
      throw new IllegalOperationError( 'doCreateCastle must be overridden' );
      return null;
   }

   protected function doCreatePipe() : DisplayObject
   {
      throw new IllegalOperationError( 'doCreatePipe must be overridden' );
      return null;
   }

   private function addTile( dO : DisplayObject , rect : Rectangle ) : void
   {
      var sprite : BitmapData = snapShot( dO );
      _pt.x = rect.x;
      _pt.y = rect.y;
      if (rect.width > 0 || rect.height > 0)
      {
         sprite = tile( sprite , rect );
      }
      bitmap.copyPixels( sprite , sprite.rect , _pt );
   }

   private function snapShot( dO : DisplayObject ) : BitmapData
   {
      var snapshot : BitmapData = new BitmapData( dO.width, dO.height, true, 0 );
      snapshot.draw( dO );
      return snapshot;
   }

   private function tile( bmpd : BitmapData , rect : Rectangle ) : BitmapData
   {
      var _t : Shape = _tile;
      var g : Graphics = _t.graphics;
```

```
            g.clear();
            g.beginBitmapFill( bmpd , null , true , false );
            g.drawRect( 0 , 0 , rect.width , rect.height );
            g.endFill();
            return snapShot( _t );
        }
    }
}
```

Having provided the abstract class, you proceed to fulfill the specifics of the factory methods involved via the subclass. You call this MarioLevelEditor (see **Listing 6-20**).

Listing 6-20. MarioLevelEditor subclasses AbstractMarioEsqueLevelEditor to supply its implementation.

```
package
{
    public class MarioLevelEditor extends AbstractMarioEsqueLevelEditor
    {
        public function MarioLevelEditor()
        {
            super();
        }

        override protected function doCreateSolidBrick() : DisplayObject
        {
            return new SolidBrick();
        }

        override protected function doCreateBreakableBrick() : DisplayObject
        {
            return new BreakableBrick();
        }

        override protected function doCreateStone() : DisplayObject
        {
            return new Stone();
        }

        override protected function doCreateMoneyBox() : DisplayObject
        {
            return  new MoneyBox();
        }

        override protected function doCreateCloud() : DisplayObject
        {
            return new Cloud();
```

```
        }

        override  protected function doCreateHill() : DisplayObject
        {
           return  new Hill();
        }

        override protected function doCreatePipe() : DisplayObject
        {
           return new Pipe();
        }

        override protected function doCreateBush() : DisplayObject
        {
           return new Shrubs();
        }
    }
}
```

The interface in **Listing 6-19** is extensive and would be a pain to modify in a client, if the interface changed. To ease the burden this would cause, you create a middleman—the director—that knows about the given interface exposed by the builder (see **Listing 6-21**). A director adheres to the interface of an abstract builder and greatly minimizes the interface that a client must be concerned with. Of course, each director may change to provide different implementations; therefore you need to provide a superclass to promote polymorphism while also implementing code common to each subclass.

Listing 6-21. AbstractMarioLevelDirector

```
package
{
    public class AbstractMarioLevelDirector
    {
        protected var _builder : AbstractMarioEsqueLevelEditor

        public function AbstractMarioLevelDirector( builder :
            ➡ AbstractMarioEsqueLevelEditor )
        {
          _builder = builder;
        }

        public function getLevel() : BitmapData
        {
           return _builder.getLevel();
        }
    }
}
```

With the abstract director in place, you can begin creating implementations in your subclasses. Each implementation controls the representation of the product. You do this by deferring all requests to the passed-in reference of a builder object.

Listing 6-22. LevelOne subclasses AbstractMarioLevelDirector.

```
package
{
   public class LevelOne extends AbstractMarioLevelDirector
   {
      private const _width : int = 400;
      private const _height : int = 300;
      private var rect : Rectangle = new Rectangle( 0 , 0 , 0 , 0 );

      public function LevelOne( builder : AbstractMarioEsqueLevelEditor )
      {
         super( builder );
      }

      public override  function getLevel() : BitmapData
      {
         _builder.width = _width;
         _builder.height = _height;
         _builder.backgroundColor = 0 0000FF;
         _builder.createMap();
         buildPipes();
         buildFloor();
         buildScenicBushes();
         buildClouds();

         buildMoneyBox();
         buildScenicBricks();
         return _builder.getLevel();
      }

      private function buildScenicBushes() : void
      {
         assignRect( 100 , _height - 28 * 2 - 32 );
         _builder.createBush( rect );
      }

      private function buildMoneyBox() : void
      {
         assignRect( 50 , _height - 51.25 - 95 );
         _builder.createMoneyBox( rect );
```

```
    }

    private function buildScenicBricks() : void
    {
        assignRect( 50 - 28 , _height - 51.25 - 95 );
        _builder.createBreakableBrick( rect );
        assignRect( 50 + 28 , _height - 51.25 - 95 );
        _builder.createBreakableBrick( rect );
    }

    private function buildPipes() : void
    {
        assignRect( 250 , _height - 28 * 2 - 65 );
        _builder.createPipe( rect );
    }

    private function buildFloor() : void
    {
        assignRect( 0 , _height - 56 , _width , _height - 56 );
        _builder.createSolidBrick( rect );
    }

    private function buildClouds() : void
    {
        assignRect( 0 , 40 );
        _builder.createCloud( rect );
        assignRect( 200 );
        _builder.createCloud( rect );
    }

    private function assignRect( x:int = 0, y:int = 0, w:int = 0, h:int = 0 ) : void
    {
        rect.x = x;
        rect.y = y;
        rect.width = w;
        rect.height = h;
    }
  }
}
```

With the builder and director complete, its time to put them to use, as demonstrated in **Listing 6-23**.

Listing 6-23. DocumentClass instantiates both director and builder to produce your Level

```
package
{
    public class DocumentClass extends Sprite
    {
        private var _bitmap : Bitmap

        public function DocumentClass()
        {
            var stg : Stage = this.stage;
            stg.scaleMode = StageScaleMode.NO_SCALE;
            stg.align = StageAlign.TOP_LEFT;
            var levelEditor : AbstractMarioEsqueLevelEditor = new MarioLevelEditor();
            var director : AbstractMarioLevelDirector = new StageTwo( levelEditor );
            // LevelOne(levelEditor);
            _bitmap = new Bitmap( director.getLevel() );
            addChild( _bitmap );
        }
    }
}
```

Because the builder can't build the product without directions from the director, you can create numerous variations from the same builder resources. Suppose you want to adjust the product representation as shown in Figure 6-6 (see also **Listing 6-24**).

Figure 6-6. A different representation of Stage 1-0

Listing 6-24. StageTwo is a director subclass with a different set of implementations.

```
package
{
    public class StageTwo extends AbstractMarioLevelDirector
    {
        private const _width : int = 400;
        private const _height : int = 300;
        private var rect : Rectangle = new Rectangle( 0 , 0 , 0 , 0 );

        public function StageTwo( builder : AbstractMarioEsqueLevelEditor )
        {
            super( builder );
        }

        public  override  function getLevel() : BitmapData
        {
            _builder.width = _width;
            _builder.height = _height;
            _builder.backgroundColor = 0 0000FF;

            _builder.createMap();
            buildPipes();
            buildFloor();

            buildClouds();
            buildStairs();
            return _builder.getLevel();
        }

        private function buildMoneyBox() : void
        {
            assignRect( 50 , _height - 51.25 - 95 );
            _builder.createMoneyBox( rect );
        }

        private function buildStairs() : void
        {
            var totalWide : int = _width;
            var floorTall : int = _height - 28 * 2;
            var row : int = 6;
            var col : int = 1;
            while (--row)
            {
```

```
              var dist : int = totalWide - row * 28;
              assignRect( dist , floorTall - col * 28 , row * 28 , 28 );
              _builder.createStone( rect );
              col++;
          }
      }

      private function buildPipes() : void
      {
          assignRect( 50 , _height - 28 * 2 - 65 );
          _builder.createPipe( rect );
      }

      private function buildFloor() : void
      {
          assignRect( 0 , _height - 56 , _width , _height - 56 );
          _builder.createSolidBrick( rect );
      }

      private function buildClouds() : void
      {
          assignRect( 0 , 40 );
          _builder.createCloud( rect );
          assignRect( 40 , 40 );
          _builder.createCloud( rect );
          assignRect( 400 , 30 );
          _builder.createCloud( rect );
      }

      private function assignRect( x:int = 0, y:int = 0, w:int = 0, h:int = 0 ) : void
      {
          rect.x = x;
          rect.y = y;
          rect.width = w;
          rect.height = h;
      }
   }
}
```

The builder allows variations among internal representations. Each director can use a builder as it sees fit.

FAQ

- You could use the stage in Flash to do the same thing, probably much faster. What makes this approach any better?

    The example certainly could be created on the stage. The example demonstrates varying representations, which is far easier to do with graphics than with internal data. The focus of the example is the sequence of steps the director follows to vary the representation of the product.

    Although you may be able to re-create this example on the stage more quickly, you wouldn't be able to do so if there were no graphics involved to place at author-time.

    Imagine an RIA that allows a user to create a FLV reel from any number of provided FLVs. Users can cut and stitch the FLVs into a seamless .flv file that they can download. Using a builder with the exposed methods to cut and stitch bytes together, you can use the director to reflect the users' choices.

    There are many additional reasons to use a Builder design pattern.

- The example varies the representation using common assets. Can each concrete builder change those assets?

    This example bundles your assets in one .swc file for simplicity, but the truth is that you should only use what you know you need. This reduces file sizes and limits excess files.

    When you're using the Builder pattern, each concrete builder can introduce its own assets by overriding factory methods. If there are many assets that require variation, you can use abstract factories as well.

- What is another reason to use a builder?

    Suppose you were refactoring the code shown in **Listing 6-25**. This code is very rigid and shows what often occurs when there is uncertainty about how to uniformly modify the preparations among a series of objects and their varying attributes. The Builder pattern would be a great aid in adding uniformity and abstracting the assembly in the code.

Listing 6-25. Logic and preparation tied together

```
override public function createProduct( string : String ) : DisplayObject
    {
        switch(string)
        {
          case    STARTUP_SCREEN:
            currentClass = new SystemStartup();
            currentClass.x = (System.SECTION_WIDTH) * .5 - 70 - 4;
            currentClass.y = 103.5 - 70;
            currentClass.nextState = VIDEO_WELCOME;
            return currentClass;
            break;
          case    VIDEO_WELCOME:
```

```
              currentClass = new Introduction();
              currentClass.x = 835 - 5;
              currentClass.y = 55;
              currentClass.nextState = CLEARANCE_SCREEN;
              return currentClass;
              break;
      case    DEMONSTRATION_SCREEN:
              currentClass = new Demonstration();
              currentClass.x = 835 - 4;
              currentClass.y = 75;
              currentClass.nextState = NULL_SCREEN;
              return currentClass
      case          NULL_SCREEN:
              currentClass = new NullState();
              currentClass.x = (1600 - currentClass.width) * .5 - 4;
              currentClass.y = (600 - currentClass.height) * .5;
              currentClass.nextState = NULL_SCREEN;
              return currentClass;
              break;
      }
  }
```

Note: Here's a hint to get you on your way toward refactoring **Listing 6-25**: use four builders, one director, and one factory method.

Related Patterns

The following patterns are related to the Builder pattern:

- Factory Method
- Template Method
- Abstract Factory

The Simple Singleton Pattern

The Simple Singleton pattern provides a global reference to an object that requires uniqueness. Figure 6-7 shows the class diagram.

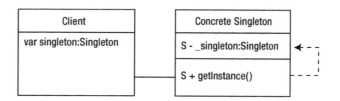

Figure 6-7. Simple Singleton pattern class diagram

This pattern has the following parts:

- Concrete singleton
- Class member
- Client

The pattern's benefits are as follows:

- Grants global access to an object
- Maintains access to its unique instance
- Is easy to create

It also has this drawback:

- Can't be extended (change is a constant)

A Comprehensive Look

Chapter 4 explained that not all object-oriented languages are built equally, and therefore not all patterns can be implemented equally. For this reason, a design pattern's intentions must be taken into consideration when you implement that pattern. Because the Simple Singleton pattern's intentions can't be met in the ActionScript 3.0 language simply by using the static modifier, you can't, and shouldn't, consider the standard implementation of the Simple Singleton an AS 3.0 design pattern.

The intentions of the Simple Singleton design pattern are as follows:

- It ensures that only one instance of an object is in use.
- It must contract an access point that the one instance has acquired.
- The singular instance should have the flexibility to offer change without adding more namespaces to the system.

But creating a singleton using the static keyword achieves only the first two of these three intentions. This is why I refer to this implementation as Simple Singleton, because it intends to maintain a global reference to a given object.

Ensuring global access for an instance requires the instance to be a class member. You learned in Chapter 2 that in order to access a class member, you must access the value from the Class object itself. Therefore, it's safe to assume there are many references to a concrete class strewn throughout the code of a system that references the member. This nearly guarantees that any change you make to the object occurs as a modification rather than an extension.

The only other remaining solution would be to track down every occurrence of the static reference and replace it with another static instance. You can see how that might force developers into breaking the open-closed principle (open for extension, closed for modification). This inflexibility is, again, why I call this implementation Simple Singleton and say that it isn't a design pattern in AS 3.0.

Vignette

A southern brand of fried chicken is regarded by locals as the world's best chicken. This gives the proprietor of the restaurant an idea. He wants his chicken to be eaten by everyone, not just people in the local vicinity. Certain that he can't get the entire world to come to his town, the proprietor decides to bring his variety of chicken to the world. He wants to be known globally and have his specialty chicken within reach of any consumer.

Knowing that his chicken will never change, he packages it and ships it to a global supermarket chain. Anyone who wants a taste of this chicken now has global access to it. The prepackaged chicken, made by the original chef, ensures great taste each and every time. The packaging helps to ensure this, with its fancy ability to lock in freshness. And the chef was required to sign an exclusive contract with the supermarket, ensuring that the chicken will always be available for clients.

The chef's chicken does so well that he receives letters from around the world asking him to create an alternate product to promote a healthy diet. The chef works to extend his already famous product, and the result is grilled chicken.

Grilled chicken provides a much healthier alternative to the original chicken. Excited by the opportunity this offers the world, the chef wants to supply the new product in place of the original chicken. Unfortunately, the contract specifies that stores have exclusive rights of the chef's original recipe, and no substitutions can be made—the supermarkets are making a tremendous profit.

The chef really wants the world to experience his new chicken variety, and he considers putting the new chicken in the old packaging. This way, people would experience the chicken, remain happy, and benefit from the healthier recipe. Unfortunately, this approach would also cause confusion: some people might receive the original recipe while others got the new recipe, and this might make the product appear inconsistent.

Unwilling to change a good thing, the chef signs another contract with the supermarket. Instead of swapping the new product for the previous one, he now offers two products. The chef can take consolation in knowing that neither product will change.

The AS 3.0 Cast

In AS 3.0, the Simple Singleton pattern's parts are as follows:

- Concrete instance: The object of a singular instance. All instances can be instantiated and have their data modified via an object using the expressed interface. The concrete instance has a unique method that acts as a wrapper around a class member instance.
- Class member Instance: A reference associated with the class and not the object. This reduces memory allocation given any number of instances of a given class. Although it's public, a class member can be accessed in a manner that doesn't require an instance. You achieve such a class reference by using the static modifier.

- Client: The simple singleton's messenger. The client can be any aspect of the application or system that has prior knowledge of the abstract product. It also must know the fully qualified name of the static class and its static method.

Example

The Simple Singleton pattern is regularly used in large-scale projects. What makes this particular object work is also the reason it's not a design pattern for AS 3.0. The only way you can get the instance as a global variable and/or prevent a unique instance from any other instantiation from overwriting such a reference is to make the reference a class member. As you learned in Chapter 2, class members can only be accessed via the fully qualified class name.

The convenience of the singleton object explains why it continues to flourish. But as you'll soon see, and likely will agree, the Simple Singleton approach may not be as helpful as you think.

A simple singleton is also used as a means of achieving a goal, by providing global reach from one object's namespace to another. Generally, it's used to communicate with a major portion of a shell or model for things such as sound management or tracking.

The code in **Listing 6-26** is an excerpt of a class from an RIA that lets you use a user's Facebook profile throughout the application. Currently, the user's profile is only accessible to the current class. This is because the RIA was never intended to remember the user's information. The current class was intended to let users share the application's link with their friends while displaying a message to the user who used their profile.

Listing 6-26. FaceBooklogin

```
package
{
   public class FaceBookLogin extends EventDispatcher
   {
      protected var _faceBook : IFaceBook;
      protected var _shortProfile : ShortProfileInformation;
      private var _hasProfile : Boolean = false;
      private var _ready : Boolean;

      public function FaceBookLogin( target : IEventDispatcher = null )
      {
         super( target );
         _ready = false;
         _shortProfile = new ShortProfileInformation();
      }

      public function init() : void
      {
         _ready = false;
         // a class that uses my FaceBookGraphAPI;
```

```
      _faceBook = new FaceBookFacade();

      _faceBook.addEventListener( FacebookEvent.CONNECT , faceBookConnectHandler ,
      ➥ false , 0 , true );
   }

   public function get facebook() : IFaceBook
   {
      return _faceBook;
   }

   public function get hasProfile() : Boolean
   {
      return _hasProfile;
   }

   public function get shortProfile() : ShortProfileInformation
   {
      return _shortProfile;
   }

   protected function faceBookConnectHandler( event : FacebookEvent ) : void
   {
      if (event.success)
      {
         FacebookCall( _faceBook.queryUserInformation() ).addEventListener(
      ➥ FacebookEvent.COMPLETE , userInfoLoaded );

         dispatchEvent( new FacebookEvent( FacebookEvent.CONNECT, false, false ) );
      }
   }

   protected function userInfoLoaded( event : FacebookEvent ) : void
   {
      var aFaceBookCall : FacebookCall = event.target as FacebookCall;
      aFaceBookCall.removeEventListener( FacebookEvent.COMPLETE , userInfoLoaded );

      dispatchEvent( new FacebookEvent( FacebookEvent.COMPLETE , false , false ) );

      var profile : ProfileInformation = _faceBook.getUserProfile();
      _shortProfile.usrIdentifier = profile.userName;
      _shortProfile.faceBook = true;
      _hasProfile = true;
   }
```

```
    }
}
```

The Simple Singleton pattern offers a solution to the problem at hand. How can you capture the information in this class so it remains usable throughout the site, as well as update current text fields with parts of a user's profile? A simple singleton lets you acquire user data globally, while ensuring that the results remain unchanged. To do this, you use a class member to keep a pointer to the memory of the object's instantiation. This allows you to obtain all methods via the interface of the object when it's retrieved from the class. It's appropriate to have Facebook information in FaceBookClass, so you create a static variable to reference the pointer:

```
public static var _fbReference:FaceBook;
// This class member will hold any subclass of Facebook
```

The static attribute of the reference enables global access to the class by way of its Class object. You set the static attribute to a variable rather than a constant so its pointer can be manipulated:

```
FaceBook.fbReference = new FaceBook();
//this changes the previous pointer to that of a new Facebook initialization.
```

To limit an object's ability to modify _fbReference, you declare the static variable as being private in scope, and use a getter for outside objects to obtain the reference. The problem is that now you can't subclass the FaceBook object and set the variable with the extension. So, you set the access modifier to protected, the better option. This allows your object to use the static reference because it's in the same hierarchy. This also means that if another FaceBook object is instantiated, it's granted appropriate privileges to overwrite the static reference, because it also has access to that variable.

You need to ensure that the FaceBook instance occurs one time and one time only; otherwise your information can and will be overwritten. The Simple Singleton pattern offers a solution to needing an access point that the class checks if an instance exists. If an instance has already been created, that instance will be the object returned to the client; otherwise a new instance is created, stored in a class member, and then returned to the client. The conditional statement is shown in **Listing 6-27**.

Listing 6-27. FaceBook class as a simple singleton

```
package
{
   public class FaceBook extends FaceBookLogin
   {
      static protected var $_fbInstance : FaceBookLogin;

      public function FaceBookA( target : IEventDispatcher = null )
      {
         super( target );
      }

      static public function getInstance() : FaceBookLogin
      {
         if ($_fbInstance)
         {
```

```
            $_fbInstance = new FaceBook();
        }
        return $_fbInstance;
    }
  }
}
```

The getInstance method is declared as a class member, creates a unique instance of the FaceBook class, and stores it as a class property. If an instance already exists when getInstance is called, the unique instance is returned to the client. This wrapper ensures the existence of only one instance.

With the creation of your singleton, you can use the instance as a global object. To obtain the reference, all you have to do is refer to the getInstance class method:

```
FaceBook.getInstance()
//returns the FaceBook object and stores it to return the same reference every time.
```

Once this object is created, you can insert the method into the appropriate classes (see **Listing 6-28**).

Listing 6-28. Class using FaceBook.getInstance

```
private var _faceBook : FaceBook
...cont

override public function intro() : void
{
        _faceBook = FaceBook.getInstance();
        trace( "_faceBook" , _faceBook );

        var _userInfo : ProfileInformation = _faceBook.getUserProfile();
        trace( "_userInfo" , _userInfo );

        var obj : Object = _userInfo.fullProfile;

        for (var key:String in obj)
        {
           trace( key + ' ' + obj );
        }
        if (!_faceBook.hasProfile)
        {
           _faceBook.addEventListener( FacebookEvent.COMPLETE , updateTextFields );
        }
        else
        {
           // ... text fields update implementation not shown.
        }
```

```
                // ... truncated code
}
```

As shown in **Listing 6-28**, a class can acquire the FaceBook object and then access the user's profile information. Otherwise, it can attach an event listener for the moment a user logs in to Facebook.

When you add this to other classes that contain code similar to that in **Listing 6-28**, the same FaceBook object is always returned. This is due to the conditional statement in **Listing 6-27**.

Now, suppose your project manager informs you that you need to modify the application. The FaceBook feature, which was never intended to be a primary aspect of the application, has become so popular that the client wants to include the user's profile image, as well as pluck random updates from their feeds. This doesn't require much work, because FaceBookFacade already includes this behavior. You just need to add another few lines of code to hook into it.

Adhering to the open-closed principle, you create a new subclass of FaceBook called FaceBookExtendedProfile. FaceBookExtendedProfile gets the user's avatar and status, and adds them to the current ProfileInformation (see **Listing 6-29**).

Listing 6-29. FaceBookExtendedProfile obtains the user's status and avatar and appends them to shortProfile.

```
package
{
    public class FaceBookExtendedProfile extends Facebook
    {
        public function FaceBookExtendedProfile()
        {
        }

        protected override function userInfoLoaded( event : FacebookEvent ) : void
        {
            super.userInfoLoaded( event );
            var profile : ProfileInformation = _faceBook.getUserProfile();
            acquireAvatar( profile.userAvatarURL );
            acquireStatus( profile.status );
        }

        protected function acquireStatus( xml : XML ) : void
        {
            shortProfile.statusXMLlist = xml..user_status;
        }

        protected function acquireAvatar( AvatarURL : String ) : void
        {
            if (AvatarURL.length < 1)
            {
                var bitmapData : BitmapData = new BitmapData( 100 , 100 , true , 0 );
```

```
        shortProfile.avatar = bitmapData.clone();
        return
    }

    var loader : Loader = new Loader()
    loader.contentLoaderInfo.addEventListener( Event.COMPLETE,onAvatarAcquired );

    var urlRequest : URLRequest = new URLRequest( AvatarURL );
    var ldrContext : LoaderContext = new LoaderContext();
    ldrContext.checkPolicyFile = true;
    loader.load( urlRequest , ldrContext );
}

private function onAvatarAcquired( event : Event ) : void
{
    var ldrInfo : LoaderInfo = event.target as LoaderInfo
    ldrInfo.removeEventListener( Event.COMPLETE , onAvatarAcquired );
    var ldrContent : Bitmap = ldrInfo.content as Bitmap;
    _bitmapData = ldrContent.bitmapData;
    _shortProfile.avatar = _bitmapData;
}
}
}
```

The subclass FaceBookExtendedProfile now extends FaceBook. With the updates implemented, you only need to replace the static variable $_fbInstance with an instance of FaceBookExtendedProfile.

Because FaceBookExtendedProfile extends FaceBook, it has the appropriate privileges to modify the $_fbInstance reference. You add $_fbInstance=this; to the constructor to swap $_fbInstance with an instance of your new subclass (see **Listing 6-30**).

Listing 6-30. Revised FaceBookExtendedProfile

```
package
{
    public class FaceBookExtendedProfile extends Facebook
    {
        public function FaceBookExtendedProfile()
        {
            super();
            $_fbInstance = this;
        }
        //… cont
    }
}
```

With the extension complete, you need to consider how to use it. Because you're attempting to modify the pointer of the $_fbInstance, you must instantiate FaceBookExtendedProfile before any calls are made to FaceBook.getInstance(). Otherwise, the incorrect reference will be returned to the client. The next dilemma is the confusion of an unsuspecting developer who attempts to modify the FaceBook class without realizing that the class is being overridden by FaceBookExtendedProfile.

This places you in a predicament with no good options. OOP is about reuse and cohesion, but all you're left with are Band-Aid fixes. Given the circumstances, the only thing to do is to copy and paste the new behaviors of FaceBookExtendedProfile into the old FaceBook class, breaking the open-closed principle.

The issue with a simple singleton, as you've seen, is its inability to be subclassed. This is due to referencing a variable with a concrete Class object. Although use of static members is inflexible, they can be used in making a reference globally accessible. As this benefit of accessibility is seen as a tremendous asset, developers use static references all the time in many areas of code. However, these references make code inflexible when changes are introduced. This is why Simple Singleton isn't the Singleton design pattern.

The Singleton Pattern

The Singleton pattern provides a global means to access a unique object while ensuring the extensibility of that object. Figure 6-8 shows the class diagram.

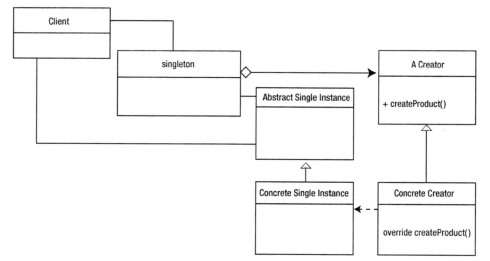

Figure 6-8. Singleton pattern class diagram

This pattern has the following parts:

- Concrete singleton
- Singleton interface
- Abstract Factory Method pattern
    - Abstract product
    - Concrete product

- Abstract creator
- Concrete creator
- Client

The pattern's benefits are as follows:

- Grants global access to an object
- Maintains access to its unique instance
- Reduces the need for multiple global variables
- Permits subclasses

It also has this drawback:

- Requires configuration

A Comprehensive Look

The singleton is an object that enables access to a specific location in memory that preserves the integrity of an OO system. Rather than stitch a series of variables throughout an application, the Singleton pattern provides an ingenious to create and retrieve an instance.

The Singleton design pattern ensures that a particular object can have exactly one instance and one instance only, unless specified otherwise. To ensure the single instance, the sole means of instantiating an object is through the pattern. This prevents the instance from being modified anywhere else in the code. The added benefit is that the singleton becomes the exclusive access point from which the object can be acquired for use.

Using the Singleton pattern also provides flexibility through the use of inheritance. Although each object that uses the Singleton is required to remain a unique instance, the ability to be subclassed can't be denied. This would be counterproductive given the open-closed design principle.

Vignette

The proprietor of the world's best fried chicken, whom you met in the last example, continues to search for a way to bring his chicken to everyone in the world. The answer comes to him after he wakes from a terrible dream in which he couldn't enhance his product without having to enter into new contracts. This was because he ensured that his products would never change, but he wasn't the enforcer between his product and the clients.

With this realization, the chef decides to take charge of ensuring that he is the contract's access point for those who want to taste his chicken. This way, he can improve his recipe and ensure that the changes are made without adding confusion among consumers. His name will become synonymous with slogan "The ONLY world's best chicken, and he'll make sure of that."

The AS 3.0 Cast

In AS 3.0, the Singleton pattern's parts are as follows:

- Abstract creator: Defines the type that is used in its particular factory.
- Concrete creator: A factory subclass that contains the logic necessary to instantiate the appropriate object in a genus of products expected by the superclass.
- Abstract product: Exposes the interface that all concrete products of the given genus inherit.
- Concrete product: Extends the abstract product to express itself as a member of the type to be used in the logic of the creator.
- Singleton interface: Exposes the contract by which the client can obtain the unique instance. The interface possesses a unique method that acts as a wrapper around a class member instance.
- Concrete singleton: Implements the behaviors and necessary factories to use.
- Class member Instance: A reference associated with the class and not the object. This reduces memory allocation given any number of instances of a given class. Although public, a class member can be accessed in a manner that doesn't require an instance. You get such a class reference using the static modifier.
- Client: Any aspect of the application or system that has prior knowledge of the abstract product, as well as the fully qualified name of the singleton class and its static method.

When It's Useful

The Singleton pattern is useful in these situations:

- When exactly one instance of an object in an application is required
- When you need global access to solve a workflow issue (analytics, managers, etc.)

Example

The Singleton pattern structures code so that while enforcing a unique instance of an object, it lets a subclass become that unique instance, without requiring modification of existing code. A secondary role of the Singleton pattern is to reduce the number of global variables in an application by consolidating namespaces. To achieve such flexibility among unique instances, the structure of the singleton relies on uniform creation via parameterization. You create varying products by using a unified process: the abstract factory.

Although FaceBookExtendedProfile and FaceBook from **Listing 6-27** and **Listing 6-29** have varying implementations, they don't have different interfaces. Therefore, although these interfaces don't exhibit change, they should be interchangeable in a singleton's instance. You know that to achieve the singleton's global access, you use a static method. And because class methods can only reference class members, you need to hold the reference as a static member. Any message to your static method must return the object referenced by the static member _instance. In order to ensure that _instance points to a reference, you need a conditional statement, which you saw earlier in the discussion of the Simple Singleton pattern. This gives you global access to an object of a unique instance, intended for use in the application.

Listing 6-31 shows the internal mechanism of the FaceBookSingleton instance, which currently lacks an interface and an object to instantiate. To maintain flexibility, you need to parameterize an object to be instantiated by the getInstance method, while maintaining anonymity for the object to create. At the same time, you expose a uniform return type.

Listing 6-31. Internals of the FaceBookSingleton object

```
package
{
    public class FaceBookSingleton
    {
        static private var $_instance : _____;

        static public function getInstance() : _____;
        {
        if ( !$_instance )
        {
            $_instance = new _____;
        }
        return $_instance;
        }
    }
}
```

You use an the abstract factory to create an interface to create the product. You know the factory must return a given product and that this product is a subclass of a FaceBook interface.

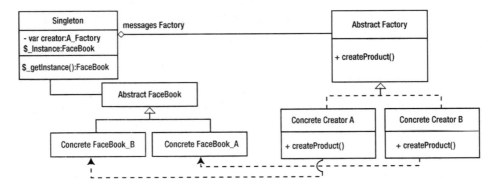

Figure 6-9. The Singleton making use of the Abstract Factory

Listing 6-32. FaceBook

```
package
{
    public class FaceBook extends EventDispatcher
```

```
    {
        [Event(name="Connect", type=" FaceBookEvent")]
        [Event(name="Complete", type=" FaceBookEvent")]

        static public const COMPLETE : String = "complete";
        static public const CONNECT : String = "connect";
        protected var _faceBook : iFaceBook;
        protected var _shortProfile : ShortProfileInformation
        protected var _hasProfile : Boolean

        public function Login( target : IEventDispatcher = null )
        {
            _shortProfile = new ShortProfileInformation()
            _hasProfile = false
        }

        public function init() : void
        {
            _ready = false
            _faceBook = new FaceBookFacade()
            // a class that utilizes my FaceBookGraphAPI
            _faceBook.addEventListener( FacebookEvent.CONNECT , faceBookConnectHandler );
        }

        public function get facebook() : IFaceBook
        {
            return _faceBook
        }

        public function get hasProfile() : Boolean
        {
            return _hasProfile
        }

        public function get shortProfile() : ShortProfileInformation
        {
            return shortProfile
        }

        protected function faceBookConnectHandler( event : FacebookEvent ) : void
        {
        }
    }
}
```

Using FaceBook as an abstract class allows you to declare your interface. Your past classes become subclasses of the new abstraction. By abstracting the two classes, you can extract commonalities and offer default implementations that occur between both concrete classes.

Listing 6-33. FaceBookProfile

```
package
{
   public class FaceBookProfile extends FaceBook
   {
      public function FaceBookProfile()
      {
         super( null );
      }

      override protected function faceBookConnectHandler( event : FacebookEvent )
         ➥: void
      {
         if (event.success)
         {
            FacebookCall( _faceBook.queryUserInformation() ).addEventListener(
         ➥ FacebookEvent.COMPLETE , userInfoLoaded );

            dispatchEvent( new FacebookEvent( FacebookEvent.CONNECT ) )
         }
      }

      protected function userInfoLoaded( event : FacebookEvent ) : void
      {
         var aFaceBookCall : FacebookCall = event.target as FacebookCall;
         aFaceBookCall.removeEventListener( FacebookEvent.COMPLETE , userInfoLoaded );

         dispatchEvent( new FacebookEvent( FacebookEvent.COMPLETE ) )
         var profile : ProfileInformation = _faceBook.getUserProfile();
         _shortProfile.usrIdentifier = profile.userName;
         _shortProfile.faceBook = true;
         _hasProfile = true
      }
   }
}
```

Listing 6-34. FaceBookExtendedProfile

```
package
{
   public class FaceBookExtendedProfile extends Facebook
```

```
{
   public function FaceBookExtendedProfile()
   {
   }

   protected override function userInfoLoaded( event : FacebookEvent ) : void
   {
      super.userInfoLoaded( event )
      var profile : ProfileInformation = _faceBook.getUserProfile();
      acquireAvatar( profile.userAvatarURL )
      acquireStatus( profile.status )
   }

   protected function acquireStatus( xml : XML ) : void
   {
      shortProfile.statusXMLlist = xml..user_status
   }

   protected function acquireAvatar( AvatarURL : String ) : void
   {
      if (AvatarURL.length < 1)
      {
         var bitmapData : BitmapData = new BitmapData( 100 , 100 , true , 0 );
         shortProfile.avatar = bitmapData.clone();
         return
      }

      var loader : Loader = new Loader()
      loader.contentLoaderInfo.addEventListener( Event.COMPLETE,onAvatarAcquired );

      var urlRequest : URLRequest = new URLRequest( AvatarURL )
      var ldrContext : LoaderContext = new LoaderContext()
      ldrContext.checkPolicyFile = true;
      loader.load( urlRequest , ldrContext )
   }

   private function onAvatarAcquired( event : Event ) : void
   {
      var ldrInfo : LoaderInfo = event.target as LoaderInfo
      ldrInfo.removeEventListener( Event.COMPLETE , onAvatarAcquired )
      var ldrContent : Bitmap = ldrInfo.content as Bitmap
      _bitmapData = ldrContent.bitmapData
      _shortProfile.avatar = _bitmapData
   }
```

```
        }
    }
```

Now that you have your product, you just need to construct the creator and abstract creator that are passed in to the Singleton. This creates an abstraction among passed-in objects that can be used with the Singleton pattern.

All you're concerned with for this application is the appropriate instantiation of your object, so the abstract creator only has a factory method that returns an instance of FaceBook (see **Listing 6-35**). And as you know, with factory methods you should use a method containing the prefix make or create. This example uses a method called makeUniqueFB (see **Listing 6-36** and **Listing 6-37**).

Listing 6-35. AFaceBookCreator

```
package
{
    public class AFaceBookCreator
    {
        public function makeUniqueFB() : FaceBook
        {
        }
    }
}
```

Listing 6-36. FaceBookShortProfileFactory subclasses AFaceBookCreator and retains the knowledge of the concrete class to instantiate, FaceBook.

```
package
{
    public class FaceBookShortProfileFactory extends AFaceBookCreator
    {
        public override function makeUniqueFB() : FaceBook
        {
            return new FaceBook()
        }
    }
}
```

Listing 6-37. FaceBookExtendedProfile subclasses AFaceBookCreator and retains the knowledge of the concrete class to instantiate, FaceBookExtendedProfile.

```
package
{
    public class FaceBookExtendedProfile extends AFaceBookCreator
    {
        override public function makeUniqueFB() : FaceBook
        {
            return new FaceBookExtendedProfile()
```

```
            }
        }
}
```

Finally, you need to enable the factory to be parameterized into a singleton to create the appropriate single instance (see **Listing 6-38**).

Listing 6-38. FaceBookSingleton accepts an abstract factory that contains the appropriate product.

```
package
{
    public class FaceBookSingleton
    {
        static private var $_factory : AFaceBookCreator;
        static private var $_instance : FaceBook;

        static public function getInstance() : FaceBook
        {
            if ( !$_instance )
            {
                $_instance = $_factory.makeUniqueFB();
            }
            return $_instance;
        }

        static public function setFactory( FBFactory : AFaceBookCreator ) : void
        {
            $_factory = FBFactory;
        }
    }
}
```

The bolded code in **Listing 6-38** adds the behavior required by the Singleton pattern to provide the flexibility required by an OO application. The appropriate factory is supplied to the singleton before the getInstance method. After the factory is passed in, the existing code can remain unchanged and continue to bind itself to the interface of the returned product.

FAQ

- Why is this approach better than using the Simple Singleton pattern?

    The immediate answer is the flexibility it offers. In many languages, a static class can't be overridden, preventing the use of polymorphism. The Simple Singleton pattern ensures that only one object instance is unique, as well as the access point to this object, by inserting this behavior into the object. Doing so gives a class behaviors that let it behave as a wrapper to itself.

By providing its own wrapper to secure itself, the product reduces loose coupling by the client. This reduces any reusable code to the remnants of objects used for a specific project.

- Why do other books show the Simple Singleton pattern as the Singleton design pattern?

    The answer is a bit complicated. As I stressed in Chapter 4, design patterns use UML to avoid referring to any specific language. This is because every language is different. Some OO languages use *abstractions*, whereas others use *interfaces*; and some allow methods to be *virtual* while others must be *static*.

    The language that interprets each pattern plays a large role in how the pattern appears. The most important thing is understanding the problem the pattern solves and not using the model as the only source.

- What makes this approach so flexible?

    In short, the pattern's indirection makes it so flexible. Although this pattern allows unique instances to remain accessible, extendable, and global, it requires a lot of complexity. This indirection can be both good and bad.

- Can more than one object be accessed from the singleton?

    Yes, as long as it fits the needs of your application and doesn't overly complicate the code. The Singleton pattern aims to reduce the number of global variables in an application by allowing them to be acquired from a single access point.

Related Patterns

The following patterns are related to the Singleton pattern:

- Abstract Factory
- Builder

Summary

It's very easy to overlook the chance to use a creational pattern and fall back on the new keyword. This is a "Get it done" mentality; and although I can sympathize with it as a developer, it doesn't save you any time on the next project. The quick implementations may be the last nail in the coffin.

This doesn't mean you should afraid of the keyword new, but consider how important it is for the declaration to be in the body where it resides. This is the deciding factor when you're considering whether your code should use a creational pattern.

Abstraction is crucial. Specifics are always necessary in an application, but their placement is critical. The design patterns discussed in this chapter rely heavily on abstraction that makes code easier to change.

Key Points

- The new keyword may decrease the flexibility of your code as well as prevent internal reuse.
- The Factory Method pattern relies on inheritance to localize preparation and creational logic.

- The Abstract Factory pattern bundles families of related or dependent objects.
- The Singleton pattern allows for extension.
- The Builder pattern varies the internal representation of its product.
- A singleton should remain extensible.
- A pattern can become the client of other patterns.
- Simple Factory isn't the Factory Method pattern or the Singleton pattern—it's not even a pattern.

Chapter 7

Behavioral Patterns

Each object used in a rich Internet application (RIA) application adds a specialized behavior. It may be computational or managerial, but regardless of the specifics, the objects aim to facilitate specific goals in a system.

Code that should be encapsulated is too often hard-coded in a class, due to the ease of maintaining scope. Time constraints, lack of practice, and unfamiliarity with better techniques are all reasons a developer may allow non-encapsulated behaviors to add unnecessary lines of code to classes. Doing so can make a class more difficult to maintain and adjust, and decreases the code's reusability.

Behavioral patterns abstract the objects that are to be messaged. This loosens the couplings between the invoker and the implemented behavior, enabling substitutions between them.

Behavioral patterns offer generalizations that make the relationships of invoker and receiver more flexible. Some behavioral patterns localize an object's state that a behavior depends on, or is determined by, and others preserve the scope to which the behavior belongs. A few conceal computations and calculations of which an object would be unaware. Strictly speaking, behavioral patterns don't focus on the encapsulations of behaviors and calculations. They're concerned with the *assignment* of those encapsulations to the objects that require them.

This chapter discusses the following patterns: Strategy, Template Method, Command, Chain of Responsibility, Iterator, State, Memento, and Observer.

The Strategy Pattern

The Strategy pattern encapsulates a set of algorithms uniformly (sibling subclasses that inherit a common interface) to achieve interchangeability among them. **Figure 7-1** shows the class diagram.

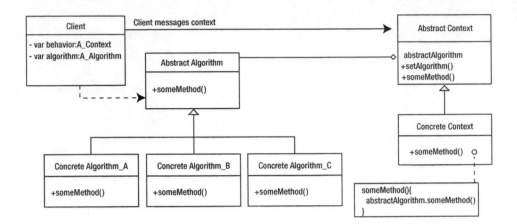

Figure 7-1. Strategy pattern class diagram

This pattern has the following parts:

- Abstract strategy
- Concrete strategy
- Abstract context
- Concrete context
- Client

The pattern's benefits are as follows:

- Algorithms can be used among varying systems
- Algorithms can be more easily maintained
- Algorithms can be interchanged both during development and at runtime

And it has these drawbacks:

- Clients must be aware of the strategies.
- Strategies are more objects to manage.

A Comprehensive Look

The word *algorithm* may mean something different to a Flash programmer than it does to a computer science major. The term, which sounds mathematical, is defined as "the sum of any and all techniques used to arrive at the desired goal." In fact, an algorithm may lack any mathematical computations. Essentially, an algorithm represents the actions taken, *by any means necessary,* to get from point A to point B.

Because there can be numerous ways to arrive at point B, encapsulating behaviors allows the implementations to vary freely. And thus the destination doesn't always have to be the same.

In order to be polymorphic, each algorithm must possess the same hierarchy; and to remain uniform in their use, the algorithms must expose a shared interface. This way, the data required by the strategy can be passed into that strategy. It's the responsibility of the abstract algorithm to create both the abstract methods and interfaces that each subclass inherits.

The abstract context, on the other hand, requires knowledge of the abstract algorithm in order to properly arrive at the expected solution and expose the interface to which the client interfaces.

The context and strategy objects must work together to satisfy their needs by providing the appropriate access. There are two ways for this to occur: the context can pass in data to the strategy, or the context can pass itself as the data and allow the strategy to use its interface.

The client in this relationship can identify the behavior of the context. This enables various outcomes without changing the data in the context.

Vignette

Teachers (*the client*) use various strategies and methods to teach students of varying abilities. They need to differentiate instruction in order to meet the learning needs of all their students. The concepts in the curriculum remain the same, but the way they're demonstrated and lessons implemented differs based on how a student grasps the information.

For example, when teaching a child how to perform a simple calculation, such as addition, a teacher might begin with the use of manipulatives (*strategy A*) that help the student understand the concept through a hands-on activity. Children use the physical objects rather than numbers on a page. From there, the teacher puts images of those objects on paper, next to each number in the equation, reinforcing the concept (*strategy B*). Finally, the teacher substitutes examples containing only numbers for those containing numbers and pictures (*strategy C*).

The AS 3.0 Cast

In AS 3.0, the Strategy pattern's parts are as follows:

- Abstract strategy: Exposes the interface a given family of subclassed algorithms inherits and houses any functionality they share. The interface enables the context to retrieve any necessary data or behaviors that make up this set of algorithms.
- Concrete strategy: A specialized algorithm that performs a varied but specialized implementation among a set of algorithms.
- Abstract context: Exposes the interface that can be used by the client. In addition, the abstract context knows which type of behavioral objects can be supplied by the client and retains this reference to defer requests. The abstract context may optionally provide an additional interface that a strategy can use to access pertinent data.
- Concrete context: A specialized context, that through the use of composition, works with a strategy that is submitted by a client, in order to fulfil a behavior.
- Client: Any aspect of the application or system that has prior knowledge of the concrete strategy to be used by the context, as well as the context the client may message.

When It's Useful

The Strategy pattern is useful when you want to preserve the reuse of algorithms that make up a behavior. Such algorithms are validations, expressions, easing formulas, button logic, and network communications.

The Strategy pattern eliminates conditionals among an object state in order to target the appropriate method, via method uniformity.

Example

Often, a web site lets a user contact the company for which the site advertises. Because contact forms vary, it's valuable to possess the various validation algorithms as individual strategies.

Suppose you have a form field that contains four text fields, which ask users for their first name, last name, e-mail address, and e-mail confirmation. These text fields may require various validations depending on the client or the particular project. For this example, you want to ensure that all required fields are filled in, that the provided e-mail address is valid, that the confirmation e-mail and the original e-mail match, and that no text field contains an expletive.

You begin by devising the abstraction shown in **Listing 7-1**, which all the validations extend. This makes them uniform and enables polymorphism.

Listing 7-1. AFormValidationBehavior devises the uniformity for a family of algorithms.

```
package
{
   public class AFormValidationBehavior extends Object
   {
      protected var _formContactForm : IForm

      public function AFormValidationBehavior( form : IForm = null )
      {
         if (form)
         {
            _formContactForm = form
         }
      }

      public function get formContactForm() : IForm
      {
         return _formContactForm;
      }

      public function set formContactForm( formContactForm : IForm ) : void
      {
         _formContactForm = formContactForm;
      }

      public function validate() : void
      {
         throw new IllegalOperationError( 'validate must be overridden' )
      }
```

```
    }
}
```

The form requires a means of abstraction to which it can be referred. In this case, you use `IForm` and `IValidate` to reduce the number of excess classes displayed in this code. They contain the getters in the contact form. An example of this can be seen below in **listing 7-2**.

Listing 7-2. Abstract form that all validations analyze

```
package
{
    public class ContactForm extends Sprite implements IForm, IValidate
    {
        protected var _email : FormObject;
        protected var _confirmEmail : FormObject;
        protected var _firstName : FormObject;
        protected var _LastName : FormObject;
        protected var _formCollections : Vector.<FormObject>;
        protected var _analysis : AFormValidationBehavior;

        public function ContactForm()
        {
            _email = new FormObject();
            _confirmEmail = new FormObject();
            _firstName = new FormObject();
            _lastName = new FormObject();

            _formCollections = Vector.<FormObject>( [ _email ,
                                                      _confirmEmail ,
                                                      _firstName ,
                                                      _lastName ] );

            _email.packet.data = "iBen@Spilled-Milk.com";
            _confirmEmail.packet.data = "iBen@Spilled-Milk.com";
            _firstName.packet.data = "Ben";
            _lastName.packet.data = "Smith";
        }

        public function get email() : FormObject
        {
            return _email;
        }

        public function set email( email : FormObject ) : void
        {
            _email = email;
```

```
   }

   public function get firstName() : FormObject
   {
      return _firstName;
   }

   public function set firstName( firstName : FormObject ) : void
   {
      _firstName = firstName;
   }

   public function get lastName() : FormObject
   {
      return _lastName;
   }

   public function set lastName( lastName : FormObject ) : void
   {
      _lastName = lastName;
   }

   public function get analysis() : AFormValidationBehavior
   {
      return _analysis;
   }

   public function set analysis( analysis : AFormValidationBehavior ) : void
   {
      _analysis = analysis;
      _analysis.formContactForm = this;
      trace( _analysis );
   }

   public function validate() : void
   {
      _analysis.validate();
   }

   public function get formCollections() : Vector.<FormObject>
   {
      return _formCollections;
   }
```

```
      public function get confirmEmail() : FormObject
      {
         return _confirmEmail;
      }

      public function set confirmEmail( confirmEmail : FormObject ) : void
      {
         _confirmEmail = confirmEmail;
      }
   }
}
```

Listing 7-3 through **Listing 7-7** show the various algorithms in the form-validation family.

Listing 7-3. Algorithm that validates that all required fields are properly filled

```
package
{
   public class RequiredValidation extends AFormValidationBehavior
   {
      private static const ERROR : String = "All required fields must be filled in";

      public function RequiredValidation( form : ContactForm = null )
      {
         super( form );
      }

      override public function validate() : void
      {
         for each ( var fObj:FormObject in _formContactForm.formCollections )
         {
            var fp : FormPacket = fObj.packet;
            if ( fp.isRequired )
            {
               var cleanser : RegExp = /\s{1,}/gi;
               var clone : String = fp.data.replace( cleanser , '' );

               if ( clone == '' || clone == fp.prompt ) ;
               {
                  fp.hasErrors = true;
                  fp.addError( ERROR );
                  trace( 'error' );
               }
            }
         }
```

```
      }
   }
}
```

Listing 7-4. Algorithm that validates the provided e-mail address

```
package
{
   public class EmailValidation extends AFormValidationBehavior
   {
      static protected const Email_Expression : RegExp = ➥
                          /^[a-z][\w.-]+@\w[\w.-]+\.[\w.-]*[a-z][a-z]$/i

      static protected const Error : String = "A Valid Email is Required"

      public function EmailValidation( form : ContactForm = null )
      {
         super( form );
      }

      override public function validate() : void
      {
         var email : FormObject = this._formContactForm.email
         var emailData : FormPacket = email.packet
         var emailAddy : String = emailData.data

         if (!Email_Expression.test( emailAddy ))
         {
            emailData.hasErrors = true
         }
      }
   }
}
```

Listing 7-5. Algorithm that validates that both the original e-mail address and the confirmation e-mail match

```
package
{
   public class ConfirmedEmailValidation extends AFormValidationBehavior
   {
      static protected const ERROR : String = "Emails Must Match"

      public function ConfirmedEmailValidation( form : ContactForm = null )
      {
         super( form );
```

```
        }

        override public function validate() : void
        {
            var email : FormObject = this._formContactForm.email
            var emailData : FormPacket = email.packet
            var emailAddy : String = emailData.data

            var confirmEmail : FormObject = this._formContactForm.confirmEmail
            var confirmEmailData : FormPacket = confirmEmail.packet
            var confirmEmailAddy : String = confirmEmailData.data

            var match : Boolean = confirmEmailAddy == emailAddy
            if (!match)
            {
                trace( 'error' )
                emailData.hasErrors = true
                emailData.addError( ERROR )
            }
        }
    }
}
```

Listing 7-6. The profanity-filter abstract algorithm defines the template method, for which subclasses are expected to provide an appropriate filter listing.

```
package
{
    public class AProfanityFilter extends AFormValidationBehavior
    {
        protected static const Error : String = 'Please refrain from using obscenities';
        protected var profanityAr : Vector.<String>

        public function AProfanityFilter( form : ContactForm = null )
        {
            super( form );
            doProfanity()
        }

        protected function doProfanity() : void
        {
            throw new IllegalOperationError( 'doProfanity must be overridden' )
        }

        override public function validate() : void
```

```
    {
        var field : Vector.<FormObject>= this._formContactForm.formCollections
        for each (var form:FormObject in field)
        {
            var fp : FormPacket = form.packet
            var data : String = fp.data
            if (recourse( data ))
            {
                fp.hasErrors = true
                fp.addError( Error )
            }
        }
    }

    protected function recourse( str : String , count : uint = 0 ) : Boolean
    {
        var tmpAr : Array;
        var expressionString : String = (count < profanityAr.length - 1) ? ➥
                            '\\b' + profanityAr[count] + '\\b' : profanityAr[count]

        var regExp : RegExp = new RegExp( expressionString , 'gix' )
        tmpAr = (regExp.exec( str ));
        if (tmpAr != null)
        {
            return true
        }
        else
        {
            if (count < profanityAr.length - 1)
            {
                return recourse( str , ++count )
            }
        }
        return false
    }
    }
}
```

Listing 7-7. Profanity-filter default algorithm that validates by means of RegExp

```
package
{
    public class DefaultProfanityFilter extends AProfanityFilter
    {
        public function DefaultProfanityFilter( form : ContactForm = null )
```

```
        {
            super( form );
        }

        override protected function doProfanity() : void
        {
            profanityAr = Vector.<String>( [ 'Listing of profanities goes here' ] );
        }
    }
}
```

Listing 7-8 shows how each algorithm can be substituted for one another to be used with the contact form, in order to validate the appropriate fields. Using the interface IValidate, which exposes only two methods, safeguards the internals.

Listing 7-8. Substitution of algorithms made by the client

```
var form : IValidate = new ContactForm()

    form.analysis = new RequiredValidation()
    form.validate()

    form.analysis = new EmailValidation()
    form.validate()

    form.analysis = new ConfirmedEmailValidation()
    form.validate()

    form.analysis = new DefaultProfanityFilter()
    form.validate()
```

Related Patterns

The following patterns are related to the Strategy pattern:

- State
- Template

The Template Method Pattern

The Template Method pattern defines the skeleton of an algorithm in an operation, deferring steps to subclasses for implementation. **Figure 7-2** shows the class diagram.

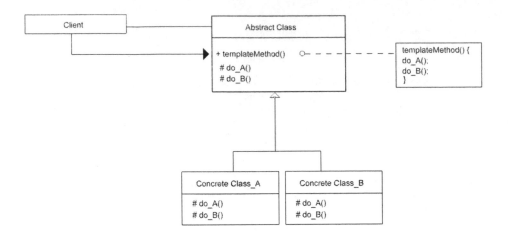

Figure 7-2. Template Method pattern class diagram

This pattern has the following parts:

- Abstract class
- Concrete class
- Client

The pattern's benefits are as follows:

- Hooks that promote overriding
- Fixed ordering among algorithmic steps
- Specific extension points

A Comprehensive Look

The operations in an abstract class, that define the skeletal composition of the template method, are similar to the bullet points in a topic outline that emphasize a building block of the topic. These bare-boned operations outline the skeleton of an algorithm that a subclass elaborates on. Thus these points form the template, which each subclass needs to model itself to arrive at an end behavior.

Although the subclasses implement specifics, they don't dictate the order in which the operations are used. This is left up to the abstraction in an effort to localize and maintain the logic among operations.

The Template Method pattern defines the order of the skeletal operations to create uniformity among its subclasses. Primitive operations, which are overridden, are often indicated using the prefix do. (You must prevent subclasses from overriding the template method itself.) The template method increases class cohesion, and provides the necessary hooks into which subclasses can tap.

Vignette

The phrase "Mother knows best" may not always hold true, but a mother does know how she chooses to raise her children. She protects and nurtures them, but she also provides structure. If a mother changes her rules on a daily basis, her children don't know what path to follow; this is why it's very important for the mother to solidify this path, and ensure that her children remain on it.

But a mother can't be there every second of the day. On occasion, the duties of a mother may be passed to a babysitter for a few hours. The babysitter isn't the mother, doesn't know what's best for the children, and has no idea what the parents plan for their children's future. This is because the babysitter is an individual and doesn't have the same concerns as the mother. Plus, watching the children is just a way for the babysitter to earn a few extra dollars.

To ensure that the babysitter represents the mother's presence, the mother must enforce guidelines to be followed while caring for her children. This is accomplished via itemized rules as well as precautionary actions to be taken if anything goes wrong. These actions are detailed and given due diligence on the part of the mother, but what isn't expressed is the means by which these actions are to be carried out.

The AS 3.0 Cast

In AS 3.0, the Template Method pattern's parts are as follows:

- Abstract class: Exposes the interface and defines the order of operations necessary to fulfill the obligations of an algorithm. The abstraction must ensure the prevention of its template method.
- Concrete class: Defines the specific implementations of behaviors specified by its abstraction.
- Client: The messenger of the concrete class, which by messaging may trigger the template method. This may be the concrete class itself.

When It's Useful

The Template Method pattern is useful for doing the following:

- Providing uniformity among subclasses
- Preventing alteration of sequences
- Enforcing factory methods
- Providing additional hooks to which subclasses may specialize

Example

You've seen how modularity can promote flexibility. While modules remain in a hierarchy, they can be interchanged, allowing for greater flexibility. Interfaces tie modules together by allowing clients to message their behaviors using a common signature, but an interface doesn't achieve uniformity of an algorithm to be performed. The Template Method localizes the steps of an algorithm so you can make changes in one place rather than many, thus subclassing the abstraction.

Sections of a web site often use template methods to enforce expected behaviors when a section initiates or exits. Consider these sections of an ActionScript 3.0 web site: Portfolio, News, About You, Home, and Contact. Each section is written as its own module, and the modules are tied together by their common interface.

Often an abstract class known as `ABaseClass` defines this interface and extends the `flash.display.Sprite` object for its interactive properties. `ABaseClass`'s duties are those of any abstract class: it supplies default behaviors and declares any abstract methods expected to be overwritten by its subclasses. It also creates the inherited interface used by all subclasses that are messaged by the application framework.

Listing 7-9 shows an abstract class that defines an interface that is implemented by all subclasses. ABaseSection also implements a few defaults that are shared among the subclasses. The problem demonstrated in this abstract class is the expectation that subclasses override behaviors, which may already implement a default behavior.

Listing 7-9. ABaseSection acting as an abstract class among modular site sections

```
package
{
    public class ABaseSection extends Sprite
    {
        protected var _paused : Boolean;
        protected var _width : Number;
        protected var _height : Number;
        protected var _shell : IShell;

        public function ABaseSection()
        {
        }

        /*
         * Init is the first to be triggered override and load assets
         */
        public function init( shell : IShell ) : void
        {
            _shell = shell;
            shell.addEventListener( ShellEvent.EXIT_SECTION , outro );
        }

        /*
         * Pause expects videos, animations, timers, sounds etc... to pause.
         */
        public function pause() : void
        {
            _paused = true;
        }

        /*
         * Unpause expects videos, animations, timers, sounds etc... to resume.
         */
        public function unpause() : void
        {
            _paused = false;
```

```
        }

        public function intro() : void
        {
        }

        /*
         * destroy expects memory to be released.
         */
        public function destroy() : void
        {
            shell.removeEventListener( ShellEvent.EXIT_SECTION , outro );
        }

        public function updateLayout( width : Number , height : Number ) : void
        {
            _wide = width;
            _height = height;
        }

        protected function outro() : void
        {
        }
    }
}
```

Any subclass that does as intended and overrides these abstract methods may forget to use the default implementation of the superclass. The problem is that not only do your subclasses require their own logic for their section of the web site, but the superclass in this case, also expects them to recognize when they need to call a superclass method. The dilemma becomes apparent when a subclass extends the abstraction, as shown in **Listing 7-10**.

Listing 7-10. Home is a specialized type of section and overrides the intro operation to support its own code

```
package
{
    public class Home extends AbstractSection
    {
        public var introCopyAnimation : MovieClip;
        public var background : Bitmap;
        public var backgroundContainer : Sprite;

        public function Home()
        {
            backgroundContainer = new Sprite();
```

```
      background = new HomeBackground();
      backgroundContainer.addChild( background );
      addChild( backgroundContainer );
   }

   override public function intro() : void
   {
      background.intro();
      introCopyAnimation = new IntroCopyAnimation();
      introCopyAnimation.x = (stage.stageWidth - introCopyAnimation.width) * .5;
      introCopyAnimation.y = 175;
      addChild( introCopyAnimation );

      addEventListener( HomeEvent.ACTIVATE , activate );
      addEventListener( HomeEvent.DEACTIVATE , deactivate );
      background.addEventListener( HomeEvent.NAVIGATION_ACTIVATE , navigate );
      background.addEventListener( HomeEvent.NAVIGATION_DEACTIVATE , navigate );
      background.addEventListener( HomeEvent.NAVIGATE_TO_SECTION , navigate );
   }

   override public function updateLayout( width : Number , height : Number ) : void
   {
      if (introCopyAnimation)
      {
         introCopyAnimation.x = (stage.stageWidth - introCopyAnimation.width) * .5;
         introCopyAnimation.y = 175;
      }

      super.updateLayout( width , height );
      BestFit.scaleToFill( background , width , height );
      background.x = (_width - background.width) * .5;
      background.y = (_height - background.height) * .5;
      backgroundContainer.scrollRect = new Rectangle( 0 , 0 , width , height );
   }

   override public function destroy() : void
   {
      background.destroy();
      removeEventListener( HomeEvent.ACTIVATE , activate );
      removeEventListener( HomeEvent.DEACTIVATE , deactivate );
      background.removeEventListener( HomeEvent.NAVIGATION_ACTIVATE , navigate );
      background.removeEventListener( HomeEvent.NAVIGATION_DEACTIVATE , navigate );
      background.removeEventListener( HomeEvent.NAVIGATE_TO_SECTION , navigate );
      super.destroy();
```

```
        }
    }
}
```

The reason the Home section will malfunction is because the Home section overrides the parent's operation and the requests aren't properly forwarded to the superclass, which fulfills common behavior among all classes. This is only one subclass; but what if the developers creating the other sections make similar mistakes? The sections' behaviors may be so varied so that the only thing they share is the interface. Therefore, each class is expected to implement its own logic for the interface. The lack of criteria to meet the algorithm defined by the abstract class gets in the way of a uniform structure between the algorithm and the subclasses.

You can handle this by localizing the sequence of steps necessary for an algorithm that lets subclasses implement the code they require, while focusing only on their behaviors and not on what is expected of them by the abstract class. The abstract class must possess the appropriate logic related to the sequences expected of an algorithm, in order to fulfill the appropriate behavior. Adding the skeletal operations lets each subclass define appropriate behaviors without having to consider the when and the why.

Additionally, these abstract operations provide hooks (or callback methods), which can be overridden. This prevents possible effects on the superclass's default functionality. To preserve the integrity of the entire algorithm in the superclass, you mark it final so no subclass can override it.

The revised ABaseSection in **Listing 7-11** uses the Template Method pattern to maintain the appropriate structure of the algorithms the interface suggests. The relationship, which previously required subclasses to defer requests to the superclass, is no longer necessary because the superclass handles this independently of the subclasses. This is referred to as the Hollywood principle ("don't call you, we'll call you"): the subclass shouldn't contact the superclass, because the superclass will be in touch with the subclass.

Listing 7-11. ABaseSection utilizes template methods to devise a consistency among the steps of an operation.

```
package
{
    public class ABaseSection extends Sprite
    {
        protected var _paused : Boolean;
        protected var _width : Number;
        protected var _height : Number;
        protected var _shell : IShell;

        public function ABaseSection()
        {
        }

        final public function init( shell : IShell ) : void
        {
            _shell = shell;
```

```
      _shell.addEventListener( ShellEvent.EXIT_SECTION , outro );
      doLoadAssets()
   }

   final public function pause() : void
   {
      _paused = true
      doPauseVideo()
      doPauseAnimations()
      doPauseTimers()
      doPauseSounds()
   }

   final public function unPause() : void
   {
      _paused = false
      doUnPauseVideo()
      doUnPauseAnimations()
      doUnPauseTimers()
      doUnPauseSounds()
   }

   final public function intro() : void
   {
   }

   /*
    * destroy expects memory to be released.
    */
   final public function destroy() : void
   {
      shell.removeEventListener( ShellEvent.EXIT_SECTION , outro )
      doDestroy()
   }

   final public function updateLayout( width : Number , height : Number ) : void
   {
      _wide = width
      _height = height
      doUpdateLayout()
   }

   final protected function outro() : void
   {
```

```
    doOutro()
}

protected function doLoadAssets() : void
{
    throw new IllegalOperationError( 'doLoadAssets must be overridden' )
}

protected function doPauseVideo() : void
{
    throw new IllegalOperationError( 'doPauseVideo must be overridden' )
}

protected function doPauseAnimations() : void
{
    throw new IllegalOperationError( 'doPauseAnimations must be overridden' )
}

protected function doPauseTimers() : void
{
    throw new IllegalOperationError( 'doPauseTimers must be overridden' )
}

protected function doPauseSounds() : void
{
    throw new IllegalOperationError( 'doPauseSounds must be overridden' )
}

protected function doUnPauseVideo() : void
{
    throw new IllegalOperationError( 'doUnPauseVideo must be overridden' )
}

protected function doUnPauseAnimations() : void
{
    throw new IllegalOperationError( 'doUnPauseAnimations must be overridden' )
}

protected function doUnPauseTimers() : void
{
    throw new IllegalOperationError( 'doUnPauseTimers must be overridden' )
}

protected function doUnPauseSounds() : void
```

```
    {
        throw new IllegalOperationError( 'doUnPauseSounds must be overridden' )
    }

    protected function doDestroy() : void
    {
        throw new IllegalOperationError( 'doDestroy must be overridden' )
    }

    protected function doUpdateLayout() : void
    {
        throw new IllegalOperationError( 'doUpdateLayout must be overridden' )
    }

    protected function doOutro() : void
    {
        throw new IllegalOperationError( 'doOutro must be overridden' )
    }
    }
}
```

In ActionScript 3.0, you can use the Template Method pattern to improve the structure of your code and localize uniform behavior. By exposing an interface that can't be overridden, subclasses are strong armed to override only protected methods.

FAQ

- Does a Template Method ever contain only one step?

  Yes, especially in AS 3.0. This helps protect your data. Because you can't specify virtual or abstract modifiers for methods in AS 3.0, it isn't clear which methods need to be overridden. This may invite methods marked as protected or public from being overridden. Thus, may encourage overriding operations among interfaces as they use the `public` modifier.

  Instead, by using the Template Method pattern, you can emphasize the method that should be overridden. Because this method is no longer part of the interface, it allows better data hiding because you can mark it `protected`.

  This approach encourages data hiding in the class's behaviors. The Template Method will help you to make better use of the `private` and `protected` modifiers.

- Is a template method supposed to be declared as final?

  Yes. No subclass should be able to modify it, because that would interfere with the intended sequence that makes up the algorithm. Also, as in the answer to the first question, if you don't mark the template method final, you leave the interface open to be overridden.

Related Patterns

The following patterns are related to the Template Method pattern:

- Factory Method
- Strategy

The Command Pattern

The Command pattern encapsulates a request as an object. This abstracts the receiver from being invoked in the application. **Figure 7-3** shows the class diagram.

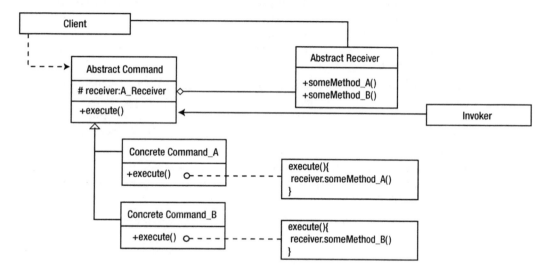

Figure 7-3. Command pattern class diagram

This pattern has the following parts:

- Abstract command
- Concrete command
- Invoker
- Receiver
- Client

The pattern's benefits are as follows:

- Decouples the receiver and the invoker, so the invoker has no bindings among another objects
- Enables undo and redo capabilities

A Comprehensive Look

Anyone who has used an AS 3.0 tweening engine understands the potential of the callback. It lets you trigger or message a method on a tween's completion. In ActionScript 2.0, the most difficult aspect of the callback was keeping the scope of the object the callback was targeting.

AS 3.0 takes heavy advantage of this pattern in order to achieve method closures, which is why it's so important to remove event listeners. AS 3.0 doesn't offer let you tap into these method closures.

The Command pattern captures a request for a given object within its own encapsulation so the request can be passed or stored. Thus objects that are destined to be wrapped inside a command object can be sequenced and queued to be messaged later.

You do this using the Command object, which contains an object, known as a receiver, to message. This way, you conceal the interface of the receiver to be messaged and the intended invoker. The invoker doesn't need to be aware of anything other than the Command object's interface. The interface of the Command object is eloquently named execute. This "execute" method, when messaged, defers the request to its receiver and thus targets the appropriate method.

Concrete Commands are written so that they're aware of the interfaces to the objects that they're holding. When the command method "execute" is messaged, the appropriate interface of the receiver will be invoked. The interfaces of the receivers intended for messaging vary, so the concrete commands must properly accommodate them. Thus commands and receivers share parallel hierarchies.

The larger the application, the more interfaces are likely to be used and tightly coupled, which can potentially decrease the possibility of code reuse. The Command pattern can conceal such interfaces, so the invoker only knows about the Commander's particular interface. This provides extremely loose coupling between the sender and the receiver of the message.

The end result is a highly abstracted relay of message requests and invoked behaviors.

Vignette

Johnny's mother repeatedly informs her son to quit playing video games, make his bed, and clean his room. If Johnny refuses his mother's requests, it's just a matter of time before the games are unplugged and he's grounded. Usually, his mother's presence and repeated actions invoke his behavior, which is to turn off the game and do his chores.

One Saturday, his mother has to run some errands. Before leaving, she says, "Johnny, I want to see your room cleaned and your bed made when I return in two hours." Johnny replies, "Yeah, yeah", and continues to stare intently at his game.

After a while, a sound from outside causes Johnny to run to the window. Unaware of how much time has passed, he's worried that his mother is home. Luckily, it's the next-door neighbor pulling into the driveway. The fear of being grounded causes him to panic and his heart to race, and triggers Johnny's behavior just as his mother's presence would. Johnny decides to turn off the console, clean his room, and make his bed.

The AS 3.0 Cast

In AS 3.0, the Command pattern's parts are as follows:

- Abstract command: Exposes the abstract method execute that all subclasses must implement appropriately. The abstract command also houses the reference of the receiver to which its subclasses are bound.
- Concrete command: The encapsulated request. The concrete command specifies the appropriate method that requires messaging. The concrete command can be either extremely intelligent or absent of any logic necessary to relay the receiver.
- Abstract receiver: Exposes an interface to which a family of commands can relay messages. The receiver's interface creates sets of commands that can be used in an application.
- Concrete receiver: Holds a specific behavior that it's requested to perform. As long as a class has an interface, any class can be a receiver.
- Client: The concrete command. The client that uses the Command pattern can be any object that initializes the appropriate command with a receiver. The client instantiates and initializes the receiver.
- Invoker: The object that invokes the execute behavior of a concrete command.

When It's Useful

The Command pattern is useful for the following:

- Queuing requests to execute later
- Parameterizing a class as a receiver to decouple the request from the action
- Implementing undo/redo commands

Example

A sprite is placed on the stage to act as a button. When a mouse rolls over the button, a specified sound plays. When the mouse moves off the button, the sound stops. The code is shown in **Listing 7-12**.

Listing 7-12. SoundButton uses a SoundObject to pause and play on hover and rollout.

```
package
{
   public class SoundButton extends Sprite
   {
      private var _snd : Sound;
      private var _sndChannel : SoundChannel;

      public function SoundButton()
      {
         addEventListener( MouseEvent.MOUSE_OVER , onHover );
         addEventListener( MouseEvent.MOUSE_OUT , onOut );
```

```
        }

        public function get snd() : Sound
        {
           return _snd;
        }

        public function set snd( sound : Sound ) : void
        {
           _snd = sound;
        }

        private function onHover( me : MouseEvent ) : void
        {
           _sndChannel = _snd.play();
        }

        private function onOut( me : MouseEvent ) : void
        {
           _sndChannel.stop();
        }
     }
}
```

This simple example works; but if the button needs to do anything other than exchange your sound reference for another MP3, you have to modify the code. The button was written specifically to operate on sound. Binding the receiver limits code reuse.

If you extract the actions that occur on the mouse events to the container that holds the SoundSprite, you give another class information it shouldn't know. This isn't good OOP practice, so you leave the code as it is in the SoundButton.

But now you have a problem: the client makes a last-minute request to have the button play an animation instead of a sound. The SoundButton class no longer does what you need. With your handy editor, you copy and paste the SoundButton code into a new class, which you name SWFButton (see **Listing 7-13**).

Listing 7-13. SWFButton uses the MovieClip type.

```
package
{
   public class SWFButton extends Sprite
   {
      private var _swf : MovieClip;

      public function SWFButton()
      {
         addEventListener( MouseEvent.MOUSE_OVER , onHover );
```

```
        addEventListener( MouseEvent.MOUSE_OUT , onOut );
    }

    public function get swf() : MovieClip
    {
        return _swf;
    }

    public function set swf( mc : MovieClip ) : void
    {
        _swf = mc;
    }

    private function onHover( me : MouseEvent ) : void
    {
        _swf.play()
    }

    private function onOut( me : MouseEvent ) : void
    {
        _swf.stop();
    }
  }
}
```

Now, when the mouse rolls over the button, you forward the play or stop request to your SWF instance.

The client thinks that although the animation is nice, it doesn't grab the user's attention the way the sound did: they want the animation and the sound to play together. You could perform the same copy-and-paste routine, writing more duplicate code. Or you can use the Command pattern to decouple the sender of the request from the receiver, allowing for greater flexibility.

In other words, you conceal the contents you're messaging—movie clip, sound, both, end so on—in an object that exposes only one behavior: execute. This frees your button from being bound to any particular receiver.

To begin, you create an abstract class that represents a given command behavior on a particular receiver interface. It's the command's role to create any necessary logic that may be required, to take the responsibility off your button class.

The abstract command object needs to know the interface of the object it's to make the request of, and to unify any behaviors that can message the intended interface. Your first goal is to refer to Sound and MovieClip as similar objects that they can play and pause, and to allow both types to create their own means of pausing and playing (see **Listing 7-14** through **Listing 7-17**).

Listing 7-14. IPauseable interface

```
package
{
    public interface IPauseable
    {
        function pause() : void;

        function resume() : void;
    }
}
```

Listing 7-15. ExtendedMovieClip can pause and resume.

```
package
{
    public class ExtendedMovieClip extends MovieClip implements IPauseable
    {
        final public function pause() : void
        {
            this.stop();
        }

        final public function resume() : void
        {
            this.play();
        }
    }
}
```

Listing 7-16. ExtendedSound can pause and resume.

```
package
{
    public class ExtendedSound extends Sound implements IPauseable
    {
        private var _sndPosition : Number;
        private var _sndChannel : SoundChannel;

        final public function pause() : void
        {
            _sndPosition.playheadPosition;
            _sndChannel.stop();
        }

        final public function resume() : void
```

```
      {
          sndChannel = _snd.play( _sndPosition , 0 );
      }
   }
}
```

Listing 7-17. ExtendedMovieClipAndSound can pause and resume.

```
package
{
   import flash.display.Sprite;

   public class ExtendedMovieClipAndSound extends Sprite implements IPauseable
   {
      private var _mc : ExtendedMovieClip;
      private var _snd : ExtendedSound;

      final public function pause() : void
      {
         _mc. pause();
         _snd. pause();
      }

      final public function resume() : void
      {
         _mc. resume();
         _snd.resume();
      }
   }
}
```

Now that you've created a common interface, you can specify a type of receiver for our abstract Command pattern (see **Listing 7-18** through **Listing 7-23**).

Listing 7-18. ICommand interface

```
package
{
   public interface ICommand
   {
      function execute() : void
   }
}
```

Listing 7-19. AbstractPauseableCommand implements ICommand.

```
package
{
    public class AbstractPauseableCommand implements ICommand
    {
        protected var _receiver : IPauseable

        public function AbstractPauseableCommand( aReceiver : IPauseable ) : void
        {
            _receiver = aReceiver;
        }

        final public function execute() : void
        {
            doExecution();
        }

        final public function set receiver( aReceiver : IPauseable ) : void
        {
            _receiver = _aReceiver;
        }

        final public function get receiver() : IPauseable
        {
            return _receiver ;
        }

        protected function doExecution() : void
        {
            throw new IllegalOperationError( 'doExecution must be overridden' );
        }
    }
}
```

Listing 7-20. PauseCommand extends AbstractPauseableCommand and applies its implementation to the hook as defined in the superclass.

```
package
{
    public class PauseCommand extends AbstractPauseableCommand
    {
        override protected function doExecution() : void
        {
            _receiver.pause();
```

```
        }
    }
}
```

Listing 7-21. ResumeCommand extends AbstractPauseableCommand and applies its implementation to the hook as defined in the superclass.

```
package
{
    public class ResumeCommand extends AbstractPauseableCommand
    {
        override protected function doExecution() : void
        {
            _receiver.resume();
        }
    }
}
```

Listing 7-22. ReusableButton uses both commands.

```
package
{
    public class ReusableButton extends Sprite
    {
        private var _exitCommand : ICommand;
        private var _hoverCommand : ICommand;

        public function ReusableButton()
        {
            addEventListener( MouseEvent.MOUSE_OVER , onHover )
            addEventListener( MouseEvent.MOUSE_OUT , onOut )
        }

        final public function get hoverCommand() : ICommand
        {
            return _hoverCommand;
        }

        final public function set hoverCommand( command : ICommand ) : void
        {
            _hoverCommand = command;
        }

        final public function get exitCommand() : ICommand
        {
            return _exitCommand;
```

```
        }

        final public function set exitCommand( command : ICommand ) : void
        {
            _exitCommand = command;
        }

        final private function onHover( me : MouseEvent ) : void
        {
            _hoverCommand.execute();
        }

        final private function onOut( me : MouseEvent ) : void
        {
            _exitCommand.execute();
        }
    }
}
```

Listing 7-23. The client uses the commands and the receiver.

```
package
{
    public class Client extends Sprite
    {
        // ...
        var whateverPauseable : IPauseable
        // ... rBtn is an instance of your ReusableButton
        rBtn.exitCommand = new PauseCommand( whateverPauseable );
        rBtn.hoverCommand = new ResumeCommand( whateverPauseable );
    }
}
```

As you can see, you pass in the whateverPauseable instance of IPauseable. This may be an ExtendedSound, an ExtendedMovieClip, or even an ExtendedMovieClipAndSound. The concept that it can be anything is the source of the command's power. Without having to bind your ReusableButton to a specific object that may change, you can increase the longevity of your button in an ever-changing field.

FAQ

- Can reusable buttons be coupled to IPauseable instances?

  In this example yes, because you don't add excessive logic in the concrete commands that wrap the IPauseable. But imagine if the instance that was being passed in wasn't intended to pause and resume on rollover, but rather to adjust the tint of a sprite.

  Suggesting that this behavior pauses and resumes would confuse any developer. Instead, you'd construct more commands in a similar fashion, continuing to reuse ReusableButton.

- Is a command limited to exposing only the ICommand interface?

  No, but creating too many varying interfaces for specific commands will slowly bring ReusableButton back to reusability, similar to that of SoundButton. The more specific the command interfaces, the more bound to a specific type your code becomes.

  Rather than use a MOUSE_OVER command and a MOUSE_OUT command, you can enable your command to understand a Boolean value passed in to the execute method. A parameter of True resumes the clip, and False pauses it.

Related Patterns

The following patterns are related to the Command pattern:

- Template Method
- Chain of Responsibility
- Adapter
- Memento

The Chain of Responsibility Pattern

The Chain of Responsibility pattern lets you forward a request to any number of successors required to fulfill the request. **Figure 7-4** shows the class diagram.

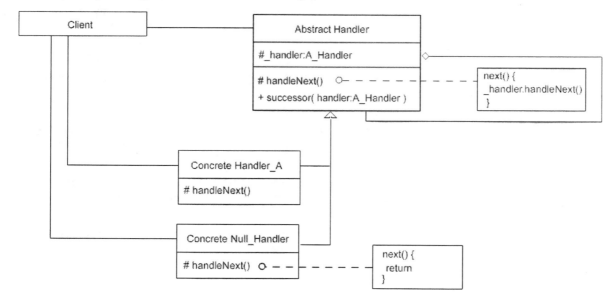

Figure 7-4. Chain of Responsibility pattern class diagram

This pattern has the following parts:

- Abstract handler
- Concrete handler

- Null handler
- Client

The pattern's benefits are as follows:

- Enables any number of receivers to respond to a request
- Lets you arrange the order dynamically or statically
- Allows a chain to connect parallel receivers in series, unlike events
- Decouples the messenger from the receiver(s) that handle the request

And it has these drawbacks:

- A message may go unhandled, depending on the assembly and the parameter being forwarded.
- Appropriate termination is required.

A Comprehensive Look

The Chain of Responsibility pattern links like-typed objects together to relay a message from the client to each successor in the chain. This decouples the message client from the receiving element meant to handle the request.

The client possesses no knowledge of who the recipient will be once the message is dispatched. Any number of receivers may choose to handle the request, but there is an expected handler. This receiver is said to be an *implicit receiver*, because it exists and will receive the message (but only the receiver knows this).

Developers who are familiar with the AS 3.0 event system should be aware of this concept. AS 3.0 passes around events without knowing who will receive the request. Handling the request may or may not prevent further forwarding, as also required in the Chain of Responsibility pattern.

Unlike in the AS 3.0 event system, the Chain of Responsibility pattern lets you manipulate the order of the handlers, as well as the handlers responsible in a chain. The client initiates the message to the first handler in the chain. From there, the concrete handlers may or may not choose to handle the request but are expected to forward it further along the chain.

In order to prevent the messaging from continuing, a Null handler must be used, to not only prevent the request from being passed to an undefined successor, but also ensure the chain isn't infinite. The Null handler caps the end of the chain to signify the end not only to the application but also to the developer.

The client remains unaware whether the request was handled, and if so by which handler. This provides a high degree of flexibility among the various handlers in the chain.

Vignette

Children often play clever games, and one of them is very reminiscent of the Chain of Responsibility pattern. The game has a few names, such as Operator, Grapevine, and Telephone. The goal of the game is to pass a message to the next player (the player's immediate neighbor), and so on, until the message has been passed from the first receiver of the message to the last available player.

The roles of the players are exactly like those in Chain of Responsibility. The player at the beginning of the line initiates messaging in the chain and injects the necessary data. Each player in the line acts as a receiver and may optionally handle the message but will absolutely forward the request.

As the message travels, each player forwards the message they received to the next player. Because children love to fabricate (some more than others), they may choose to alter the message. Not every player will distort the message: some will forward the message as received, thus abstracting the details of which player in the sequence was responsible for what.

The game concludes when the final receiver is reached and the message is compared to the original. Although this isn't expected in the Chain of Responsibility pattern, it demonstrates that the messenger is unaware of what the receivers do with the message.

The AS 3.0 Cast

In AS 3.0, the Chain of Responsibility pattern's parts are as follows:

- Abstract handler: Defines the interface that all handlers possess and supplies default behaviors that are common among its subclasses. The abstract handler may or may not, depending on its implementation, possess a reference of the successor.
- Concrete handler: Has the option to handle the request or continue to propagate it further down the chain.
- Null handler: Provides a fail-safe link. When dealing with the Chain of Responsibility pattern, one of the possible drawbacks is that the sequence must come to an end. If this isn't properly implemented, an error may occur. Using the Null handler is useful to implement the appropriate end to the request so a concrete handler that happens to be the last in the line doesn't require unnecessary logic.
- Client: Initiates the message and passes it to the first link in the chain. The client has knowledge of the interface to the abstract handlers.

When It's Useful

The Chain of Responsibility pattern is useful in the following cases:

- When there may be multiple receivers that can optionally handle the same request
- When you're creating an event system
- To inject data among a series of objects

Example

Depending on a scenario, you can bubble events and potentially use this approach to decouple objects. But bubbling events can only go so far. Consider the scenario shown in **Figure 7-5**.

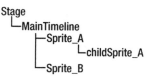

Figure 7-5. The display list and its contents

In **Figure 7-5**, two sprites reside in parallel in the root of an application. One of those sprites contains a nested sprite, childSprite_A. As a member of the flash.display.Sprite hierarchy, childSprite_A can potentially dispatch a MouseEvent when the mouse rolls into the clip's boundaries. For brevity, this example doesn't go into the three phases of the event; you only look at the bubbling phase.

As the event is dispatched, much as in the chain of command, it continues to propagate until one of the handlers prevents it from continuing. Because MouseEvents can't be cancelled, Stage acts as the terminating link; but on the way to Stage, the event passes through Sprite_A and MainTimeline.

Suppose Sprite_B needs to know if an event is dispatched to childSprite_A. Sprite_B can put the DocumentClass (MainTimeline) in the position of intercepting the propagation. **Listing 7-24** shows DocumentClass.

Listing 7-24. DocumentClass

```
package
{
 public class DocumentClass extends MovieClip
   {
       const SquareSpriteWidth : int = 58;
       const SquareSpriteHeight : int = 58;

       public function DocumentClass()
       {
          var sprite_A : Sprite = new CSprite();
          sprite_A.name = 'sprite_A';

          var sprite_B : Sprite = new CSprite();
          sprite_B.name = 'sprite_B';
          sprite_B.y = SquareSpriteHeight;

          var child_A : Sprite = new CSprite();
          child_A.name = 'childSprite_A';
          child_A.x = SquareSpriteWidth

          addChild( sprite_B );
          addChild( sprite_A );
          sprite_A.addChild( child_A );

          addEventListener( MouseEvent.MOUSE_OVER , onHover );
       }

       private function onHover( me : MouseEvent ) : void
       {
          sprite_B.someMethod();
       }
```

```
      }
}
```

The code in **Listing 7-24** demonstrates how a concrete class can listen for an event, and defer the handling to an object that wasn't initially part of the propagation chain. Although this approach is effective, the concrete class requires specifics that don't pertain to it. This decreases the cohesive quality of your class, and spreads code that should be localized.

The Chain of Responsibility pattern lets you achieve this level of localization by appending any number of objects to a chain. To do so, you need a uniform way for Sprite_B to be a part of the chain as a handler. This will rid DocumentClass of any unnecessary handling.

Further tapping into the built-in event system doesn't achieve the desired behavior, because you have no way to modify the event chain without using Sprite_B as the DisplayObjectContainer of Sprite_A. This means you need to add an additional event listener to childSprite_A, allowing it to become a client of the message in a new chain (see **Listing 7-25** through **7-29**).

Listing 7-25. IEventHandler

```
package
{
    public interface IEventHandler
    {
        function addHandler( IEventHandler ) : void;

        function forwardEvent( event : Event ) : void;
    }
}
```

Listing 7-26. AbstractEventHandlerSprite implements IEventHandler.

```
package
{
    public class AbstractEventHandlerSprite extends Sprite implements IEventHandler
    {
        private var _eventHandler : IEventHandler;
        static protected const WIDTH : int = 58;
        static protected const HEIGHT : int = 58;

        public function AbstractEventHandlerSprite()
        {
            this.graphics.lineStyle( 1 , 0xFFFFFF , 1 )
            this.graphics.beginFill( 0x000000 );
            this.graphics.drawRect( 0 , 0 , WIDTH , HEIGHT )
        }

        final public function addHandler( eventHandler : IEventHandler ) : void
        {
```

```
         doAddHandler( eventHandler );
      }

      final public function forwardEvent( event : Event ) : void
      {
         doHandleEvent( event );
         doForwardEvent( event );
      }

      protected function doAddHandler( eventHandler : IEventHandler ) : void
      {
         _eventHandler = eventHandler;
         trace( eventHandler + ' added' );
      }

      protected function doHandleEvent( event : Event ) : void
      {
         throw new IllegalOperationError( 'doHandleEvent must be overridden' );
      }

      protected function doForwardEvent( event : Event ) : void
      {
         _eventHandler.forwardEvent( event );
      }

      public function get wide() : Number
      {
         return WIDTH;
      }

      public function get tall() : Number
      {
         return HEIGHT;
      }
   }
}
```

Listing 7-27. HandlerSprite is a successor of InitiatorSprite.

```
package
{
   public class HandlerSprite extends AbstractEventHandlerSprite
   {
      public function HandlerSprite()
      {
```

```
         super();
      }

      override protected function doHandleEvent( event : Event ) : void
      {
         trace( this.name + '  I received the doHandleEvent' );
      }
   }
}
```

Listing 7-28. InitiatorSprite initiates the message.

```
package
{
   public class InitiatorSprite extends HandlerSprite
   {
      public function InitiatorSprite()
      {
         super();
         addEventListener( MouseEvent.MOUSE_OVER , onHover , false , 0 , true );
      }

      private function onHover( me : MouseEvent ) : void
      {
         this.forwardEvent( me );
      }
   }
}
```

Listing 7-29. DocumentClass initiates the Handlers and devises their order of succession.

```
package
{
   public class DocumentClass extends Sprite
   {
      public function DocumentClass()
      {
         var sprite_A : Sprite = new HandlerSprite();
         sprite_A.name = 'sprite_A';

         var sprite_B : AbstractEventHandlerSprite = new HandlerSprite();
         sprite_B.name = 'sprite_B';
         sprite_B.y = sprite_B.tall;

         var child_A : AbstractEventHandlerSprite = new InitiatorSprite();
         child_A.name = 'childSprite_A';
```

```
        child_A.x = child_A.wide

        addChild( sprite_B );
        addChild( sprite_A );
        sprite_A.addChild( DisplayObject( child_A ) );

        child_A.addHandler( sprite_B );
        // pass sprite_B as the successor of child_A
    }
  }
}
```

Currently, when you run this application it appears to work, but it suddenly breaks when you move the mouse over the nested child. This happens because the forwardEvent method is targeted on Sprite_B, which doesn't have a successor. You could add information in the AbstractEventHandler, but I find it's easier to follow a chain when a physical object marks the end. This object is the Null handler (see **Listing 7-30** and **Listing 7-31**)). This object's sole purpose is to prevent your loop from failing, and it's never added to Stage, so it's appropriate that its type is that of Object.

Listing 7-30. NullHandler reveals the end of the chain. The addition of the NullHandles ensures no conditional statements must be added in order to know when to stop the message from being forwarded.

```
package
{
    public class NullHandler extends Object implements IEventHandler
    {
        public function NullHandler()
        {
        }

        final public function addHandler( handler : IEventHandler ) : void
        {
            return;
        }

        final public function forwardEvent( event : Event ) : void
        {
            trace( 'end of the chain' );
            return;
        }
    }
}
```

Listing 7-31. DocumentClass from **Listing 7-29** now makes use of the NullHandler instance

```
package
{
```

```
public class DocumentClass extends Sprite
{
   public function DocumentClass()
   {
      // ....
      child_A.addHandler( sprite_B );
      // pass sprite_B as the successor of child_A;
      sprite_B.addHandler( new NullHandler );
      // pass NullHandler as the successor of sprite_B;

      // .. running process traces:
      // childSprite_A  I received the doHandleEvent
      // sprite_B  I received the doHandleEvent
      // end of the chain
   }
}
}
```

FAQ

- Why do you extend a sprite and implement IEventHandler to form AbstractEventHandlerSprite rather than implement IEventHandler into both HandlerSprite and InitiatorSprite?

  The main reason is to establish a class that holds the default code. This reduces the amount of code that must be manually written each time you create a flash.display.Sprite handler. I stress Sprite, because you only use Sprite. The reason to use IEventHandler is given next.

- How can you add a MovieClip as an IEventHandler?

  Because this example only uses sprites, you must assume that after doing your due diligence of OOA and OOD, this application is only intended for sprites. Therefore the code is as simple as necessary for this application.

  When you introduce another handler type from a hierarchy other than sprites, you have two options, but only one of them uses design patterns and OOP.

  First, you can copy and paste the current AbstractEventHandlerSprite code into a new AbstractEventHandlerMovieClip class. You must make sure you add the IEventHandler Implementation so your MovieClip and Sprite can be interchangeable to the IEventHandler interface.

  Second, the OOP and design patterns solution uses the Strategy pattern. You must refactor the code and create a new interface for the abstract classes, but some work is necessary.

Related Patterns

The Composite pattern is related to the Chain of Responsibility pattern.

The Iterator Pattern

The Iterator pattern provides sequential access to elements in an aggregate without knowing how the elements are structured. **Figure 7-6** shows the class diagram.

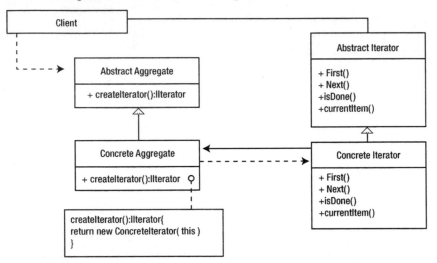

Figure 7-6. Iterator pattern class diagram

This pattern has the following parts:

- Abstract iterator
- Concrete iterator
- Abstract aggregate
- Concrete aggregate
- Client

The pattern's benefits are as follows:

- Makes elements of a collection accessible to any number of clients
- Separates maintaining a collection from the objects that require the elements

A Comprehensive Look

You want to store objects in list formation, but as it has been mentioned, classes shouldn't be exposed to information that doesn't pertain to them. Therefore, when you think of lists that contain sets of information, you need to consider them in the context of reducing unnecessary information. Think of how you can use them, but decrease what isn't needed.

AS 3.0 provides various lists through the use of arrays, vectors, objects, and dictionaries. When you try to acquire the elements of an array, the array is often used along with a loop, which should be a localized behavior to the collection. This gives a class that wants to use the elements the freedom to create the logic required to obtain said element. This logic, which retrieves the appropriate element, is the behavior of the object known as an *iterator*.

The iterator's responsibility is to maintain the current aggregate and process its successor. There are two types of iterators: internal and external. You can give the internal iterator an algorithm that it applies to every element. The external iterator enables a higher level of control by exposing its interface in such a way that the client can traverse the aggregate. Both have potential benefits and drawbacks. The iterator must ensure that any modification to the aggregate doesn't negatively impact operations currently traversing the collection.

An example of a collection is the following:

```
var array : Array= [ 1 , 2  , 3 , 4 , 5 ]
```

ActionScript 3.0 provides the internal iterator via `for...each...in`, `every`, `some`, and `map` loops, as shown in **Listing 7-32** and **Listing 7-33**.

Listing 7-32. Internal iterator encapsulating the traverse logic from the client

```
var originalArray : Array= [ 1 , 2  , 3 , 4 , 5 ];

for each( var integer : int  in originalArray )
{
        trace( integer );
}

//... 1
//... 2
//... 3
//... 4
//... 5
```

Listing 7-33. Internal iterator traversing a collection and applying an algorithm to each element

```
//...
var array : Array = [ 1 , 2 , 3 , 4 , 5 ];
     array.every( tracer );
//... cont

public function tracer( aggregate : int  , index : int , collection : Array ) : Boolean
{
        trace( aggregate );
        return true;
}

//... 1
//... 2
//... 3
```

```
//... 4
//... 5
```

Although ActionScript is kind enough to provide the internal iterator, it fails to offer an external iterator. Internal Iterators conceal the operations required to traverse the elements of the collection, but they don't let you manually control the traversing. In other words, the iterator traverses all elements in an aggregate without you being able to control the incrementing of the index.

Vignette

An old-fashioned jukebox offers numerous songs that can be played for money. These days, updated jukeboxes are designed to give the nostalgic feeling of an old-time jukebox, making it difficult to distinguish an older model from a newer one. If you've never peered inside a jukebox, you may be unaware of how one works. Does it contain records, MP3s, CDs, or HDDs? You don't know because the workings of the machine aren't the point—you want the music.

To you, it makes no difference how the jukebox plays, only that it does play. Unfortunately, you did not participate in the collection of songs the jukebox contains. However, you can conveniently move forward and backward through the collection the jukebox supplies. This way, you can work with the presented information as you see fit.

The AS 3.0 Cast

In AS 3.0, the Iterator pattern's parts are as follows:

- Abstract iterator: Exposes the interface used by the concrete iterator that is necessary for traversing each aggregate
- Concrete iterator: Knows the current position in the aggregate's traversal and creates the implementations for achieving the intended behavior of the exposed interface
- Abstract aggregate: Defines the interface for maintaining a collection and provides the factory method that manufactures an iterator
- Concrete aggregate: Implements the specific details required of the aggregate interface
- Client: Can be any aspect of the application or system that works with the aggregate to either maintain a collection or obtain the iterator it can traverse

When It's Useful

The Iterator pattern is useful when you want to do the following:

- Enable a collection to be traversed simultaneously
- Reveal the content of any aggregate in a uniform manner

Example

To create an external iterator, you must provide an interface that a client can use to access the current and next aggregate. The typical iterator interface exposes the ability to see if the end of the collection has been reached, the ability to retrieve the successor of the current element, the ability to reset the position, and the ability to retrieve the current element. You can bundle these four methods into one exposed method, but I prefer to use all four. These methods are shown in **Listing 7-34** and form the minimal behavior of the iterator. You can create more specialized versions that can iterate in the reverse direction, or even enable a carousel of elements with no identifiable end.

Listing 7-34. Typical iterator interface

```
package
{
    public interface IIterator
    {
        function next() : void;

        function hasNext() : Boolean

        function reset() : void

        function currentItem() : *
    }
}
```

The collection itself, requires the appropriate interface to add and remove elements, as well as reveal the length of the the collection. The inteface for the Aggregate is labeled IAggregate as depicted in **Listing 7-35**

Listing 7-35. Interface of the collection

```
package
{
    public interface IAggregate
    {
        function count() : int;

        function append( item : * ) : Boolean;

        function remove( item : * ) : Boolean;
    }
}
```

Lastly, a collection possesses the factory method to return it's current aggregate as an Iterator to be traversed. Listing 7-36 reveals the IIterate interface which makes use of the current IAgregate interface.

Listing 7-36. Interface of a factory method for the collection

```
package
{
    public interface IIterate extends IAggregate
```

```
    {
        function createIterator( string : String = null ) : IIterator;
    }
}
```

Now that you have the interfaces, you must create the abstractions to which you can add your default behaviors and abstract methods, and finally provide your abstract class with commonalities required by your collections.

Because AS 3.0 provides various ways to use collections—vectors, arrays, and so on—you must ensure that your concrete iterators, and any abstract collection, take this into account. To do so, you construct an abstract collection that an additional layer of abstract classes will subclass. These subclasses are specific to the collections you use (see **Listing 7-37** through **7-39**).

Listing 7-37. Abstract collection

```
package
{
    public class AbstractCollection implements IIterate
    {
        protected var _iterator : IIterator

        public function AbstractCollection()
        {
        }

        final public function count() : int
        {
            return doCount();
        }

        final public function append( element : * ) : Boolean
        {
            return doAppend( element );
        }

        final public function remove( element : * ) : Boolean
        {
            return doRemove( element );
        }

        final public function createIterator( string : String = null ) : IIterator
        {
            return doCreateIterator( string );
        }
```

```
    protected function doCount() : int
    {
        throw new IllegalOperationError( ' doCount must be overridden' );
        return 0;
    }

    protected function doAppend( element : * ) : Boolean
    {
        throw new IllegalOperationError( ' doAppend must be overridden' );
        return false;
    }

    protected function doRemove( element : * ) : Boolean
    {
        throw new IllegalOperationError( ' doRemove must be overridden' );
        return false;
    }

    protected function doCreateIterator( string : String ) : IIterator
    {
        return null;
    }
  }
}
```

Listing 7-38. Abstract Iterator

```
package
{
    public class AbstractIterator extends Object implements IIterator
    {
        protected var _cursor : int = 0;

        final public function next() : void
        {
            doNext();
        }

        final public function hasNext() : Boolean
        {
            return doHasNext();
        }

        final public function reset() : void
        {
```

```
          doReset();
      }

      final public function currentElement() : *
      {
          return doCurrentElement();
      }

      protected function doNext() : void
      {
          throw new IllegalOperationError( 'doNext must be overridden ' );
      }

      protected function doHasNext() : Boolean
      {
          throw new IllegalOperationError( 'doHasNext must be overridden ' );
          return false;
      }

      protected function doReset() : void
      {
          throw new IllegalOperationError( 'doReset must be overridden ' );
      }

      protected function doCurrentElement() : *
      {
          throw new IllegalOperationError( 'doCurrentElement must be overridden ' );
          return null;
      }
   }
}
```

Listing 7-39. Abstract array collection that all subclasses that use an array can extend

```
package
{
   public class AbstractArrayCollection extends AbstractCollection
   {
      protected var _collection : Array;

      public function AbstractArrayCollection()
      {
          super();
          _collection = new Array();
      }
```

```
public function each( func : Function ) : void
{
   var tmpIt : IIterator = doCreateIterator( null );
   var _count : int = 0;
   do
   {
      func.call( this , tmpIt.currentElement() , _count , _collection );
      tmpIt.next();
      _count++
   }
   while (tmpIt.hasNext());
}

override protected function doCount() : int
{
   return _collection.length;
}

override protected function doAppend( element : * ) : Boolean
{
   _collection[_collection.length] = element;
   return true;
}

override protected function doRemove( element : * ) : Boolean
{
   return false;
}

override protected function doCreateIterator( string : String ) : IIterator
{
   throw new IllegalOperationError( ' doCreateIterator must be overridden' );
}
   }
}
```

Now that you have the abstract class for arrays defined, you can use your concretes to use the array collections and return a specific iterator that the collection requires by overriding your factory method.

Next you need to extend the abstract iterator to one that is solely focused on arrays as being the collection to iterate. Let's call this iterator ArrayIterator (see **Listings 7-40** through **7-43**).

Listing 7-40. `ArrayIterator` subclasses `AbstractIterator` to use arrays

```
package
{
    public class ArrayIterator extends AbstractIterator
    {
        protected var _collection : Array;

        public function ArrayIterator( collection : Array )
        {
            _collection = collection;
        }

        override protected function doNext() : void
        {
            _cursor++;
        }

        override protected function doHasNext() : Boolean
        {
            return _cursor < _collection.length;
        }

        override protected function doReset() : void
        {
            _cursor = 0;
        }

        override protected function doCurrentElement() : *
        {
            return _collection[_cursor];
        }
    }
}
```

Listing 7-41. Concrete `ArrayCollection` overriding the factory method to return an array iterator

```
package
{
    public class ArrayCollection extends AbstractArrayCollection
    {
        public function ArrayCollection()
        {
            super();
        }
```

```
      override protected function doCreateIterator( string : String ) : IIterator
      {
         return new ArrayIterator( _collection );
      }
   }
}
```

Listing 7-42. The DocumentClass demonstrates the use of internal and external iteration of elements within the ArrayCollection

```
package
{
   public class DocumentClass extends Sprite
   {
      public function DocumentClass()
      {
         var arrayCollection : AbstractArrayCollection = new ArrayCollection();
         arrayCollection.append( 1 );
         arrayCollection.append( 2 );
         arrayCollection.append( 3 );
         arrayCollection.append( 4 );
         arrayCollection.append( 5 );

         var it : IIterator = arrayCollection.createIterator();

         do
         {
            trace( it.currentElement() );
            it.next();
         }
         while (it.hasNext());

         arrayCollection.each( test );
      }

      function test( element : int , index : int , arrayCollection : Array ) : Boolean
      {
         trace( element , index , arrayCollection );
         return true;
      }
   }
}
```

Listing 7-43. The Iterated results from **Listing 7-42**

```
//... The above code traces out the following.
        //Utilizing your External Iterator
//... 1
//... 2
//... 3
//... 4
//... 5
        //Utilizing your ArrayCollection Internal Iterator and passed function Test
//... 1 0 1,2,3,4,5
//... 2 1 1,2,3,4,5
//... 3 2 1,2,3,4,5
//... 4 3 1,2,3,4,5
//... 5 4 1,2,3,4,5
```

In AS 3.0, there are built-in collections from which a user can choose, and it may be easier for other developers to use these instead of your new array collection—especially if they're unfamiliar with the ArrayCollection class. The good thing about separating the iterator from the collection is that having created your ArrayIterator, you can use it along with any built-in AS 3.0 collection by instantiating a new iterator and passing in its appropriate collection (see Listing **7-44**).

Listing 7-44. Built-in AS 3.0 array, traversed by instantiating ArrayIterator within the constructor of DocumentClass

```
public function DocumentClass()
{
   var ar : Array = [ 1 , 2 , 3 , 4 , 5 , 6 ];

   var itr : IIterator = new ArrayIterator( ar );
   do
   {
      trace( itr.currentElement() + ' via AS3.0 Array ' );
      itr.next();
   }
   while (itr.hasNext());
}


//... traces
//... 1 via AS3.0 Array
//... 2 via AS3.0 Array
//... 3 via AS3.0 Array
//... 4 via AS3.0 Array
//... 5 via AS3.0 Array
//... 6 via AS3.0 Array
```

FAQ

- Which object is supposed to possess the algorithm, in **Listing 7-33**, that is to be used with the internal iterator?

  The answer lies in the question. The algorithm is a strategy that can be instantiated and used by the internal iterator. This lets you reuse the algorithm with other internal iterators, and allows the strategy to relieve the client and/or the collection from knowing such specifics.

Related Patterns

The Iterator pattern is related to the following patterns:

- Composite
- Factory Method
- Memento

The State Pattern

The State pattern lets you change an object's behavior to reflect a change in its state. **Figure 7-7** shows the class diagram.

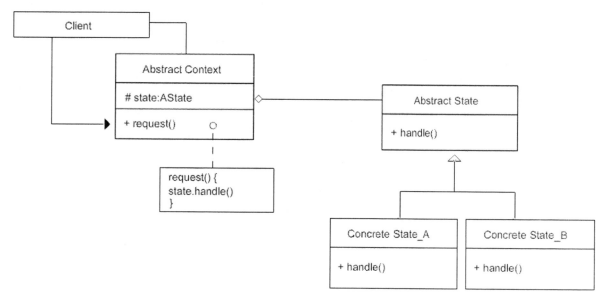

Figure 7-7. State pattern class diagram

This pattern has the following parts:

- Abstract context
- Abstract state
- Concrete state
- Client

The pattern's benefits are as follows:

- Localizes operations
- Maximizes cohesion
- Reduces if...else... dependencies

And it has these drawbacks:

- The localization of state specifics causes delocalization among behaviors.
- The pattern requires additional classes.

A Comprehensive Look

A *state* is a specific variable that can possess a value in a program. This value can be simple and appear insignificant, yet any change to it can determine the operation of a behavior in context.

Consider the effect of destroying a Loader instance in AS 3.0. The means by which you attempt to rid the system of this instance will vary depending on if the Loader has been used or is currently in use. Consider the destroyLoader method shown in **Listing 7-45**.

Listing 7-45. A typical way to destroy a built-in Loader

```
protected function destroyLoader() : void
{
  loader.contentLoaderInfo.removeEventListener( Event.OPEN , handleOpen )
  loader.contentLoaderInfo.removeEventListener( Event.INIT , handleInit )
  loader.contentLoaderInfo.removeEventListener( Event.COMPLETE , handleLoadComplete );
  loader.contentLoaderInfo.removeEventListener( IOErrorEvent.IO_ERROR , ➥
  handleLoadIError );
  if ( isLoaded )
  {
    loader.unloadAndStop();
  }
  else
  {
    loader.close();
    loader.unloadAndStop();
  }

  loader = null;
}
```

As you can see, you destroy the Loader instance with the aid of a conditional statement. You determine if the Loader is currently loading something, and, if so, you're required to close the Loader before you remove any reference to it. This is a pain.

Unfortunately, the Loader class can't close and unload itself without the client specifying the condition. This reduces the cohesion of the client and unnecessarily increases the number of lines of code. The issue in the case of the `Loader` is the lack of change among its behaviors' functionality; the behaviors are state dependent, as demonstrated in **Listing 7-45**. This is where the State pattern offers a solution.

The State pattern localizes appropriate behaviors in their own encapsulations that implement the appropriate operations of the given state, thereby reducing the complexities of the messaged object that the client doesn't need to know about. This pattern uses two components: a state object and the context object.

Because the client remains unaware of the state-dependent behaviors of the object it's messaging, the messaged object must ensure that the appropriate behaviors reflect the context's state. The context defines the interface the client uses, and each request is delegated to an encapsulated behavior known as the *state object*. A finite number of state objects represent all possible states of the context. In the `Loader` example, the states are `Loader.LOADED`, `Loader.LOADING`, and `Loader.BARREN`.

You have three states, which means you need to create three state objects. All of these states make implementations of the interface, but it's mandatory that their behaviors reflect their state. In order to make them interchangeable and uniform, they stem from an abstraction, which lets the context use the appropriate implementation at runtime.

What determines the transitions among the states depends entirely on the application. If the application is linear, the context can create the appropriate logic. If it's more dynamic and varies at runtime, then you have more flexibility to allow each state to enable the appropriate transition. (Here, *transition* refers to the swapping of state objects; don't confuse it with animation.)

To enable a state object to trigger the succession of states, it can optionally contain a reference to the context object. If the state object defines the transition's successor, the state requires the context to expose an additional interface that it can use. This allows state-specific operations to transition to an appropriate state when required. In the `Loader` example, you have a transition from a loading state to a loaded state when the image loading has completed.

Vignette

Human emotions often vary without rhyme or reason. Although external factors can influence a response, no one can predict the resulting behavior. Each person is different, so even if the stimulus remains constant, the internal changes are often specific to the subject.

A person's state may not be known, but their behavior and mood reflect their current state of mind. Happy, sad, and angry moods can be recognized by the behaviors you exhibit.

Of course, even if your moods vary, others can still recognize you and will continue to interact with you as they always have. This will just get a different response when they do.

The AS 3.0 Cast

In AS 3.0, the State pattern's parts are as follows:

- Abstract state: Exposes the interface that the state objects inherit.
- Concrete state: Implements the behaviors of the interface that reflect the state appropriately.
- Abstract context: Exposes the interface that clients message, and in turn delegates requests to the appropriate state object.

- Concrete context: Implements the specifics of the logic that states may transition. It also may contain the factory method that manufactures the appropriate state object.
- Client: Any aspect of the application or system that works with the abstract context. It's unaware of the state objects because it never works with them directly.

When It's Useful

The State pattern is useful in these situations:

- To reduce nested conditional statements that reflect a state
- To localize behavior specific to a state

Example

Suppose you're creating a simple calculator application whose state can be addition, subtraction, multiplication, or division. The calculator's state is set by the client. (It would be wise to use a model in this case, because the entire application is the calculator; but for brevity, this example uses the client.)

The mode the user chooses adjusts the state of the context. First you need to define the interface of the calculator context. As always, the abstract class contains any default or necessary references used by the subclass. You call this abstract class AbstractCalculatorContext (see **Listing 7-46**).

Listing 7-46. AbstractCalculatorContext defines the abstract operations.

```
package
{
    public class AbstractCalculatorContext
    {
        protected var _state : AbstractStateObject;

        public function AbstractCalculatorContext()
        {
        }

        final public function addition() : void
        {
            doAddition();
        }

        final public function subtraction() : void
        {
            dosubtraction();
        }

        final public function division() : void
        {
            doDivision();
```

```
        }

        final public function multiplication() : void
        {
            doMultiplication();
        }

        final public function setDilineatedValues( values : Vector.<Number> ) : void
        {
            doSetDilineatedValues( values );
        }

        protected function doAddition() : void
        {
            throw new IllegalOperationError( 'doAddition must be overridden' );
        }

        protected function dosubtraction() : void
        {
            throw new IllegalOperationError( 'dosubtraction must be overridden' );
        }

        protected function doDivision() : void
        {
            throw new IllegalOperationError( 'doDivision must be overridden' );
        }

        protected function doMultiplication() : void
        {
            throw new IllegalOperationError( 'doMultiplication must be overridden' );
        }

        protected function doSetDilineatedValues( values : Vector.<Number> ) : void
        {
            throw new IllegalOperationError( 'doSetDilineatedValues must be overridden' )
        }
    }
}
```

In order to make the behaviors uniform, you also need to create an abstract state object that defines the interface used by its subclasses. This abstract class is also known by the calculator abstract class, which is called AbstractStateObject. (see **Listing 7-47**).

Listing 7-47. `AbstractStateObject` declares a single abstract method as its interface.

```
package
{
   public class AbstractStateObject
   {
      public function calculate( values : Vector.<Number> ) : void
      {
         throw new IllegalOperationError( 'calculate must be overridden' );
      }
   }
}
```

As shown in the listing, the `calculate` interface accepts any number of values, which are acted on by the appropriate subclass calculations.

Because the user chooses the successor, and not the states themselves, you know it's a fixed transition, and the successor can be chosen by the context to determine which calculation to use for the state. This is shown in **Listing 7-48**, where the concrete context instantiates the appropriate state object.

Listing 7-48. Calculator context declares succeeding transitions

```
package
{
   public class CalculatorContext extends AbstractCalculatorContext
   {
      public function CalculatorContext()
      {
      }

      override  protected function doAddition() : void
      {
         this._state = new AdditionState();
      }

      override  protected function dosubtraction() : void
      {
         this._state = new SubtractionState();
      }

      override  protected function doDivision() : void
      {
         this._state = new DivisionState();
      }

      override  protected function doMultiplication() : void
```

```
   {
      this._state = new MultiplicationState();
   }

   override protected function doSetDilineatedValues( values : Vector.<Number> )➥
                                                                      : void
   {
      this._state.calculate( values );
   }
}
}
```

CalculatorContext uses a finite number of state objects to adjust the behavior of the calculator. To provide further flexibility, you can encapsulate the creation process using a factory method that returns the appropriate AbstractStateObject (see **Listing 7-49**).

Listing 7-49. CalculatorContext with the declaration of the factory method

```
package
{
   public class CalculatorContext extends AbstractCalculatorContext
   {
      protected static const Addition_Mode : int = 0;
      protected static const Subtraction_Mode : int = 1;
      protected static const Multiplication_Mode : int = 2;
      protected static const Division_Mode : int = 3;

      public function CalculatorContext()
      {
      }

      override  protected function doAddition() : void
      {
         this._state = doCreateAbstractStateObject( Addition_Mode );
      }

      override  protected function doSubtraction() : void
      {
         this._state = doCreateAbstractStateObject( Subtraction_Mode );
      }

      override  protected function doDivision() : void
      {
         this._state = doCreateAbstractStateObject( Division_Mode );
      }
```

```
        override  protected function doMultiplication() : void
        {
            this._state = doCreateAbstractStateObject( Multiplication_Mode );
        }

        override protected function doSetDilineatedValues( values : Vector.<Number> ) ➟
                                                                                     : void
        {
            this._state.calculate( values );
        }

        protected function doCreateAbstractStateObject( EnumType : int ) ➟
                                                             : AbstractStateObject
        {
            throw new IllegalOperationError( 'doFactoryMethod must be overridden' );
            return null;
        }
    }
}
```

Listing 7-50. Subclass CalculatorContextStateLogic applies the manufacturing logic.

```
package
{
    public class CalculatorContextStateLogic extends CalculatorContext
    {
        override protected function doCreateAbstractStateObject( EnumType : int ) ➟
                                                             : AbstractStateObject
        {
            var product : AbstractStateObject;
            switch(EnumType)
            {
                case 0:
                    product = new AdditionState();
                    break;
                case 1:
                    product = new SubtractionState();
                    break;
                case 2:
                    product = new MultiplicationState();
                    break;
                case 3:
                    product = new DivisionState();
                    break;
            }
```

```
                return product;
            }
        }
    }
```

All that remains is to implement the behaviors that reflect the appropriate state among the interfaces the client can use. The implementation for the addition state is shown in **Listing 7-51**.

Listing 7-51. Addition state implementing its behavior in the calculator interface

```
package
{
    public class AdditionState extends AbstractStateObject
    {
        public function AdditionState()
        {
        }

        override public function calculate( values : Vector.<Number> ) : void
        {
            var sum : Number = 0;
            for each ( var number:Number in values);
            {
                sum += number;
            }
            trace( sum );
        }
    }
}
```

Because a change in state can alter the implementation of the behavior, the client doesn't need to be concerned with how the calculations are performed. This is handled by the state object that the context delegates (see **Listing 7-52**).

Listing 7-52. The client uses the calculator object without worrying about what state it's in.

```
package
{
    public class Client extends Sprite
    {
        public function Client()
        {
            var ti_92Plus : AbstractCalculatorContext = new CalculatorContextStateLogic()

            ti_92Plus.addition();
            ti_92Plus.setDilineatedValues( Vector.<Number>( [ 2 , 2 ] ) );
            ti_92Plus.setDilineatedValues( Vector.<Number>( [ 3 , 9 ] ) );
```

```
        }
      }
    }
```

FAQ

- Isn't this pattern a lot like the Strategy pattern?

  They appear similar at first glance because they both use varying implementations that are encapsulated. They're also interchangeable because they rely on polymorphic structures. The main distinction between the two is the goal to achieve or the obstacle to overcome.

  In the case of the State pattern, the goal is to allow context behaviors to vary and reflect the state of the context. The Strategy pattern lets a client assign the appropriate context behavior without modifying the state. The difference is the dependency between the state and behaviors.

Related Patterns

The State pattern is related to the Strategy pattern.

The Memento Pattern

The Memento pattern externalizes the internal state of an object for later state restoration. **Figure 7-8** shows the class diagram.

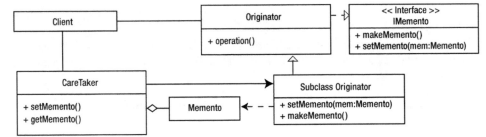

Figure 7-8. Memento pattern class diagram

This pattern has the following parts:

- Memento
- Caretaker
- Originator
- Client

The pattern's benefits are as follows:

- State reversion
- Increased cohesion

And it has these drawbacks:

- Memory consumption
- Additional classes
- Speed of object initialization, depending on how often mementos are initialized

A Comprehensive Look

Data hiding is a very important principle of OOP; it ensures that no object can change the state of an object without the object's consent. This allows the object to regulate its own states. For this reason, a class may contain extraneous information that pertains to state maintenance, but that decreases the cohesion among its behaviors. Sometimes an object requires help in concealing such information in order to maintain its states.

This help is in the form of the memento. The memento externalizes the internal state of an object and safeguards its contents from anything other than the originator. Otherwise, anything else would break the principle of data hiding.

The memento can hold any state information the originator allows/requires, but only the originator can supply and obtain the contents of the memento. Depending on the information held in the memento and on the number of mementos in use, mementos can be costly in terms of memory; therefore mementos should remain passive and be created only when necessary.

Mementos aren't held in the originator because that would be similar to maintaining their mementos, which is a similar burden. Rather than the originators retaining the memento, they pass the mementos to a caretaker.

The caretaker retains mementos for safekeeping. It can only store mementos; it can't view their contents. If the originator's state needs to be restored, it obtains the state from the caretaker. The caretaker invokes the factory method, which prompts the creation of a memento from the originator; and it can do so more than once if multiple states are required for the application. You can easily do this by using the Façade pattern (see Chapter 8), or with The Observer Pattern (Discussed at the end of this chapter).

Additionally, a memento may contain incremental changes to create a history of the originator's changes. If such changes are linear and can be restored in the same order in the stack, then only the retained state should be concerned with those changes, not the originator's current state. This reduces the amount of memory used.

Mementos can work well with the Command pattern, specifically commands that define both execute and un-execute. In a scenario that uses such a command, the command may become the caretaker.

Vignette

You can use a string tied around your finger as a means of remembering something. The string signifies that you need to remember—it doesn't fulfill the task of stating what it is you have to remember.

Everyday life requires focus that often drowns out other aspects of the world, resulting in the need to use the string. But what is this string for? you may ask yourself, wishing someone could remind you.

The AS 3.0 Cast

In AS 3.0, the Memento pattern's parts are as follows:

- Originator: Creates and uses a memento. The originator may be any class in the application that needs to be able to revert its state. The originator implements the IMemento interface or extends from an abstraction if possible, to expose the necessary interface for the caretaker. Additionally, the originator must notify the caretaker when a memento is needed for state reversion.
- Caretaker: Invokes the originator. The caretaker is the messenger of the originator that either obtains or sets a memento for the originator. The caretaker depends on the originator, because it has no way of knowing when the originator has updated its state. Additionally, the caretaker must be informed by the application when restoration to a state is required.
- Memento: A black box. The memento must not reveal its contents to anything other than the originator, because doing so breaches the concept of data hiding. The memento conceals its interface either by using custom namespaces or by declaring its definition as internal.
- Client: The messenger of the originator. Well, not necessarily of the originator, but of the class that implements the IMemento interface, making it an originator. Remember, the originator doesn't retain its own state, not because it can't, but because it has other behaviors it needs to perform. These behaviors continue to be messaged by the client, which as always can be any aspect of the application or system. It also notifies the caretaker if a state must be reset or supplied to the originator.

When It's Useful

The Memento pattern is useful when an object's state may need to be restored: user input, drawing applications, forms, and so on.

Example

Most applications rely heavily on user interactions to engage and captivate an audience. Unlike our applications (*cough*), humans have flaws and are likely to make mistakes that they want to undo. Rather than expect your objects to maintain a change in their state, the objects set the changes aside for safekeeping, until the object requires them back.

Have you ever had to complete a form online that called for you to enter a lot of text? The text fields in AS 3.0 are great for this type of behavior in an application, but they don't allow the user to undo data entry, short of using the backspace. The memento can supply this functionality (see **Listing 7-53**).

Listing 7-53. The IMemento interface defines a narrow interface to obtain and set a memento.

```
package
{
```

```
    public interface IMemento
    {
        function setMemento( memento : Memento ) : void

        function makeMomento() : Memento
    }
}
```

The IMemento interface lets any object possess the interface required to externalize a state (see **Listing 7-54** through **Listing 7-59**).

Listing 7-54. FormField implements IMemento to take advantage of resetting its state

```
package
{
    public class FormField extends TextField implements IMemento
    {
        use namespace originatorOnly
        public function FormField()
        {
        }

        public function setMemento( memento : Memento ) : void
        {
            this.text = memento.string;
            this.setSelection( memento.cursor , memento.cursor );
        }

        final public function makeMemento() : Memento
        {
            var memento : Memento = doMakeMemento();
            memento.string = this.text;
            memento.cursor = this.caretIndex;
            return memento;
        }

        protected function doMakeMemento() : Memento
        {
            throw new IllegalOperationError( 'doMakeMomento must be overridden' );
            return null;
        }
    }
}
```

Listing 7-55. The `originatorOnly` namespace protects the memento interface from being used beyond the originator.

```
package
{
    internal namespace originatorOnly
    {
    }
}
```

Listing 7-56. The originator is a subclass of `FormField` and implements the factory logic.

```
package
{
    public class Originator extends FormField
    {
        use namespace originatorOnly;
        public function Originator()
        {
            super();
        }

        override protected function doMakeMemento() : Memento
        {
            var memento : Memento = new Memento();
            return memento;
        }
    }
}
```

Listing 7-57. The `Memento` object should be as minimal as possible, because the bytes add up.

```
package
{
    public class Memento extends Object
    {
        private var _string : String;
        private var _cursor : int;

        public function Memento()
        {
            trace( getSize( this ) + ' bytes' );
        }

        originatorOnly function get string() : String
        {
```

```
            return _string;
        }

        originatorOnly function set string( str : String ) : void
        {
            _string = str;
        }

        originatorOnly function get cursor() : int
        {
            return _cursor;
        }

        originatorOnly function set cursor( cursor : int ) : void
        {
            _cursor = cursor;
        }
    }
}
```

Listing 7-58. The caretaker creates the logic to determine when a new state snapshot is required.

```
package
{
    public class Caretaker extends Sprite
    {
        public var _stack : Vector.<Memento>;
        private var _originator : Originator;
        private var _backSpaceMonitor : Array = [];

        public function Caretaker( orginator : Originator )
        {
            _originator = orginator;
            _originator.addEventListener( KeyboardEvent.KEY_DOWN , onKeyDown );
            _originator.addEventListener( KeyboardEvent.KEY_UP , onKeyUP );
            _stack = new Vector.<Memento>();
        }

        public function onKeyUP( event : KeyboardEvent ) : void
        {
            if (!event.ctrlKey)
            {
                if (event.keyCode == Keyboard.BACKSPACE)
                {
                    _backSpaceMonitor[_backSpaceMonitor.length] = true;
```

```
            }
            if ( _backSpaceMonitor.length > 1)
            {
                _backSpaceMonitor.shift();
                return;
            }
            else
            {
                addStack( _originator.makeMemento() );
            }
        }
    }

    public function onKeyDown( event : KeyboardEvent ) : void
    {
        if (event.ctrlKey && event.keyCode == Keyboard.Z)
        {
            _originator.setMemento( retrieveStack() );
        }
    }

    private function addStack( memento : Memento ) : void
    {
        _stack[_stack.length] = memento;
    }

    private function retrieveStack() : Memento
    {
        return _stack.pop();
    }
  }
}
```

Listing 7-59. DocumentClass initializes the originator and the caretaker.

```
package
{
    public class DocumentClass extends Sprite
    {
        var caretaker : Caretaker;
        var ff : FormField;

        public function DocumentClass()
        {
            stage.align = StageAlign.TOP_LEFT;
```

```
        stage.scaleMode = StageScaleMode.NO_SCALE;

        ff = new Originator();
        ff.width = 300;
        ff.height = 500;
        ff.type = TextFieldType.INPUT;
        ff.border = true;
        addChild( ff );

        caretaker = new Caretaker( Originator( ff ) );
    }
  }
}
```

In order not to pollute DocumentClass (or any class, for that matter) with listeners, you pass in the originator to the Caretaker instance. This not only increases the cohesiveness of the containing class, but also emphasizes that the caretaker must invoke the originator's factory method to prevent the application from seeing and possibly modifying the memento.

FAQ

- This example shows how you can retrieve a state when a user presses Ctrl+z, which makes sense here because caretaker already listens for keypresses being dispatched from originator. But how would a reset or undo in a drawing application force the caretaker to submit a saved state?

  For the reason mentioned, the caretaker doesn't expose an interface that will do this. If the ability to reset or step backward is required, the caretaker can optionally implement this functionality to be triggered by the application. This makes the caretaker dependent on the reset or undo button as well.

- Does this example use the Façade pattern or the Observer pattern to retrieve the memento?

  This question makes a nice transition, because Observer is the next pattern discussed. The current example uses AS 3.0 event notification for simplification, which isn't exactly the Observer pattern, as you soon see.

Related Patterns

The Memento pattern is related to these patterns:

- Command
- Iterator

The Observer Pattern

The Observer pattern establishes a one-to-many type of relationship in which objects dependent on information can subscribe to a source for direct notifications. **Figure 7-9** shows the class diagram.

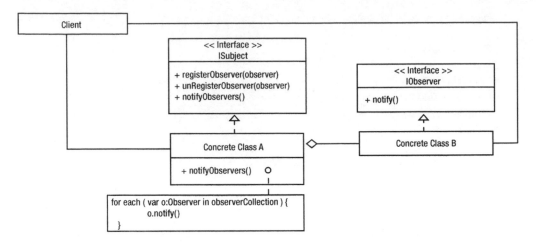

Figure 7-9. Observer pattern class diagram

This pattern has the following parts:

- Abstract subject
- Concrete subject
- Abstract observer
- Concrete observer
- Client

The pattern's benefits are as follows:

- Synchronizes state-dependent objects
- Uses a one-to-many relationships
- Lets subjects and observers also be observers and subjects

And it has these drawbacks:

- Object lookup speeds can affect performance.
- It may cause redundant notifications.

A Comprehensive Look

The Observer pattern lets an object that is dependent on the state of another object maintain synchronization when there is a change in state. An object called an *observer* registers itself with an object possessing a given state, for reasons known only to the observer. The object with which it's registered is known as the *subject* because it's the subject whose state is being observed.

The subject not only exposes an interface, allowing observers access to its states, but also informs all of its observers that a particular value has been updated. This allows the observers to retrieve the updated information to reflect their own states.

The most important aspects of the Observer pattern are the interfaces of the subject and the observer. These vary greatly on the extent to which you wish to implement them, and allow them to be dependent on each other. The simplest subject interface is one that adds and removes an observer. The simplest observer interface is one that can be notified. This requires the abstract classes of both observer and subject to have the default behaviors to perform the duties of these interfaces. This couples the relationship between the two objects.

The alternative is for the subject to declare an interface that allows observers to supply the intended state to watch, and an interface that lets observers to un-watch all or particular aspects. The observer may also let the subject be passed in, allowing state retrieval.

The means by which states are retrieved by observers is called a *push and pull*. The push and pull are two individual behaviors that obtain data.

- During the push, the subject notifies observers and provides the values each observer requires, pushing its details onto observers.
- During the pull behavior, the subject notifies the observers. It's up to the observers to retrieve the data, pulling it from the subject.

Both procedures have advantages and disadvantages. Pushing requires the subject to be aware of the interfaces among its observers, but pushing can send information regarding an update of an aspect. Pulling allows the subject to remain unaware of the dependent objects' interfaces, but requires each observer to be intelligent enough to figure out what may have changed.

Vignette

"If a tree falls in the woods and no one's around, does it make a sound?" The answer, according to harmonics (physics), is yes; but because no one is there, the sound waves aren't interpreted, at least not by human ears. You know the tree falling generates a sound, so perhaps the question should be, "If a tree falls in the woods and no one's around, how do you know the tree fell?"

Perhaps this is a question of existentialism, but it's also the reason for newspapers. You can't experience every event firsthand; you need a source for information. Whether your interests are sports, stocks, the daily funnies, or all of these, you can subscribe to updates.

You may subscribe to the paper out of necessity. Business, local, and weather information pertain to information that can impact your life. Being a subscriber to these notifications helps you to behave appropriately.

The benefit of the newspaper is its ability to spread information via a singular channel that can reach the entire town that the local paper covers. The paper, combined with the media you subscribe to on a regular basis, including TV and the Internet, demonstrates your need to remain updated and informed.

The AS 3.0 Cast

In AS 3.0, the Observer pattern's parts are as follows:

- Subject: Implements `ISubject`. Subjects aren't merely subjects, but rather are objects that possess a state that another object needs. The interface inheritance makes a subject a subject. The subject layers additional behaviors that notify dependent objects about state manipulations.

- Observer: Implements IObserver. Observers become observers by adopting and implementing the IObserver interface. They may retain a reference to the subject for added control over the means of obtaining state information from its subject.
- Change manager: Optional object that reduces the couplings among subjects and observers. Push notifications mean the subject must have knowledge of the observer. Pull notifications mean observers must have knowledge of the subject. A change manager acts as a mapping between the two, preventing such couplings.
- Client: Messages subjects and observers. Both subjects and observers are objects with behaviors of their own that don't pertain to being a subject or an observer. It just so happens that the two are dependent on each another. The client in the system continues to message the two objects as if they were neither subjects nor observers.

When It's Useful

The Observer pattern is useful when you're doing the following:

- Devising a model
- Using multiple views to reflect a singular state

Example

AS 3.0 lets you use observers to monitor an aspect of a subject by using the EventDispatcher's built-in method addEventListener. The word *event* denotes an action that can manipulate a particular state. The EventDispatcher uses the push method, so details of what has changed often appear in the notification. You can optionally use the pull method by maintaining a reference to the subject that dispatched the notification.

Twitter is the epitome of the Observer pattern, so this example attempts to simulate the act of following a particular Twitter user. A subject changes its status at random intervals using Lorem Ipsum (placeholder text) that is then broadcast to any status-dependent observers. See **Listing 7-60** through **Listing 7-64**.

Listing 7-60. ISubject interface that enables observers to be added to and removed from the subject

```
package
{
   public interface ISubject
   {
      function addObserver( observer : IObserve , aspect : Function ) : Boolean

      function removeObserver( observer : IObserve ) : Boolean
   }
}
```

Listing 7-61. IObserve interface defining an operation to be notified

```
package
{
```

```
      public interface IObserve
      {
        function notify( str : String ) : void
      }
}
```

Listing 7-62. Subject Implements the ISubject interface and updates its status regardless of whether there are observers.

```
package
{
   public class Subject extends Object implements ISubject
   {
      static const LoremIspum : String = "Lorem ipsum dolor sit amet, consectetur
                    adipiscing elit. Morbi condimentum leo sit amet augue pulvinar non
                    dictum neque vehicula. Morbi feugiat diam consectetur sapien porta
                    mattis..."

      static const LoremIpsumAr : Array = LoremIspum.split( " " );
      protected var _dict : Dictionary;
      private var timer : Timer;

      public function Subject()
      {
         _dict = new Dictionary( false );
         timer = new Timer( 550 );
         timer.repeatCount = 1;
         timer.addEventListener( TimerEvent.TIMER_COMPLETE , onComplete );
         timer.start();
      }

      public function removeObserver( observer : IObserve ) : Boolean
      {
         _dict[observer] = null;
         delete _dict[observer];
         return true;
      }

      public function addObserver( observer : IObserve , aspect : Function ) : Boolean
      {
         _dict[observer] = getTimer();
         return true;
      }

      protected function notifyObservers( Enum : String ) : void
```

```
   {
      for (var observer:* in _dict)
      {
         observer.notify( Enum );
      }
   }

   private function onComplete( event : TimerEvent ) : void
   {
      timer.stop();
      timer.delay = Math.random() * 1000;
      timer.reset();
      var startIndex : int;
      var endIndex : int;
      startIndex = Math.random() * LoremIpsumAr.length;
      var pool : int = LoremIpsumAr.length - startIndex;
      endIndex = Math.random() * ((pool < 140) ? pool : 140);
      var status : String = "";
      while (startIndex < endIndex)
      {
         status += LoremIpsumAr[startIndex] + " ";
         startIndex++;
      }

      notifyObservers( status );
      timer.start();
   }
  }
}
```

Listing 7-63. Observer lacks any behaviors for this example other than those of IObserve

```
package
{
   public class Observer extends Object implements IObserve
   {
      public function Observer()
      {
      }

      // status updates from the Subject will trace out here
      public function notify( str : String ) : void
      {
         trace( str );
      }
```

```
        }
  }
```

Listing 7-64. DocumentClass creates the subject with an instance of an observer.

```
package
{
    public class DocumentClass extends Sprite
    {
        public function DocumentClass()
        {
            var observer : IObserve = new Observer()
            var subject : ISubject = new Subject()

            subject.addObserver( observer , null );
        }
    }
}
```

This example, although simple, illustrates the essence of the subscriber/notifier method known as the Observer pattern. The subject, an avid Twitter status updater, makes great use of the one-to-many principle by giving any and all subscribers an opportunity to be notified of status updates. When an update occurs, the notification pushes the state to those who depend on it. Of course, the example illustrated a one-to-one relationship, so let's rectify that to better demonstrate one to many (see **Listing 7-65** through **Listing 7-67**).

Listing 7-65. The TwitterUser class becomes the abstract class of both observer and subject so names can be represented.

```
package
{
    public class TwitterUser extends Object
    {
        private var _twitterName : String

        public function TwitterUser( userName : String )
        {
            _twitterName = username;
        }

        public function get twitterName() : String
        {
            return _twitterName;
        }

        public function set twitterName( twitterName : String ) : void
        {
```

```
        _twitterName = twitterName;
    }
  }
}
```

Listing 7-66. Subject and observer both extend `TwitterUser`

```
public class Subject extends TwitterUser implements ISubject
public class Object extends TwitterUser implements IObserver
```

Listing 7-67. Revisiting `DocumentClass` with many observers monitoring the subject's status

```
package
{
    public class DocumentClass extends Sprite
    {
        public function DocumentClass()
        {
            var subject : ISubject = new Subject( "FeZEC" );

            var observer_1 : IObserve = new Observer( "Andrew" );
            var observer_2 : IObserve = new Observer( "Mike" );
            var observer_3 : IObserve = new Observer( "Ed" );
            var observer_4 : IObserve = new Observer( "Lucas" );
            var observer_5 : IObserve = new Observer( "Edy" );

            subject.addObserver( observer_1 , null );
            subject.addObserver( observer_2 , null );
            subject.addObserver( observer_3 , null );
            subject.addObserver( observer_4 , null );
            subject.addObserver( observer_5 , null );
        }
    }
}
```

FAQ

- Can observers observe more than one subject?

  Absolutely. Because a subject maintains a collection of observers, it's easier for each observer to do so. The observers just need to tell the subject to add them.

  Subjects can also be observers of other subjects. They need to implement the `IObserve` interface to be able to register themselves with a subject.

- If AS 3.0 has the Observer pattern built in, why is it important to know about the Observer pattern?

  All developers should be aware of the foundations on which they build. This gives you greater understanding of how to take advantage of the tools at your disposal. The AS 3.0 Observer model uses the Chain of Responsibility and Composite patterns, which potentially decrease performance. Knowing about the Observer pattern lets you construct alternatives, such as AS 3.0 signals that bypass as much of the built-in event notification as possible.

- Isn't the Chain of Responsibility pattern the event system in AS 3.0?

    The Chain of Responsibility pattern in AS 3.0 is responsible for relaying events. `EventDispatcher` is responsible for managing and maintaining all subject subscriptions among their observers.

Related Patterns

The Observer pattern is related to these patterns:

- Singleton

Summary

OOD heavily relies on behavioral patterns, because the ultimate goal is to define how objects collaborate with one another. For this reason, these patterns are often implemented in applications and in the AS 3.0 language itself. This isn't a coincidence: it's due to the flexibility they offer.

As you may have noticed, behavioral patterns work very well with one another, and with the patterns you learned about previously.

Key Points

- The Strategy pattern offers interchangeability among a family of algorithms.
- The Template Method pattern localizes and protects the steps that make up an expected algorithm.
- The Chain of Responsibility pattern forwards requests in succession to decouple the client from the receiver.
- The Command pattern encapsulates the request to be carried out, decoupling the invoker from the request.
- The Memento pattern externalizes an object's state.
- Iterators can be external or internal.
- The State pattern may appear to change its class.
- Observers use push and pull methods to notify dependent objects about changes.
- Behavioral patterns are concerned with the assignments of behaviors.

Chapter 8

Structural Patterns

You have inadvertently witnessed the use of structure among your objects via interface inheritance and object composition, which allowed objects to possess the ability to obtain new functionality from other objects. In essence, these enabled an object's power. Continuing with this thought, the weaker the structure, or the flimsier the support, the less empowered the objects.

Consider how reusable a Concrete class is without any inherited interface. The structure that utilizes this object is forced to bind itself to a single implementation and not to that of an interface. Of course, this would be unwise if change is a possibility. To remedy this scenario, you make use of a simple interface or abstraction that the Concrete class may subclass. Doing so properly enables polymorphism, abstracts your references, and offers flexibility among variations of implementations. You achieved greater benefits from the structuring among two classes rather than the one.

Structural patterns are concerned with the makeup of parts among both classes and objects that help to strengthen their associations with additional objects. This is what makes them really good at devising new functionality from already existing objects, sometimes forming compound patterns.

This chapter will cover the Decorator, the Adapter, the Composite, and the Facade.

The Decorator Pattern

Technical Overview

Intent: To embellish objects dynamically either visually or behaviorally, as shown in Figure 8-1.

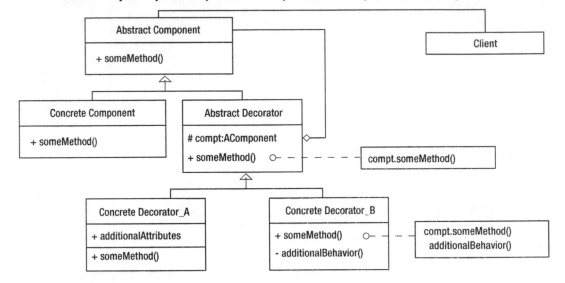

Figure 8-1. Class diagram

Parts

- Abstract Component
- Concrete Component
- Abstract Decorator
- Concrete Decorator
- Client

Benefits

- Expand on an individual object without the use of inheritance.
- Additional behaviors can be added and removed to meet the needs of an application.
- Deconstruct complex objects that attempt to foresee all cases into individual wrappers.

Drawbacks

- Many pieces appear similar, which may cause confusion.
- Decorators may require specific orders.

A Comprehensive Look

For quick illustration, the Decorator pattern is the yin among objects if the Strategy pattern is the yang, as the two have very similar goals. The Decorator pattern devises strategies that embellish the visual aspects and/or the functional aspects among objects, but in an alternate solution to those of the Strategy pattern. While strategies are utilized within an object, the strategies utilized with the Decorator pattern surround the objects they alter. This is why these strategies are known as *decorators*.

What enables a decorator to remain apart from most delegating objects is its ability to wrap a given type object and still allow the client to view the decorated object for what it was originally. This type of wrapper is said to be transparent, as it does not attempt to mask the content from the client. It's this transparent ability that allows any number of decorators to decorate an object without impacting the bindings between the decorated object and the client.

The object that is decorated is referred to as a *component*. The component that is decorated can be any object within an application. In fact, even decorators can be components of other decorators. What makes this possible is polymorphism among an interface.

A decorating object and the component that it will decorate must share an interface. This is what enables the transparency of the decorator. If many decorators will be utilized to wrap a similar interface, an abstract decorator class should be used that subclasses can extend. Because the decorator conforms to the component, the component will remain unaware of the presence of the decorator, which can preserve the integrity of your objects while still possessing the ability to lace it with new functionality.

Vignette

I'm sure there was a point in time when you purchased a poster that you were excited to hang on your wall. Perhaps it represented you at the time, or it merely tied the room together. No matter the reason, you had to have this poster. So eager to adhere it to the wall you may used push pins or even double-sided tape. These two methods would ultimately ruin your poster. The gravity on the poster would eventually cause either forms of adhesive to give, thereby tearing the poster. I was always left with the corners torn around the pushpins, forcing me to add additional holes to the poster.

Being human we learn from our mistakes; now I use frames to mount my posters to the wall. The frames allow the poster to remain intact and unchanged. Whether the frame is made of plastic, wood, or even tin, the border that surrounds the poster also adds a subtle touch.

The AS3.0 Cast

Abstract Component – The interface

The abstract component declares the interface as well as any default behaviors and/or abstract methods that its subclasses will inherit.

Concrete Component – The Concrete Behavior

The concrete component implements the behavior as defined by its superclass.

Abstract Decorator – The Decorating Interface

The abstract decorator must compliment the abstract components interface in order to defer requests to its contained component. A reference to the abstract component is contained within.

Concrete Decorator – Transparent Wrapper

The concrete decorator implements the behavior as defined by its superclass. It has the added benefit of intercepting the requests that are forwarded to its contained component. The concrete decorator can perform additional behaviors before or after deferring requests to that of its component.

Client – The Messenger of the Component

The client is any aspect of the application that messengers the component. The client knows of the abstract component and on occasion will know of the decorator.

When It's Useful

When the addition of behavioral or decorative ornaments are required at runtime.

For creating graphical composites and sounds.

For intercepting requests between a client and component.

When reducing unused complexities of a class to reduce its size.

Demonstration

Sound is a great object for a decorator to enhance, as there are many possible decorative uses that may vary from application to application. To begin, you will need to define your abstractions for both decorators and your sound.

You know that decorators must possess the same interface as your components, but I really don't want to have decorators subclass sound. Instead let's devise an interface for a sound object (see Listing 8-1).

Listing 8-1. Interface ISound Exposes the Interface within flash.media.Sound

```
package
{
    public interface ISound extends IEventDispatcher
    {
        function get bytesLoaded() : uint;

        function get bytesTotal() : int;

        function close() : void;

        function extract( target : ByteArray , length : Number ,
              ➥ startPosition : Number = -1 ) : Number;

        function get id3() : ID3Info;

        function get isBuffering() : Boolean;

        function get length() : Number;
```

```
        function load( stream : URLRequest , context : SoundLoaderContext = null ) : void;

        function play( startTime : Number = 0 , loops : int = 0 , sndTransform : ➡
SoundTransform = null ) : SoundChannel;

        function get url() : String;
    }
}
```

Once you have your interface extracted, you can then implement that interface into your AbstractSoundDecorator. This will allow the decorators to possess a similar interface to the Sound component, as shown in Listing 8-2.

Listing 8-2. AbstractSoundDecorator Implements ISound and Has the Ability to Wrap ISound Objects

```
package
{
    public class AbstractSoundDecorator implements ISound
    {
        protected static var _channel : SoundChannel;
        protected var _snd : ISound;

        public function AbstractSoundDecorator( snd : ISound ) : void
        {
            _snd = snd;
        }

        public function get bytesLoaded() : uint
        {
            return 0;
        }

        public function get bytesTotal() : int
        {
            return 0;
        }

        public function close() : void
        {
        }

        public function extract( target : ByteArray , length : Number ,
                    ➡ startPosition : Number = -1 ) : Number
        {
            return 0;
```

```
   }

   public function get id3() : ID3Info
   {
      return null;
   }

   public function get isBuffering() : Boolean
   {
      return false;
   }

   public function get length() : Number
   {
      return 0;
   }

   public function load( stream : URLRequest ,
                ➥ context : SoundLoaderContext = null ) : void
   {
   }

   final public function play( startTime : Number = 0 , loops : int = 0 ,
                      ➥ sndTransform : SoundTransform = null ) : SoundChannel
   {
      _channel = doPlay( startTime , loops , sndTransform );
      return _channel;
   }

   public function get url() : String
   {
      return "";
   }

   public function addEventListener( type : String , listener : Function ,
                   ➥ useCapture : Boolean = false , priority : int = 0 ,
                   ➥ useWeakReference : Boolean = false ) : void
   {
   }

   public function dispatchEvent( event : Event ) : Boolean
   {
      return false;
   }
```

```
public function hasEventListener( type : String ) : Boolean
{
   return false;
}

public function removeEventListener( type : String , listener : Function ,
            ➥ useCapture : Boolean = false ) : void
{
}

public function willTrigger( type : String ) : Boolean
{
   return false;
}

protected function doPlay( startTime : Number = 0 , loops : int = 0 ,
            ➥ sndTransform : SoundTransform = null ) : SoundChannel
{
   throw new IllegalOperationError( 'doPlay must be overridden' );
   return null;
}
   }
}
```

As you can see in **Listing 8-2**, your wrappers will expect a component of ISound. As you know from Chapter 3, flash.media.Sound does not contain any reference to ISound within its trait object. Therefore, to properly allow this, you need to devise an abstraction for your component, which can extend flash.media.Sound but must implement ISound to achieve this hierarchy, as shown in Listing 8-3.

Listing 8-3. Audible Extends Sound and Implements ISound

```
package
{
   public class Audible extends Sound implements ISound
   {
      public function Audible( stream : URLRequest = null ,
            ➥ context : SoundLoaderContext = null )
      {
         super( stream , context );
      }
   }
}
```

There are many decorators that could be used as decorators, including the following:

A decorator that retains the state of the audio.

A decorator that fades the audio on play.

A decorator that fades the audio on stop.

A decorator that can pause and resume a sound.

A decorator that can allow infinite loops.

A decorator that can display the MP3 ID3 tag information.

A decorator that enables multiple channels for overlapping audible sound.

This demonstration will focus on the pause and resume with the addition of infinite looping. But why build a wrapper that can offer looping when it's part of the Play method parameters? The answer is simple if you have tried to implement a pause and resume functionality along with the built-in loop parameters. Sound objects work with bytes, and when you specify a start time, the sound object plays a trimmed version of the sound. This has to do with the headers and modifying the bytes to reflect a specific position to play. The looping then continues to loop the bytes, which it currently possesses, meaning it begins from where it trimmed the bytes; see Listing 8-4 through 8-6.

Listing 8-4. InfiniteLoopDecorator

```
public class InfiniteLoopDecorator extends AbstractSoundDecorator
{
    public function InfiniteLoopDecorator( snd : ISound )
    {
      super( snd );
    }

    override protected function doPlay( startTime : Number = 0 , loops : int = 0 ,
                          ➥ sndTransform : SoundTransform = null ) : SoundChannel
    {
      removeEvents();
      _channel = _snd.play( startTime , loops );
      _channel.addEventListener( Event.SOUND_COMPLETE , repeat );
      return _channel;
    }

    private function repeat( event : Event ) : void
    {
      _channel = play( 0 , 0 , null );
    }

    private function removeEvents() : void
    {
```

```
      if ( _channel)
         _channel.removeEventListener( Event.SOUND_COMPLETE , repeat );
   }
}
```

Listing 8-5. PauseableAudibleDecorator Extends AbstractSoundDecorator

```
package
{
   public class PauseableAudibleDecorator extends AbstractSoundDecorator
            ➥ implements ISoundChannel
   {
      protected var _position : Number = 0;

      public function PauseableAudibleDecorator( snd : ISound )
      {
         super( snd );
      }

      override  protected function doPlay( startTime : Number = 0 , loops : int = 0 ,
                        ➥ sndTransform : SoundTransform = null ) : SoundChannel
      {
         stop();
         removeEvents();
         _channel = _snd.play( _position , loops , sndTransform );
         _channel.addEventListener( Event.SOUND_COMPLETE , resetPosition );
         return _channel;
      }

      private function removeEvents() : void
      {
         if ( _channel)
            _channel.removeEventListener( Event.SOUND_COMPLETE , resetPosition );
      }

      private function resetPosition( event : Event ) : void
      {
         _position = 0;
      }

      public function get leftPeak() : Number
      {
         return 0;
      }
```

```
        public function get position() : Number
        {
           return 0;
        }

        public function get rightPeak() : Number
        {
           return 0;
        }

        public function get soundTransform() : SoundTransform
        {
           return null;
        }

        public function set soundTransform( sndTransform : SoundTransform ) : void
        {
        }

        public function stop() : void
        {
           if (_channel)
           {
              _position = _channel.position;
              trace( _position );
              _channel.stop();
           }
        }
     }
  }
}
```

Listing 8-6. Client Making Use of the Decorators

```
package
{
   public class Decorator extends Sprite
   {
      private var _isPlaying : Boolean = false;
      var sound : ISound;

      public function Decorator()
      {
         sound = new Audible( new URLRequest( "music.mp3" ) );
         sound = new InfiniteLoopDecorator( sound );
         sound = new PauseableAudibleDecorator( sound );
```

```
        sound.play()
        stage.addEventListener( MouseEvent.MOUSE_DOWN , onDown );
    }

    private function onDown( event : MouseEvent ) : void
    {
        var localsnd : ISound = sound;
        var snd : ISoundChannel = ISoundChannel( localsnd );
        _isPlaying = !_isPlaying;
        if (_isPlaying)
        {
            snd.stop();
        }
        else
        {
            localsnd.play()
        }
    }
}
}
```

What makes the decorator a great tool is how it allows you to spare the added behavior from being implemented directly into your Audio class. This way, if it's to be used in a future application, which does not make use of pause and resume, or even the infinite loop, it does not need to bare the excess weight of such features.

FAQ

- Why might decorators be order-specific?

  Decorators provide an alternative to fixed inheritance but must adhere to the rules of inheritance, as the decorator must mimic the interface of the component it is to wrap.

  When a decorator adds a behavior, it may be to perform a specific operation before passing it on to the component. This is no different than a subclass overriding a method and calling the operation of the superclass.

  The more specific a decorator becomes, the greater the risk of disrupting the order in which operations were intended.

- If the rules of inheritance apply, does that mean two-three decorators should be the limit?

  Yes and no. This depends on the nature of the beast and It's difficult to determine without knowing the scenario. More often than not, visual ornaments don't require a limit, providing you're achieving the effect you desire, but this may occur when modifying functional behavior. Since each decorator is one level away from the abstract component, it's not likely to deal with the issues that many layers of inheritance can cause.

  Bear in mind, though, that wrapping many behaviors that don't run in a proper order can easily grow cumbersome and have strange effects on your system. The more specific the intercepted behavior, the more complicated the chain may become in order to remain synchronized.

Related Patterns

Visitor

Adapter

Composite

The Adapter

Technical Overview

Intent: To conform a class interface to one that is expected by a client of the system, as shown in Figure 8-2.

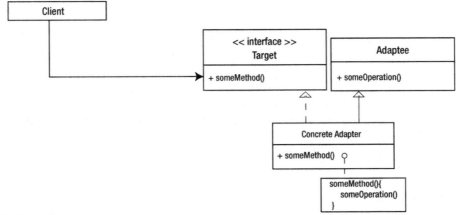

Figure 8-2. Class diagram

Parts

- Target
- Adaptee
- Adapter
- Client

Benefits

- Maintains the original interface of a class and utilizes it where another interface is expected.
- Allows the adaptee to optionally be seen by the client.

Drawbacks

- Adds more classes to an application.
- Adapters are often application-specific.

A Comprehensive Look

Over the course of time you may find yourself in a position of wanting to use a specific object that possesses a certain behavior, but the interface of that object varies from the interface currently supported by the application. Your first inclination may be to change the method names within the class to match those required by the client, but this breaks the Open/Closed Principle. This is where adapters are useful.

Adapters possess the ability to alter an interface by means of class or object scope. Most of the time you'll be working with object scope to adapt your interfaces; this is due to a feature that AS3.0 lacks called *multiple inheritance*, which enables a subclass to inherit from multiple classes. Instead, class adapters must make use of subclassing the object to adapt and implementing the interface of the target. If the target lacks a defined interface that can be implemented in the adapter, refactoring should be performed.

The benefits of this will allow for what is known as two-way adapters as your adapter has the ability to be used by your client as a target and in other areas of your application used as the previously adapted adaptee.

The alternative to the class adapter is the object adapter, which uses parameterization and delegation among an interface of the adaptees it's expecting. Because the object adapter doesn't inherit from the adaptee, the object does not require any alterations when dealing with descendants of an adaptee class, whereas class adapters do.

Object adapters specify the interface of the adaptee to which they will be supplied. This occurs most often at runtime. In order for the adapter to defer the requests of the client to the adaptee, they must possess the interface of a target that is used by the client. Much like class adapters, object adapters can become two-way by implementing the adaptee interface.

Both the class and object adapters make the appropriate referrals among the requests by the client to that of the adaptee.

Vignette

Three years ago my wife and I visited the United Kingdom for her sister's wedding. Having a lot of work to catch up on, I brought my laptop along. My planned attempts to get work done were thwarted by lack of battery life and the incompatibility of my U.S.-compliant plug with the U.K.-compliant wall socket.

The distinct receptacles of the sockets were nothing like my two-pronged cord and reminded me of a child attempting to push a star-shaped block into the circular hole of his Fisher-Price toy. Luckily this is a well known issue, so I was able to purchase the appropriate fitting that allowed me to plug my computer into a power source. One side of the device mimicked the receptacle one would find in America, whereas the other side was noticeably the male that would fit snugly within the U.K. wall socket. The purchase was obviously a worthwhile solution at the time, but, as I have yet to travel outside the country since then, I have not had the reason to use it again.

The AS3.0 Cast

Target Interface – The Intended Interface

The target interface is known by the client and must be the exposed interface of your abstract adapter.

Abstract Adapter – The Narrow Interface

The abstract adapter defines the smallest possible Interface that is required for the adaptee to be utilized by the client. This makes it easier for a developer to extend it.

Concrete Adapter – Subclass of the Abstract Adapter

The concrete adapter is optional if you make use of the un-typed property. It may also possess a reference of its own for which the abstract operations are overridden and specified.

Adaptee – An object of the application

The adaptee is can be any object within your application that must overcome constraints of its interface to be utilized by a client, bound to a varied type.

Client – The Messenger

The client is any aspect of the application that messengers the adapter and/or the adaptee. The client knows of the target interface, and may also be familiar with the interface of the adaptee.

When It's Useful

Frameworks can make great use of the adapters.

When using connecting methods of varied names.

Demonstration

Many applications, both for Web and desktop, have differing distinctions between the uses of Pause/Resume and Play/Stop. While they may have similar implementations, their indication of their roles might have distinct meanings.

Consider these terms in the scenario of a game. What nature would you expect from a method labeled Pause? Certainly you would expect the game to stop while retaining its current state.

Suppose for this demonstration you have a game and are monitoring all objects in use that must be paused, including tweening animations, movie clips, and sounds. To achieve this feat, you must devise a system that monitors all objects in your application that have reason to pause. Clearly you don't require data to pause; therefore you assign an IPause interface to objects that require it (see Listings 8-7 through 8-9).

Listing 8-7. IPause Defines the Interface Among Objects that Possess the Ability to Advance Their State

```
public interface IPause
{
        function pause():void;
        function resume():void;
}
```

Listing 8-8. Abstract Pause Conductor Defines the Interface That Is Collected and Operated On

```
package
{
```

```
public class APauseConductor extends Object
{
    private var _collection : IIterate;
    private var _iterator : IIterator;

    public function APauseConductor()
    {
        _collection = doCreateCollection();
    }

    final public function addElement( element : IPause ) : void
    {
        doAddElement( element );
    }

    final public function removeElement( element : IPause ) : void
    {
        doRemoveElement( element );
    }

    final public function pause() : void
    {
        doPause();
    }

    final public function resume() : void
    {
        doResume();
    }

    protected function doRemoveElement( element : IPause ) : void
    {
        _collection.remove( element );
    }

    protected function doAddElement( element : IPause ) : void
    {
        _collection.append( element );
    }

    protected function doCreateCollection() : IIterate
    {
        throw new IllegalOperationError( 'doCreateCollection must be overridden' );
        return null;
```

```
      }

      protected function doPause() : void
      {
         _iterator = _collection.createIterator();
         while (_iterator.hasNext())
         {
            var pauseable : IPause = _iterator.currentElement();
            _iterator.next();
            pauseable.pause();
         }
      }

      protected  function doResume() : void
      {
         _iterator.reset();
         while (_iterator.hasNext())
         {
            var resumeable : IPause = _iterator.currentElement();
            _iterator.next();
            resumeable.resume();
         }
      }
    }
  }
}
```

Listing 8-9. Concrete Conductor, Which Implements the Specifics of the Manufactured Object

```
package
{
   public class IPauseConductor extends APauseConductor
   {
      public function IPauseConductor()
      {
         super();
      }

      override protected function doCreateCollection() : IIterate
      {
         return new DictionaryCollection();
      }
   }
}
```

Let's revisit the decorated audio file, since you built it for reuse. It appears that you have the perfect solution as PauseableAudibleDecorator will properly pause your sounds. The only issue here is that

PauseableAudibleDecorator doesn't possess the proper IPause interface. Obeying the Open/Closed Principle, your solution is adaptation.

You are confronted with two means by which you can adapt your PauseableAudibleDecorator to possess the IPause interface class and object adaption. When utilizing class adaptation, you want to inherit the abilities or your adaptee and expose the interface of the target your client will message.

Listing 8-10. AudibleIPauseAdapter Inherits the PauseableAudibleDecorator's Interface and Exposes an Additional Interface of IPause

```
package
{
    public class AudibleIPauseAdapter extends PauseableAudibleDecorator
        ➡ implements IPause
    {
        public function AudibleIPauseAdapter( snd : ISound )
        {
            super( snd );
        }

        public function pause() : void
        {
            this.stop();
        }

        public function resume() : void
        {
            this.play();
        }
    }
}
```

AudibleIPauseAdapter, as seen in **Listing 8-10,** inherits from AudibleIPauseAdapter and Implements the interface IPause, which in turn is utilized to defer requests from target to adaptee.

Listing 8-11. DecoratorClass Making Use of the AudbileIPauseAdapter and Passing it into IPauseConductor

```
public class DecoratorClass extends Sprite
{
    private var _isPlaying : Boolean = false;
    var sound : ISound;
    var pauseconductor : APauseConductor;

    public function DecoratorClass()
    {
        sound = new Audible( new URLRequest( "music.mp3" ) ) ;
```

```
            sound = new InfiniteLoopDecorator(sound );
            sound = new AudibleIPauseAdapter(sound );
            sound.play();

            pauseconductor = new IPauseConductor();
            pauseconductor.addElement( IPause( sound ) );
            stage.addEventListener( MouseEvent.MOUSE_DOWN , onDown );
        }

        private function onDown( event : MouseEvent ) : void
        {
            _isPlaying = !_isPlaying;
            if (_isPlaying)
            {
                pauseconductor.pause();
            }
            else
            {
                pauseconductor.resume();
            }
        }
    }
}
```

Because you inherited your decorator, you are not impeded from wrapping your audible with more decorators, as your adapter is a two-way adapter (see Listing 8-11). Additionally, you managed to do very little work to make your adapter, due to the inherited nature, although your adapter is limited to its superclass. This means any other subclasses or decorators will require an adapter as well.

Object adapters, on the other hand, make use of delegation and object parameterization. This allows a more flexible adapter to be present in an application.

Listing 8-12. IPausePauseableAudioDecorators Accepts Parameters of any PauseableAudibleDecorator Instance, Including Subclasses

```
package
{
    public class IPauseAudibles implements IPause
    {
        protected var _pauseableAudio : PauseableAudibleDecorator;

        public function IPauseAudibles( audible : PauseableAudibleDecorator ) : void
        {
            _pauseableAudio = audible;
        }

        public function pause() : void
        {
```

```
        _pauseableAudio.stop()
    }

    public function resume() : void
    {
        _pauseableAudio.play()
    }
  }
}
```

Listing 8-12 is not a two-way adapter currently but can be by implementing the ISound interface and delegating all requests to the _pauseableAudio reference. This, of course, requires more code than that of its counterpart.

Having demonstrated what an adapter does, you can see many of the flaws of their general usage. They adapt specific objects, while many interfaces will possess stop and play functionality, such as a MovieClip. The code you already devised to conform stop and play within an adapter is specific to objects of the given hierarchy—PauseableAudibleDecorator.

This doesn't mean that adapters are a waste; it just means that you need to devise better ways to make them adaptable. Even though MovieClip does possess a stop and play method, the compiler won't allow its assignment among your typed reference because it's incompatible, though dynamic binding would allow for MovieClip to properly use the stop and play methods.

ActionScript 3.0 does allow for you to bypass compile time checking to use such dynamic binding properties of the language. It's known as the *un-typed property* or *wildcard annotation* and is represented by an asterisk: *. Any assignment to an un-typed property will never warrant compile time errors as the reference is recognized to hold any value. They will, on the other hand, be type checked at runtime. This is not something to be overused as it's a tightrope walk between dynamically and statically typed checking.

Listing 8-13. StopPlayToPauseResume Utilizes the Wildcard Annotation to Circumvent Providing a Fixed Type, which Limits its Reuse

```
public function StopPlayToPauseResume
{
        protected var _stopStart:*
        public function StopPlayToPauseResume(startStop:*)
        {
                _stopStart=startStop
        }

        public function pause() : void
        {
                _stopStart.stop()
        }

        public function resume() : void
        {
```

```
              _stopStart.play()
         }
}
```

```
//…client
var StopPlayToPauseResume:IPause = new StopPlayToPauseResume(mc)
pauseconductor.addElement( MinimalPauseAdaption )
```

Listing 8-13 demonstrates the ability of reuse among varied types to make use of dynamic binding. Unfortunately, the wildcard puts the burden on the developers to ensure they maintain an awareness of what objects are being passed in.

First, you change the name of StopPlayToPauseResume to reflect a base class to which Developers can subclass. Let's use AMinimalStopPlayToPauseResume; see Listings 8-14 through 8-17.

Listing 8-14. Reflects the New Name of StopPlayToPauseResume

```
package
{
   public class AMinimalStopPlayToPauseResume extends Object implements IPause
   {
   // ….cont
   }
}
```

Listing 8-15. Subclass MChasStartStop Extends AMinimalStopPlayToPauseResume, which will Ensure the Integrity of all MovieClips at Author-time

```
package
{
   public class MChasStartStop extends AMinimalStopPlayToPauseResume
   {
      public function MChasStartStop( mc : MovieClip )
      {
         super( mc );
      }
   }
}
```

Listing 8-16. Subclass AudioDecoratorIPauseAdapter Extends AMinimalStopPlayToPauseResume, which will Ensure the Integrity of all PauseableAudibleDecorator at Author-time

```
package
{

   public class AudioDecoratorIPauseAdapter extends AMinimalStopPlayToPauseResume
   {
      public function AudioDecoratorIPauseAdapter( startStop :
```

```
                                  ➥ PauseableAudibleDecorator )
      {
         super( startStop );
      }
   }
}
```

Listing 8-17. DocumentClass Making Use of Your New Narrow Adaption

```
package
{
   public class DocumentClass extends Sprite
   {
      private var _isPlaying : Boolean = false;
      var sound : ISound;
      var pauseconductor : APauseConductor;

      public function DocumentClass()
      {
         sound = new Audible( new URLRequest( "music.mp3" ) );
         sound = new InfiniteLoopDecorator( sound );
         sound = new PauseableAudibleDecorator( sound );
         sound.play()

         var mc : MovieClip = new SimpleMCAnimation();
         addChild( mc );

         var mcMinimalPauseAdaption : IPause = new MChasStartStop( mc );
         var soundMinimalPauseAdaption : IPause = new
            ➥ AudioDecoratorIPauseAdapter( PauseableAudibleDecorator( sound ) );

         pauseconductor = new IPauseConductor();
         pauseconductor.addElement( soundMinimalPauseAdaption );
         pauseconductor.addElement( mcMinimalPauseAdaption );
         stage.addEventListener( MouseEvent.MOUSE_DOWN , onDown );
      }

      private function onDown( event : MouseEvent ) : void
      {
         _isPlaying = !_isPlaying;
         if (_isPlaying)
         {
            pauseconductor.pause();
         }
         else
```

```
        {
            pauseconductor.resume();
        }
    }
  }
}
```

FAQ

- You mention that adapters are often application specific. Are they not reusable?

  Adapters are never devised in the object-oriented design phase and the reason why is simple: adapters were unnecessary if all went as planned in the designing stage.

  Remember that change is constant and you have to roll with it. The adapter allows you to roll with it in an elegant way that doesn't break your system or require a major overhaul among client or object.

  The answer is they are not meant to be reusable as they are devised specifically for the problem at hand; this is known as the problem domain. Unless another application suffers the exact fate as this one, you most likely won't be reusing them.

  But hey, that's a great thing; don't feel bad.

Related Patterns

Proxy

Bridge

Decorator

The Composite

Technical Overview

Intent: To devise a data structure representing a nesting relationship among objects of a part-whole hierarchy, as shown in Figure 8-3.

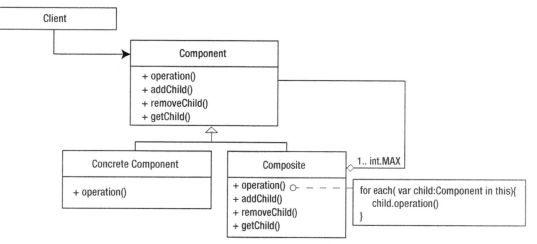

Figure 8-3. Class diagram

Parts

- Component
- Leaf
- Composite
- Client

Benefits

- Uniformity among client interactions and the data.
- New components are easy to create and integrate.

Drawbacks

- Limited type enforcements: any object that inherits from components can be added safely even if they are not meant to work with your system.
- It's difficult to follow conceptually.

A Comprehensive Look

The Composite pattern is a very convenient pattern to use with ActionScript 3.0 because the foundation of the display list was built on the idea of the composite. The composite represents a tree structure where each object is aware of any objects nested within. The structure should be as efficient as possible for traversing, adding and removing elements, ordering, etc.

For efficiency, the client should not be able to distinguish one element from another, meaning compositions of objects from individual objects. This is important because the composite will forward one request to each and every component contained within the structure without prejudice.

ActionScript 3.0's display list refers to these as `DisplayObjectContainer` and a `DisplayObject`, whereas the Composite pattern refers to them as composite and leaf. In XML, such components are referred to as nodes.

A composite is an element that contains any number of additional composites or leaves. Therefore, it must define operations that access and manipulate its nested elements.

A leaf, on the other hand, has no children. This is the main distinction between the two. In order for the two to appear as indistinguishable from the client as possible, they must both utilize inheritance to which they both gain a common interface. This enables the client to interact with either uniformly.

This interface is how the clients will see these two components. The component's interface should account for as much commonality between the leaf and the composite as possible. This further allows the client to remain unaware of the object's true identity. You will be confronted with the decision to compromise either safety or transparency for optimal conditions when considering who should define the operations of child management.

Optionally, components may possess references to their parents. This may assist in the traversing upwards among the structure and supports the addition of the chain of responsibility, which can facilitate the removal of an element. Otherwise, a composite traverses downwards and outwards towards the leaf/leaves.

Vignette

There are several divisions of the U.S. military: Army, Marines, Air Force, and Navy. Each division contains smaller divisions until a specific unit size has been reached. I can't begin to explain the hierarchy of each branch. What I do know is the President resides at the top and at the bottom the newest recruits. Everything in between is looking to pass their demands off to those of lesser rank. This is known as the chain of command.

The president will never physically tell a new recruit what to do but will pass the message to his immediate successor until the message has been received by the individuals of a particular division within a military branch.

While specific branches can be targeted, all branches can be issued the same requests in a time of war. From the top of the Armed Forces to the lowest on the poles, all will receive the same commands. This will trigger their specific operations depending on their role within the military.

Such structuring within the Armed Forces allows one message to be carried out similarly and indiscriminately among high ranking officers and the grunts. This also speeds up the dissemination of information by simultaneously passing the operation down all channels.

The AS3.0 Cast

Abstract Component – The interface

The abstract component defines the operations common to both the leaf and composite; it also defines the interface that the client will utilize to interact with the structure.

Leaf – An object

The leaf may represent any object within your application providing it possesses no children that must be traversed.

Composite – An object container

The composite maintains references to its nested elements in addition to the implementations defined by the component to manage said children.

Client – The Messenger of the Component

The client is any aspect of the application that messages the interface of the component. The client remains unaware of which element, either leaf or composite, it's manipulating.

When It's Useful

Many objects require the same message to perform similar behaviors at the same time, such as objects that manage or oversee pausing, resuming, destroying, etc.

Demonstration

In previous demonstrations I've portrayed the means by which you can pause and resume any object that possesses the IPause interface. That was an example of a "loose" type composite. You made use of an individual composition and leaf nodes, which were objects that implemented IPause. I refer to this as "loose" because your two objects did not derive from a common component other than the built-in object.

Suppose you have a MovieClip that contains a given number of nested MovieClips as well as Sprites. If you wanted to pause your MovieClip instances, you could define an operation within the main MovieClip that targets only MovieClips and ensures they stop or play depending on the situation. Such a method is shown in **Listing 8-18**.

Listing 8-18. Utilizes Recursion Among any Descendants Within a Found MovieClip in Order to Pause or Resume Any Instances of MovieClips

```
public function traverse( mc : MovieClip , bol : Boolean ) : void
{
        if (bol)
        {
           mc.play();
        }
        else
        {
           mc.stop();
        }
```

```
        if (mc.numChildren > 0)
        {
            for (var i : int = 0;i < mc.numChildren;i++)
            {
                var innerds : DisplayObject = mc.getChildAt( i );
                if (innerds is MovieClip)
                {
                    traverse( MovieClip( innerds ) , bol );
                }
            }
        }
}
```

Listing 8-18 demonstrates how a MovieClip composite operates on the leaf nodes and continues to traverse all possible nested composites. As mentioned earlier, because AS3.0's display list is built around the Composite, you are able to tap into its ability with a bit of ingenuity.

Dealing with DisplayObjects is very convenient with the Composite pattern, as DisplayObject possesses many of the necessary commonalities among the more elaborate DisplayObjects such as Sprite, MovieClip, and Bitmap. You begin this menu system by making your component for all leaf and composite objects to extend, as shown in Listing 8-19.

Listing 8-19. *Component Class*

```
package
{
    public class Component extends Sprite
    {
        private static var _counter : int = 0;
        protected var _parentComposite : Component;
        protected var _identity : int;
        protected var _arCollection : ArrayCollection;

        public function Component()
        {
            _identity = ++_counter;
        }

        final public function addComponent( cmpt : Component ) : void
        {
            doVerifyCollection();
            doAddComponent( cmpt );
        }

        final public function removeComponent( cmpt : Component ) : void
```

```
{
   if (_arCollection) ;
   doRemoveComponent();
}

final public function operate() : void
{
   doOperate();
}

final public function get parentComposite() : Component
{
   return _parentComposite;
}

final public function set parentComposite( parentComposite : Component ) : void
{
   _parentComposite = parentComposite;
}

public function get identity() : int
{
   return _identity;
}

protected function doOperate() : void
{
   throw new IllegalOperationError( 'doOperate must be overridden' );
}

protected function doAddComponent( cmpt : Component ) : void
{
   throw new IllegalOperationError( 'doAddComponent must be overridden' );
}

protected function doRemoveComponent() : void
{
   throw new IllegalOperationError( 'doRemoveComponent must be overridden' );
}

private function doVerifyCollection() : void
{
   if (!_arCollection)
      _arCollection = new ArrayCollection();
```

```
         }
      }
   }
```

The component class may look overwhelming, but it's rather simple. The component class takes advantage of being the abstract class and declares common attributes and behaviors that will be utilized by both leaf and composites. The static variable, _counter, is intended to keep track of the number of components utilized to aid in the removal of the appropriate object. Its assigned value is stored in the _identity attribute.

To make use of code you have already created, you might recognize our _arCollection from the Iterator pattern. Because the Composite pattern makes use of structured data, you may optionally rely on a means to iterate such data, and the Iterator does this very well, as you will see. Lastly, _parentComposite will maintain the parent composite for every component utilized. This will help you to notify all composites upwards, which can then notify their components of updates, just like the chain of command (see Listing 8-20).

Listing 8-20. *Leaf Component*

```
package
{
   public class Leaf extends Component
   {
      public function Leaf()
      {
         super();
      }

      override protected function doOperate() : void
      {
         // your operation goes here
      }
   }
}
```

The leaf component overrides the doOperate method that enables the leaf to handle the operation as appropriately required.

Listing 8-21. *Composite Component*

```
package
{
   public class Composite extends Component
   {
      public function Composite()
      {
         super();
```

```
    }

    override protected function doAddComponent( cmpt : Component ) : void
    {
        cmpt.parentComposite = this;
        _arCollection.append( cmpt );
        addChild( cmpt );
    }

    override protected function doOperate() : void
    {
        var it : IIterator = _arCollection.createIterator();
        while (it.hasNext())
        {
            var cnent : Component = it.currentElement() as Component;
            it.next();
            cnent.operate();
        }
    }
}
}
```

In Listing 8-20, the composite component overrides the doAddComponent and ensures the nested child has the appropriate pointer to its parent composite. The nested component is then added to the display of the composite as well as composite's collection of contained children.

In efforts to conserve memory, composites do not instantiate a collection unless an object is being added. The method addComponent within a component makes use of a template method to ensure a collection exists before allowing a component to be added. This allows a composite the opportunity to initialize a collection, if one does not exist. doAddComponent is the hook that composite taps into.

The operate method does not have to be strictly operate and should reflect the proper behavior for which it's used. In the case of disposing of objects, you could call the operate method within the dispose component. The dispose method then just needs to be properly overwritten.

Optionally, any number of methods can be implemented to make use of the Composite pattern. The Composite pattern makes controlling a large number of objects greatly simplified, as one message is forwarded to each and every component of any given composite. Along with dispose, you could add enable, disable, hide, reveal, etc.

In **Listing 8-8**, APauseConductor from the Adapter pattern made use of a collection among objects, which implemented the IPauseable object. The conductor is very reminiscent of the composite element, in that it sends out a message to every collection that it contains. In that particular example, in the adapter, it was to make use of pausing sound and movie clips. The example shows that both sound and movie clips were treated equally; however, that may not always be the desire of the developer. You will make use of the IPause interface, along with the composite pattern, to demonstrate how you can separate pauseable movies and pauseable sounds, as well as trigger each individually or simultaneously. The structure you will devise will reflect Figure 8-4.

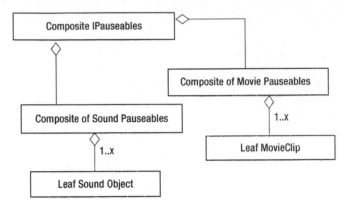

Figure 8-4. The data structure of pauseable objects

You begin by establishing the abstract component, which will contain all necessary default behaviors and attributes that will be inherited by any Component subclass; see Listing 8-22.

Listing 8-22. Component

```
package
{
   public class Component extends Object
   {
      private static var _counter : int = 0;
      protected var _parentComposite : Component;
      protected var _identity : int;

      public function Component()
      {
         _counter++;
      }

      public function get identity() : int
      {
         return _identity;
      }

      final public function get parentComposite() : Component
      {
         return _parentComposite;
      }

      final public function set parentComposite( parentComposite : Component ) : void
      {
```

```
            _parentComposite = parentComposite;
        }
    }
}
```

Next, you need to define the component that is specific to this project and possesses the specific behaviors required by your application. You'll call this PauseableComponent, as shown in **Listing 8-23**.

Listing 8-23. PauseableComponent

```
package
{
    public class PauseableComponent extends Component
    {
        public function PauseableComponent()
        {
            super();
        }

        final public function pause() : void
        {
            doPause();
        }

        final public function resume() : void
        {
            doResume();
        }

        protected function doResume() : void
        {
            throw new IllegalOperationError( 'doResume must be overridden' );
        }

        protected function doPause() : void
        {
            throw new IllegalOperationError( 'doPause must be overridden' );
        }
    }
}
```

PauseableComponent declares necessary methods particular to this application, which will also need to be overridden by any subclasses. You'll begin with the leaf, which will be labeled PauseableLeaf. Being that this application will pause both movie clips and sound, you must find a common behavior that you can specify as the parameter of your leaf; and this will be IPause, as shown in Listing 8-24.

Listing 8-24. PauseableLeaf Accepts a Parameter of IPause Objects

```
package
{
    public class PauseableLeaf extends PauseableComponent
    {
        protected var _iPause : IPause

        public function PauseableLeaf( _pauseable : IPause )
        {
            super();
            _iPause = _pauseable;
        }

        override protected function doResume() : void
        {
            _iPause.resume();
        }

        override protected function doPause() : void
        {
            _iPause.pause();
        }
    }
}
```

Lastly, you need to devise the composite that you'll call PauseableComposite. You may have noticed that neither Component nor PauseableComponent declared the operations for child management. This is because they will be placed here, in PauseableComposite. All that is left to do now is to assign the appropriate implementations shown in **Listing 8-25**.

Listing 8-25. PauseableComposite

```
package
{
    public class PauseableComposite extends PauseableComponent
    {
        protected var _arCollection : ArrayCollection;

        public function PauseableComposite()
        {
            super();
        }

        public function addComponent( pauseable : PauseableComponent ) : void
        {
```

```
            doVerifyCollection();
            _arCollection.append( pauseable );
        }

        public function removeComponent( pauseable : PauseableComponent ) : void
        {
        }

        override protected function doResume() : void
        {
            var it : IIterator = _arCollection.createIterator();
            while (it.hasNext())
            {
                var cnent : PauseableComponent = it.currentElement() as
                    ➥ PauseableComponent;
                it.next();
                cnent.resume();
            }
        }

        override protected function doPause() : void
        {
            var it : IIterator = _arCollection.createIterator()
            while (it.hasNext())
            {
                var cnent : PauseableComponent = it.currentElement() as
                    ➥ PauseableComponent;
                it.next();
                cnent.pause();
            }
        }

        private function doVerifyCollection() : void
        {
            if (!_arCollection)
                _arCollection = new ArrayCollection()
        }
    }
}
```

It's important to note that the composite element will always be the first component invoked. In any Composite pattern structure, the main node of the pattern is expected to be a composite element that contains any number of components. The message of this composite will continue through any nested composites and/or leaves until no further components can forward the message. Therefore, strategically, one could retain references to particular nodes within a data structure to be targeted specifically.

Listing 8-26. The DocumentClass that Builds the Data Structure

```
public class DocumentClass extends Sprite
{
    private var _compositeOfIPauseObjects : PauseableComponent;
    private var _sndComposite : PauseableComponent;
    private var _mcComposite : PauseableComponent;
    private var _isPlaying : Boolean = false;

    public function DocumentClass()
    {
        var sound : ISound = new Audible( new URLRequest( "music.mp3" ) );
        sound = new InfiniteLoopDecorator( sound );
        sound = new PauseableAudibleDecorator( sound );
        sound.play();

        var mc : MovieClip = new SimpleMCAnimation();
        addChild( mc );

        var mcMinimalPauseAdaption : IPause = new MChasStartStop( mc );
        var soundMinimalPauseAdaption : IPause = new
            ➡ AudioDecoratorIPauseAdapter( PauseableAudibleDecorator( sound ) );

        var mcLeaf : PauseableLeaf = new PauseableLeaf( mcMinimalPauseAdaption );
        var sndLeaf : PauseableLeaf = new PauseableLeaf(soundMinimalPauseAdaption);

        var pauseableMCComposite : PauseableComposite = new PauseableComposite();
        pauseableMCComposite.addComponent( mcLeaf );

        var pauseableSndComposite : PauseableComposite = new PauseableComposite();
        pauseableSndComposite.addComponent( sndLeaf );

        var iPauseComposites : PauseableComposite = new PauseableComposite();
        iPauseComposites.addComponent( pauseableMCComposite );
        iPauseComposites.addComponent( pauseableSndComposite );

        _compositeOfIPauseObjects = iPauseComposites;
        _sndComposite = pauseableSndComposite;
        _mcComposite = pauseableMCComposite;
        stage.addEventListener( MouseEvent.MOUSE_DOWN , onDown );
    }

    private function onDown( event : MouseEvent ) : void
    {
        if (_isPlaying)
```

```
        {
            _compositeOfIPauseObjects.pause();
        }
        else
        {
            _compositeOfIPauseObjects.resume();
        }
        _isPlaying = !_isPlaying;
    }
}
```

The code in **Listing 8-26** demonstrates the ability to pause all PauseableLeafs contained within the system. While there are only two leaves, this may not seem like such a large feat, but you are now able to toggle their ability to pause and resume at once. Optionally, if you were to retain references to pauseableMCComposite and pauseableSndComposite, you could possess a finer level of control among which a given IPause collection should pause. Consider how video games pause; often the music continues to play in the background yet animations pause to bring focus on the pause menu.

Additional methods can be added to further aid such necessity among child management as performed with XML, although such methods will vary on the data within the structure. It's quite common to see the Composite pattern make use of the already built-in functionality of the composite by the display list for convenience. This does not mean that the Composite pattern does not have its place. On the contrary, it means you use it all the time, just "loosely."

When working with data that must be maintained, managed, and simplified by the means of operating on many at once and indistinguishably, the Composite pattern is a fantastic tool.

Related Patterns

Chain of Responsibility

Iterator

Decorator

Visitor

Flyweight

Facade

Technical Overview

Intent: To provide a unified interface to a set of interfaces in a subsystem, as shown in Figure 8-5.

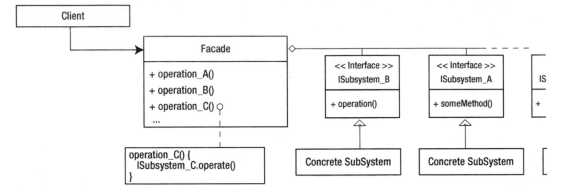

Figure 8-5. Class diagram

Parts

- Facade
- Subsystem Objects
- Client

Benefits

- Conceals the complexities of the subsystems.
- Reveals a simple interface that is more efficient.
- Subsystems can still be utilized even if a façade is in place.
- Loosens the couplings among subsystems and the client.
- Localizes the subsystems that work together.

Drawbacks:

- Additional classes.

A Comprehensive Look

In a computer language, an object is known to possess particular attributes and behaviors, which accompany it. The behaviors and attributes that it possesses ultimately define how we refer to the object itself. When I use the words "quack" and "woof" you probably think of a duck and dog. If I say "lore" and "hock" you might not realize the connection to which they refer because you are unfamiliar with these parts. We tend to give more focus to the aspects that we interface with or can observe.

There is an appropriate name for this: facade. A facade, by its definition, refers to the aspect that is publicly seen and by the most common vantage point. More accurately, it's the public entry. In programming terms, it's merely the interface that the developers and the client will use.

A facade provides two unique applications. The first is to conceal the inner workings of a complicated system from the client. This reduces the amount of possible subsystems that need to be referenced and targeted in an application. Secondly, it can reduce complexities among subsystems and the knowledge required to use them in collaborations properly by exposing a simplified interface that any developer can understand.

A facade appropriately delegates the request of the client to the appropriate subsystem.

Vignette

Ones and zeros make up the computer language known as *binary language*. Very few are able to read and write in binary, yet nearly everyone is capable of using a computer. Even we developers who understand that binary language would be helpless if it were not for the graphical user interface (GUI) of the operating system (OS), let alone our ActionScript editors. Rather than requiring users to understand binary, memory allocation, and retrieval, the system operators have provided a way to visually and textually work with the many parts of the computer such as the memory, the processor, etc. Those familiar enough with the aspects of their OS are often able to take advantage of the built-in language to achieve the lower level experiences they need.

The AS3.0 Cast

Abstract Facade – The Interface

The abstract facade provides the interface to which all subclasses will implement. Additionally, the abstract facade defines any factory objects necessary for determining the appropriate subsystem interfaces for the application.

Concrete Facade – Implements Specifics

The concrete facade specifies the implementations of the interface that facilitate the forwarding of client requests to any subsystems appropriately. The concrete facade also implements the logic to manufacture the concrete subsystems.

Concrete Subsystems – Individual Systems

The concrete subsystems may be any object within your application that increases complications within the orchestration among other objects. The concrete subsystems will never have any knowledge of the facade.

Client – The Messenger of the Facade

The client may be any aspect of your application that has knowledge of the abstract facade. On occasion, the client may have limited knowledge among the interface of one or more of the subsystems within the facade.

When It's Useful

For devising uniformity among a custom API.

For funneling multiple interfaces into a singular instance.

Demonstration

A video player is made up of three top-level objects: Video, NetStream, and NetConnection. All three objects work in collaboration to appropriately deliver a video to the user in a manner that reflects the choices he or she makes (such decisions may be to pause, replay, etc.); see Listing 8-27.

Listing 8-27. Demonstrating the Assembly among Video, NetStream, and NetConnection

```
_netConnection = new NetConnection();
_netConnection.addEventListener(
                        ➥ NetStatusEvent.NET_STATUS ,
doHandleConnectStatus );
_netConnection.connect( null );
_netStream = new NetStream( _netConnection );
_netStream.addEventListener( NetStatusEvent.NET_STATUS , doHandleNetStatus );
_netStream.client = this
_vid = new Video()
_vid.attachNetStream( _netStream )
addChild( _vid )
```

In order to handle such requests, the client needs to be aware of all three objects in order to devise the appropriate associations and delegate the appropriate behaviors to the proper object. NetStream will handle the majority of the forwarded behavior, yet Video and NetConnection are required to close a connection. Let's add a fourth object to the mix, GUI.

GUI displays the current state of the player and allows the user to control their watching experience. As a fourth component that the client may need to be aware of, your system can become overly complicated and cumbersome for another developer to manage.

The facade reduces the intricate knowledge of required subsystems by revealing a singular interface of high-level operations of which a developer and client must be aware. To enable a loosely coupled relationship between the facade and the subsystems and even the client, an abstract facade can be layered and the implementation of an abstract factory should be utilized to instantiate the appropriate subsystems.

While a video player does not truly have an overly complicated arrangement, your client knows that four video components should not be necessary. As they are also related among one another, they should be localized for any necessary maintenance. As an interface will be required for the client to communicate with your encapsulated objects, this is a good time to devise a video player facade.

You begin with an abstraction of your facade that you will modify as you layer your interface to meet the requirements of your system; see Listings 8-28 and 8-29.

Listing 8-28. AbstractVideoPlayerFacade is the Abstraction of Your Facade and Provides Default Functionality Only in This Example

```
package
{
    public class AbstractVideoPlayerFacade extends Sprite
    {
```

```
      protected var _vid : Video;
      protected var _ns : NetStream;
      protected var _nc : NetConnection;

      public function AbstractVideoPlayerFacade()
      {
         _nc = doGetNetConnection();
         _nc.connect( null );
         _ns = doGetNetStream();
         _vid = doGetVideo();
         _vid.attachNetStream( _ns );
         addChild( _vid );
      }

      public function playURL( url : String ) : void
      {
         _ns.play( url );
      }

      final public function close() : void
      {
         _nc.close();
         _vid.clear();
      }

      protected function doGetVideo() : Video
      {
         throw new IllegalOperationError( 'doGetVideo must be overridden' );
      }

      protected function doGetNetStream() : NetStream
      {
         throw new IllegalOperationError( 'doGetNetStream must be overridden' );
      }

      protected function doGetNetConnection() : NetConnection
      {
         throw new IllegalOperationError( 'doGetNetConnection must be overridden' );
      }
   }
}
```

Listing 8-29. PauseResumeVideoPlayerFacade Extends AbstractVideoPlayerFacade and Implements the Appropriate Behaviors

```
package
{
    public class PauseResumeVideoPlayerFacade extends AbstractVideoPlayerFacade
    {
        public function PauseResumeVideoPlayerFacade()
        {
            super();
        }

        public function pause() : void
        {
            _ns.pause();
        }

        public function resume() : void
        {
            _ns.resume();
        }

        override protected function doGetNetConnection() : NetConnection
        {
            return new NetConnection();
        }

        override protected function doGetNetStream() : NetStream
        {
            return new NetStream( _nc );
        }

        override protected function doGetVideo() : Video
        {
            var vid : Video = new Video();
            vid.width = 640;
            vid.height = 320;
            return vid;
        }
    }
}
```

Thus far, you have introduced four public methods that delegate the appropriate requests to the respective objects. You can continue to further support necessary interfaces as well as allow visibility among the objects for low-level operations, which your interface does not account for. Such low-level operations remain the responsibilities of Video, NetStream, and NetConnection. These objects should be extended and implement the appropriate behavior that your application requires.

The facade Is merely the interface and the necessary operations to properly defer the clients' requests to the appropriate objects. This enhances the cohesion of the client and localizes the objects that make up the video player; see Listing 8-30.

Listing 8-30. Client Use the Facade, Unaware of the Subsystems Involved

```
vid = new PauseResumeVideoPlayerFacade();
addChild( vid );
vid.playURL("superfad_preguntas.flv" );
vid.pause();
vid.play();
```

FAQ

- The facade sounds like an interface to me. How is it different from an interface?

  It's actually good that it does resemble an interface to you because that is what the facade wants you to believe. The facade acts as an interface to an object so that the client does not need to be aware of the many objects and their interfaces that, without the facade there to conceal them, it would.

  The major difference is that a facade intends to make it easier to use the many subsystems to which it coordinates, but should advanced developers require the ability to make use of the objects without the use of a facade, they can do just that.

Related Patterns

Abstract Factory

Mediator

Chapter Summary

Structural patterns shed light on ways to enable an extension of requirements by utilizing additive support. This is accomplished either with inheritance or composition to devise new associations.

The concept of adding allows objects to remain more cohesive, more reusable, and increases flexibility, and additionally, to use larger objects.

Key Points

- The Decorator pattern offers added embellishment among like interfaces.
- The Adapter pattern adapts an already existing object to a similar interface.
- The Composite delivers one message from the client to all composed Components.
- The Facade reduces the intricacies of object collaborations from a client.

Chapter 9

Q&A

The previous chapters on design patterns have covered an enormous amount, and now you get an opportunity to use that information. This chapter provides a quiz consisting of 25 questions, to provide you with immediate feedback on your understanding of the material. These questions pertain to design patterns (creational, behavioral and structural) as covered in this book.

You won't be scored or judged on your answers, so do your best to use this chapter as a way to further understand and practice using design patterns.

Notes: 1. For formatting reasons, the quiz questions don't include packages. External definitions must always have a package keyword. 2. Some questions are straightforward, and others require you to supply the implementations for incomplete listings.

Design Pattern Quiz

1. The common prefixes make, create, and get reflect which specific design pattern?

   _____

2. Primitive operations, which are prefixed with do, are used by which pattern?

   _____

3. Separate the instantiation from its assembly to promote flexibility in **Listing 9-1**.

   Listing 9-1. AbstractClass

   ```
   public class AbstractClass extends Sprite
   {
       public function AbstractClass()
       {
   ```

```
        var someMovieClip : MovieClip = new ConcreteMovieClip();
        someMovieClip.y = 25;
        someMovieClip.x = 40;
        someMovieClip.play();
        addChild( someMovieClip );
    }
}
```

Listing 9-2. AbstractClass

Listing 9-3. FactoryMethodClass.as

4. Design a decorator that enhances a bitmap with a `scrollRect` that can scroll to reveal concealed areas of the image using the mouse. The bitmap interface is `IBitmap` in **Listing 9-4**.

Listing 9-4. `IBitmap`

```
public interface IBitmap
{
    function get bitmapData() : BitmapData;
    function set bitmapData( value : BitmapData ) : void;
    function get pixelSnapping() : String;
    function set pixelSnapping( value : String ) : void;
    function get smoothing() : Boolean;
    function set smoothing( value : Boolean ) : void;
}
```

Listing 9-5. `DecoratorAbstract.as`

Listing 9-6. `MouseScrollingDecorator.as`

```
protected var _viewport : Rectangle;
protected var _pixelsPerWide : int;
protected var _pixelsPerTall : int;
private var _rectTall : int = 400;
private var _rectWide : int = 400;
```

_____

_____

_____

_____

_____

_____

_____

_____

_____

_____

_____

_____

5. Explain how you can subclass a method and provide it with an implementation without disturbing the algorithm in which the implementation is required.

_____

_____

_____

_____

_____

_____

6. Explain the benefits of an Iterator in an aggregate.

_____

_____

_____

_____

_____

7. Define a component interface that favors transparency over safety in all of its components.

Listing 9-7. IComponent.as

_____

_____

_____

_____

_____

_____

8.   This pattern ensures state synchronization. _____

9.   Mushroomy Kingdom uses the latest console platform and its power to revisit stage 1-1 with dreamy textures. **Table 9-1** lists the names that reference the linked images of the `.fla`.

Table 9-1. Stage 1-1 concretes revisited

>   New stone floor tile: `StoneFlooring`
>
>   New money box tile: `MoneMone`
>
>   New brick tile: `WhiteStone`
>
>   New pipe tile: `IndustrialPlumbing`
>
>   Cloud: `AlphaCloud`
>
>   Hill terrain: `HillSide`

Using the `AbstractMarioLevelDirector` and the `AbstractMarioEsqueLevelEditor` code and the reference names from **Table 9-1**, write the implementations to populate this scene. The dimensions aren't important.

Listing 9-8. `AbstractMarioEsqueLevelEditor.as`

```
public class AbstractMarioEsqueLevelEditor
{
    private var _bitmapD : BitmapData;
    private var _backgroundColor : uint;
    private var _width : int;
    private var _height : int;
    private var _pt : Point;
    private var _tile : Shape;

    public function AbstractMarioEsqueLevelEditor()
    {
        _tile = new Shape();
        _pt = new Point( 0 , 0 );
    }

    final public function createMap() : void
    {
        bitmap = doCreateMap();
    }

    final public function getLevel() : BitmapData
    {
        return _bitmapD;
    }
```

```
final public function createStone( rect : Rectangle ) : void
{
    addTile( doCreateStone() , rect );
}

final public function createSolidBrick( rect : Rectangle ) : void
{
    addTile( doCreateSolidBrick() , rect );
}

final public function createBreakableBrick( rect : Rectangle ) : void
{
    addTile( doCreateBreakableBrick() , rect );
}

final public function createMoneyBox( rect : Rectangle ) : void
{
    addTile( doCreateMoneyBox() , rect );
}

final public function createCloud( rect : Rectangle ) : void
{
    addTile( doCreateCloud() , rect );
}

final public function createHill( rect : Rectangle ) : void
{
    addTile( doCreateHill() , rect );
}

final public function createBush( rect : Rectangle ) : void
{
    addTile( doCreateBush() , rect );
}

final public function creatCastle( rect : Rectangle ) : void
{
    addTile( doCreatCastle() , rect );
}

final public function createPipe( rect : Rectangle ) : void
{
    addTile( doCreatePipe() , rect );
}
```

```
final public function get width() : int
{
    return _width;
}

final public function set width( width : int ) : void
{
    _width = width;
}

final public function get height() : int
{
    return _height;
}

final public function set height( height : int ) : void
{
    _height = height;
}

final public function get backgroundColor() : uint
{
    return _backgroundColor;
}

final public function set backgroundColor( backgroundColor : uint ) : void
{
    _backgroundColor = backgroundColor;
}

final public function get bitmap() : BitmapData
{
    return _bitmapD;
}

final public function set bitmap( bitmap : BitmapData ) : void
{
    _bitmapD = bitmap;
}

protected function doCreateMap() : BitmapData
{
    return new BitmapData( width , height , false , backgroundColor );
```

```
   }

   protected function doCreateSolidBrick() : DisplayObject
   {
      throw new IllegalOperationError( 'doCreateSolidBrick must be overridden' );
      return null;
   }

   protected function doCreateBreakableBrick() : DisplayObject
   {
      throw new IllegalOperationError( 'doCreateBreakableBrick must be overridden' );
      return null;
   }

   protected function doCreateMoneyBox() : DisplayObject
   {
      throw new IllegalOperationError( 'doCreateMoneyBox must be overridden' );
      return null;
   }

   protected function doCreateCloud() : DisplayObject
   {
      throw new IllegalOperationError( 'doCreateCloud must be overridden' );
      return null;
   }

   protected function doCreateHill() : DisplayObject
   {
      throw new IllegalOperationError( 'doCreateHill must be overridden' );
      return null;
   }

   protected function doCreatePipe() : DisplayObject
   {
      throw new IllegalOperationError( 'doCreatePipe must be overridden' );
      return null;
   }

   private function addTile( dO : DisplayObject , rect : Rectangle ) : void
   {
      var sprite : BitmapData = snapShot( dO );
      _pt.x = rect.x;
      _pt.y = rect.y;
      if (rect.width > 0 || rect.height > 0) ;
```

```
        {
            sprite = tile( sprite , rect );
        }
        bitmap.copyPixels( sprite , sprite.rect , _pt );
    }

    private function snapShot( dO : DisplayObject ) : BitmapData
    {
        var snapshot : BitmapData = new BitmapData( dO.width , dO.height , true , 0 );
        snapshot.draw( dO );
        return snapshot;
    }

    private function tile( bmpd : BitmapData , rect : Rectangle ) : BitmapData
    {
        var _t : Shape = _tile;
        var g : Graphics = _t.graphics;
        g.clear();
        g.beginBitmapFill( bmpd , null , true , false );
        g.drawRect( 0 , 0 , rect.width , rect.height );
        g.endFill();
        return snapShot( _t );
    }
}
```

Listing 9-9. QuizLevelEditor.as

Listing 9-10. AbstractMarioLevelDirector.as

```
public class AbstractMarioLevelDirector
{
    protected const _width : int = 400;
    protected const _height : int = 300;
    protected const _bgColor : uint = 0xacccff;
    protected var _builder : AbstractMarioEsqueLevelEditor;
```

```
public function AbstractMarioLevelDirector(builder:AbstractMarioEsqueLevelEditor);
{
    _builder = builder;
}
public function getLevel() : BitmapData
{
    return _builder.getLevel();
}
}
```

Listing 9-11. QuizLevelDirector.as

_____
_____
_____
_____
_____
_____
_____
_____
_____
_____
_____
_____
_____
_____
_____

10. Explain why it's unwise to use a Simple Singleton in an application.

_____
_____
_____
_____

11. The following code is from an unrevealed class.

Listing 9-12. Unrevealed class

```
...cont
public function makeFastFoodSandwich( menu_number : int ) : ValueMeal
{
    switch(menu_number)
    {
      case  1:
        return new DoubleStack();
        break;
      case  2 :
        return new ChickenSandwich();
        break;
      case 3:
        return new ChickenNuggets();
```

```
        break;
    case 4:
        return new Frosty();
        break;
    }
}
```
...cont

The code in Listing 9-12 uses the Factory Method pattern?   True   False

12.   Twitter is the epitome of which design pattern? _____

13.   Having parallel hierarchies means you use fewer classes than when using orthogonal hierarchies.
       True   False

14.   These three patterns can optionally intercept a request before passing it on.

       _____

       _____

       _____

15.   Show a *loose* composite that stops all MovieClips in the DisplayList.

       //traverse(this.stage);

       _____

       _____

       _____

       _____

       _____

       _____

       _____

       _____

       _____

       _____

       _____

       _____

       _____

       _____

       _____

       _____

       _____

       _____

       _____

16. Re-create the display list from AS 3.0 as a composite.

Listing 9-13. `IComponent.as` (`DisplayObject`) interface

Listing 9-14. `IComposite.as` (`DisplayObjectContainer`) interface

Listing 9-15. Leaf.as (DisplayObject)

```
public class Leaf implements _____
{
}
```

17.   What are the two most significant differences between the State pattern and the Strategy pattern?

_____

_____

_____

_____

_____

18.   Suppose a loader uses the following states: Closed, OpeningConnection, Loading, and Loaded. Given the interface of ILoader shown in **Listing 9-16**, assemble a loader using only the State pattern, ensuring that the loader can load a new request at any given point in time, as well as be destroyed, without using any conditional statements.

Listing 9-16. Loader interface

```
public interface ILoader
{
    function close();

    function load( request : URLRequest , context : LoaderContext = null ) : void;

    function loadBytes( bytes : ByteArray , context : LoaderContext = null ) : void;

    function get content() : DisplayObject;

    function get contentLoaderInfo() : LoaderInfo;

    function get ldr() : Loader;

    function dispose() : void;
}
```

Listing 9-17. AbstractLoadersContext.as

```
public class AbstractLoadersContext extends Sprite implements ILoader
{
    private var _ldr : Loader
```

```
protected var _stateLoader : ALoaderStateObject

public function AbstractLoadersContext()
{
    addChild( _ldr = new Loader() );
    _stateLoader = createState( this )
}
```

Listing 9-18. LoadersContext.as

Listing 9-19. `ALoaderStateObject.as` **extends** `Object`

Listing 9-20. `EmptyLoaderStateObject.as` **extends** `ALoaderStateObject`

Listing 9-21. `OpeningConnectionStateObject.as` **extends** `ALoaderStateObject`

Listing 9-22. `LoadingStateObject.as` extends `ALoaderStateObject`

Listing 9-23. LoadedStateObject.as **extends** ALoaderStateObject

_____

_____

_____

_____

_____

_____

_____

_____

_____

_____

_____

_____

19. Write an AbstractShape class and its subclasses, Square and Circle, so they can be drawn and cleared. Additionally, construct an AbstractCommand class that can execute and un-do said executed code. There are two possible solutions; write both.

Listing 9-24. IGraphics.as interface

_____

_____

_____

_____

_____

_____

Listing 9-25. AbstractShape.as constants WIDE and TALL are both 20 pixels. FILL_COLOR is yellow.

```
protected const WIDE : int = 20;
protected const TALL : int = 20;
private const FILL_COLOR : uint = 0xfff000;
```

_____

_____

_____

_____

_____

Listing 9-26. CircleShape.as

Listing 9-27. SquareShape.as

Listing 9-28. `AbstractShapeCommand.as`

Listing 9-29. `ShapeCommandDraw.as`

Listing 9-30. ShapeCommandUndo.as

Listing 9-31. AbstractShapeUndoCommand.as

Listing 9-32. ShapeCommandWithUndo.as

_____
_____
_____
_____

20.   The Execute method accompanies which design pattern?

_____

21.   Explain the advantage of the Abstract Factory pattern over the Factory Method pattern.

_____
_____
_____

22.   In ActionScript 3.0, what are the three design patterns used in the EventSystem to carry out events of DisplayObjects?

_____
_____
_____

23.   Three objects make up an image loader in an application: a loader, an image mask, and a description box. Using these three objects, the sequence must occur in the following order:

An image loads.

The mask transitions to reveal the image.

Text appears, giving a description.

Demonstrate how the Chain of Responsibility pattern can properly compliment the output of the following client code in **Listing 9-33**.

Listing 9-33. DocumentClass using the Chain of Responsibility pattern to accomplish its sequence

```
public function DocumentClass()
{
    var img : AbstractView = new ImageView()

    var mask : AbstractView = new MaskView()
        img.addHandler( mask )

    var tf : AbstractView = new TextFieldView()
        mask.addHandler( tf )

    tf.addHandler( IHandler( new NullHandler() ) )
}
```

```
//... [object ImageView] target hit;
//... [object MaskView] target hit;
//... [object TextFieldView] target hit;
//... [object NullHandler] target hit: end of Chain;
```

Listing 9-34. IHandler interface

_____

_____

_____

_____

_____

Listing 9-35. AbstractView

_____

_____

_____

_____

_____

_____

_____

_____

_____

_____

_____

_____

_____

_____

_____

_____

_____

_____

_____

_____

Listing 9-36. ImageView.as loads the following image: www.spilled-milk.com/000.jpg.

```
ldr.load( new URLRequest( "http://www.spilled-milk.com/000.jpg" ) )
```

Listing 9-37. MaskView

Listing 9-38. DescriptionView

_____

_____

_____

_____

_____

_____

_____

24. What pattern decouples multiple subsystems from client messaging by funneling those implementations into a simpler interface? _____

25. Choose the appropriate associations.

Model   Composite pattern

View   Subject pattern

Controller   Observer pattern

                Strategy pattern

Answers to Design Patterns Quiz

1. The common prefixes make, create, and get reflect which specific design pattern?

   The Factory Method pattern

2. Primitive operations, which are prefixed with do, are used by which pattern?

   The Template Method pattern

3. Separate the instantiation from its assembly to promote flexibility in Listing 9-1.

Listing 9-1. AbstractClass

```
public class AbstractClass extends Sprite
{
    public function AbstractClass()
    {
        var someMovieClip : MovieClip = new ConcreteMovieClip();
            someMovieClip.y = 25;
              someMovieClip.x = 40;
              someMovieClip.play();
              addChild( someMovieClip );
    }
}
```

Listing 9-2. AbstractClass

```
public class AbstractClass extends Sprite
{
    public function AbstractClass ()
    {
        var mc : MovieClip = createMovie()
        mc.y = 25;
        mc.x = 40;
        mc.play();
        addChild( mc );
    }

    protected function createMovie() : MovieClip
    {
        throw new IllegalOperationError( 'createMovie must be overridden' );
        return null;
    }
}
```

```
}
```

Listing 9-3. FactoryMethodClass.as

```
public class FactoryMethodClass extends AbstractClass
{
    override protected function createMovie() : MovieClip
    {
        return new ConcreteMovieClip();
    }
}
```

4.   Design a decorator that enhances a bitmap with a scrollRect that can scroll to reveal concealed areas of the image using the mouse. The bitmap interface is IBitmap in **Listing 9-4**.

Listing 9-4. IBitmap

```
public interface IBitmap
{
    function get bitmapData() : BitmapData;
    function set bitmapData( value : BitmapData ) : void;
    function get pixelSnapping() : String;
    function set pixelSnapping( value : String ) : void;
    function get smoothing() : Boolean;
    function set smoothing( value : Boolean ) : void;
}
```

Listing 9-5. DecoratorAbstract.as

```
public class DecoratorAbstract extends Sprite implements IBitmap
{
    protected var _decoratee : Bitmap

    public function DecoratorAbstract( decoratee : Bitmap ) : void
    {
        _decoratee = decoratee
        addChild( decoratee )
    }

    public function get bitmapData() : BitmapData
```

```
    {
        return _decoratee.bitmapData;
    }

    public function set bitmapData( value : BitmapData ) : void
    {
        _decoratee.bitmapData = value;
    }

    public function get pixelSnapping() : String
    {
        return _decoratee.pixelSnapping;
    }

    public function set pixelSnapping( value : String ) : void
    {
        _decoratee.pixelSnapping = value;
    }

    public function get smoothing() : Boolean
    {
        return _decoratee.smoothing;
    }

    public function set smoothing( value : Boolean ) : void
    {
        _decoratee.smoothing = value;
    }
}
```

Listing 9-6. MouseScrollingDecorator.as

```
public class MouseScrollingDecorator extends DecoratorAbstract
{
    protected var _viewport : Rectangle;
    protected var _pixelsPerWide : int;
    protected var _pixelsPerTall : int;
    private var _rectTall : int = 400;
```

```
        private var _rectWide : int = 400;

        public function MouseScrollingDecorator( bitmap : Bitmap )
        {
            super( bitmap );
            addEventListener( MouseEvent.MOUSE_MOVE , onMovement );
            _decoratee.scrollRect = new Rectangle( 0 , 0 , _rectWide , _rectTall );

            _pixelsPerWide = bitmap.width / _rectWide;
            _pixelsPerTall = bitmap.height / _rectTall;
            cacheAsBitmap = true;
        }

        private function onMovement( event : MouseEvent ) : void
        {
            var localRect : Rectangle = this._decoratee.scrollRect;
            localRect.x = event.localX * _pixelsPerWide;
            localRect.y = event.localY;
            _decoratee.scrollRect = localRect;
        }
}
```

5. Explain how you can subclass a method and provide it with an implementation without disturbing the algorithm in which the implementation is required.

The Template Method pattern offers the solution by marking the as final the method that defines the primitive operations that make up an algorithm. The primitive operations reveal hooks for which a subclass can provide implementations, while protecting the default implementation of the superclass.

6. Explain the benefits of an Iterator and an aggregate.

Using an iterator along with an aggregate conceals the logic that necessitates element retrieval from the aggregate, which would otherwise pollute a client with unnecessary details.

7. Define a component interface that favors transparency over safety in all of its components and leaves.

Listing 9-7. IComponent.as

```
public interface IComponent
{
        function addComponent( cmpt : Component ) : void;
        function removeComponent( cmpt : Component ) : void;
```

```
        function operation() : void;
}
```

8. This pattern ensures state synchronization. <u>The Observer pattern</u>

9. Mushroomy Kingdom uses the latest console platform and its power to revisit stage 1-1 with dreamy textures. **Table 9-1** lists the names that reference the linked images of the .fla.

Table 9-1. Stage 1-1 concretes revisited

New stone floor tile: StoneFlooring

New money box tile: MoneMone

New brick tile: WhiteStone

New pipe tile: IndustrialPlumbing

Cloud: AlphaCloud

Hill terrain: HillSide

Using the AbstractMarioLevelDirector.as and the AbstractMarioEsqueLevelEditor.as code and the reference names from **Table 9-1**, write the implementations to populate this scene. The dimensions aren't important.

Listing 9-8. AbstractMarioEsqueLevelEditor.as

```
public class AbstractMarioEsqueLevelEditor
{
      private var _bitmapD : BitmapData;
      private var _backgroundColor : uint;
      private var _width : int;
      private var _height : int;
      private var _pt : Point;
      private var _tile : Shape;

      public function AbstractMarioEsqueLevelEditor()
      {
        _tile = new Shape();
        _pt = new Point( 0 , 0 );
      }

      final public function createMap() : void
      {
        bitmap = doCreateMap();
      }

      final public function getLevel() : BitmapData
      {
        return _bitmapD;
```

```
    }

    final public function createStone( rect : Rectangle ) : void
    {
        addTile( doCreateStone() , rect );
    }

    final public function createSolidBrick( rect : Rectangle ) : void
    {
        addTile( doCreateSolidBrick() , rect );
    }

    final public function createBreakableBrick( rect : Rectangle ) : void
    {
        addTile( doCreateBreakableBrick() , rect );
    }

    final public function createMoneyBox( rect : Rectangle ) : void
    {
        addTile( doCreateMoneyBox() , rect );
    }

    final public function createCloud( rect : Rectangle ) : void
    {
        addTile( doCreateCloud() , rect );
    }

    final public function createHill( rect : Rectangle ) : void
    {
        addTile( doCreateHill() , rect );
    }

    final public function createBush( rect : Rectangle ) : void
    {
        addTile( doCreateBush() , rect );
    }

    final public function creatCastle( rect : Rectangle ) : void
    {
        addTile( doCreatCastle() , rect );
    }

    final public function createPipe( rect : Rectangle ) : void
    {
```

```
        addTile( doCreatePipe() , rect );
    }

    final public function get width() : int
    {
        return _width;
    }

    final public function set width( width : int ) : void
    {
        _width = width;
    }

    final public function get height() : int
    {
        return _height;
    }

    final public function set height( height : int ) : void
    {
        _height = height;
    }

    final public function get backgroundColor() : uint
    {
        return _backgroundColor;
    }

    final public function set backgroundColor( backgroundColor : uint ) : void
    {
        _backgroundColor = backgroundColor;
    }

    final public function get bitmap() : BitmapData
    {
        return _bitmapD;
    }

    final public function set bitmap( bitmap : BitmapData ) : void
    {
        _bitmapD = bitmap;
    }

    protected function doCreateMap() : BitmapData
```

```
    {
        return new BitmapData( width , height , false , backgroundColor );
    }

    protected function doCreateSolidBrick() : DisplayObject
    {
        throw new IllegalOperationError( 'doCreateSolidBrick must be overridden' );
        return null;
    }

    protected function doCreateBreakableBrick() : DisplayObject
    {
        throw new IllegalOperationError('doCreateBreakableBrick must be ➥
overridden');
        return null;
    }

    protected function doCreateMoneyBox() : DisplayObject
    {
        throw new IllegalOperationError( 'doCreateMoneyBox must be overridden' );
        return null;
    }

    protected function doCreateCloud() : DisplayObject
    {
        throw new IllegalOperationError( 'doCreateCloud must be overridden' );
        return null;
    }

    protected function doCreateHill() : DisplayObject
    {
        throw new IllegalOperationError( 'doCreateHill must be overridden' );
        return null;
    }

    protected function doCreatePipe() : DisplayObject
    {
        throw new IllegalOperationError( 'doCreatePipe must be overridden' );
        return null;
    }

    private function addTile( dO : DisplayObject , rect : Rectangle ) : void
    {
        var sprite : BitmapData = snapShot( dO );
```

```
        _pt.x = rect.x;
        _pt.y = rect.y;
        if (rect.width > 0 || rect.height > 0) ;
        {
            sprite = tile( sprite , rect );
        }
        bitmap.copyPixels( sprite , sprite.rect , _pt );
    }

    private function snapShot( dO : DisplayObject ) : BitmapData
    {
        var snapshot : BitmapData = new BitmapData( dO.width, dO.height , true , 0 );
        snapshot.draw( dO );
        return snapshot;
    }

    private function tile( bmpd : BitmapData , rect : Rectangle ) : BitmapData
    {
        var _t : Shape = _tile;
        var g : Graphics = _t.graphics;
        g.clear();
        g.beginBitmapFill( bmpd , null , true , false );
        g.drawRect( 0 , 0 , rect.width , rect.height );
        g.endFill();
        return snapShot( _t );
    }
}
```

Listing 9-9. `QuizLevelEditor.as`

```
public class QuizLevelEditor extends AbstractMarioEsqueLevelEditor
{
    public function QuizLevelEditor()
    {
        super();
    }

    override protected function doCreateMap() : BitmapData
    {
        return new BitmapData( width , height , false , backgroundColor );
    }
```

```
      override protected function doCreateSolidBrick() : DisplayObject
      {
          return new StoneFlooring();
      }


      override protected function doCreateBreakableBrick() : DisplayObject
      {
          return new WhiteStone();
      }


      override protected function doCreateMoneyBox() : DisplayObject
      {
          return  new MoneMone();
      }


      override protected function doCreateCloud() : DisplayObject
      {
          return new AlphaClouds();
      }


      override protected function doCreateHill() : DisplayObject
      {
          return new HillSide();
      }


      override protected function doCreatePipe() : DisplayObject
      {
          return new IndustrialPlumbing();
      }
}
```

Listing 9-10. AbstractMarioLevelDirector.as

```
public class AbstractMarioLevelDirector
{
      protected const _width : int = 400;
      protected const _height : int = 300;
      protected const _bgColor : uint = 0xacccff;
      protected var _builder : AbstractMarioEsqueLevelEditor;
```

```
    public function AbstractMarioLevelDirector( builder :
                                       ➥ AbstractMarioEsqueLevelEditor );

{
_builder = builder;
}

    public function getLevel() : BitmapData
    {
       return _builder.getLevel();
    }
}
```

Listing 9-11. `QuizLevelDirector.as`

```
public class QuizLevelDirector extends AbstractMarioLevelDirector
{
      private var rect : Rectangle = new Rectangle( 0 , 0 , 0 , 0 )

      public function QuizLevelDirector( builder : AbstractMarioEsqueLevelEditor )
      {
        super( builder );
      }

      override public function getLevel() : BitmapData
      {
        _builder.width = _width;
        _builder.height = _height;
        _builder.backgroundColor = _bgColor;
        _builder.createMap();
        buildScenicTerrain();
        buildScenicClouds();
        buildScenicBricks();
        buildFloor();
        buildPipes();
        buildMoneyBox();

        return _builder.getLevel();
      }
```

```
    private function buildMoneyBox() : void
    {
        assignRect( 210 , 40 );
        _builder.createMoneyBox( rect );
        assignRect( 80 , 130 );
        _builder.createMoneyBox( rect );
        assignRect( 180 , 130 );
        _builder.createMoneyBox( rect );
        assignRect( 230 , 130 );
        _builder.createMoneyBox( rect );
    }


    private function buildScenicBricks() : void
    {
        assignRect( 155 , 130 , 120 , 23 );
        _builder.createBreakableBrick( rect );
    }


    private function buildPipes() : void
    {
        assignRect( 330 , _height - 15 * 2 - 65 );
        _builder.createPipe( rect );
    }


    private function buildFloor() : void
    {
        assignRect( 0 , _height - 56 , _width , _height - 56 );
        _builder.createSolidBrick( rect );
    }


    private function buildScenicTerrain() : void
    {
        assignRect( 0 , 90 , _width , _height - 56 );
        _builder.createHill( rect );
    }


    private function buildScenicClouds() : void
```

```
        {
            assignRect( 0 , 0 , _width , 1 );
            _builder.createCloud( rect );
        }

        private function assignRect( x : int=0, y : int=0, w : int=0, h : int=0 ) : void
        {
            rect.x = x;
            rect.y = y;
            rect.width = w;
            rect.height = h;
        }
    }
```

10. Explain why it's unwise to use a Simple Singleton in an application.

    Using a Simple Singleton in AS 3.0 is a bad idea because it doesn't give you the ability to extend the static instance. Additionally, the Simple Singleton tightly couples code with a static reference, which makes it difficult, or slower, to reuse code in the future.

11. The following code is from an unrevealed class.

Listing 9-12. UnRevealed class

```
...cont
    public function makeFastFoodSandwich( menu_number : int ) : ValueMeal
    {
        switch(menu_number)
        {
            case 1:
                return new DoubleStack();
                break;
            case 2 :
                return new ChickenSandwich();
                break;
            case 3:
                return new ChickenNuggets();
                break;
            case 4:
                return new Frosty();
                break;
        }
    }
...cont
```

The code in **Listing 9-12** is a factory method.   True ⟨False⟩

12.   Twitter is the epitome of which design pattern? <u>The Observer pattern</u>

13.   Having parallel hierarchies means you use fewer classes than when using orthogonal hierarchies.
        True ⟨False⟩

        Quite the contrary. Any time you have parallel hierarchies, you multiply your system by the number of parallel hierarchies.

14.   These three patterns can optionally intercept a request before passing it on.

        Decorator pattern

        Chain of Responsibility pattern

        Adapter pattern

15.   Show a *loose* composite that stops all MovieClips in the DisplayList.

```
//traverse(this.stage)
public function traverse( mc : DisplayObjectContainer ) : void
{
      if (mc is MovieClip) ;
      {
          MovieClip( mc ).stop();
      }

      if (mc.numChildren > 0) ;
      {
          for (var i : int = 0;i < mc.numChildren;i++) ;
          {
              var innards : DisplayObject = mc.getChildAt( i );

              if ( innards  is  MovieClip) ;
              {
                  traverse( MovieClip( innards ) );
              }
          }
      }
}
```

16.   Re-create the display list from AS 3.0 as a composite.

Listing 9-13. `IComponent.as` (DisplayObject) interface

```
public interface IComponent
{
    function get parentComposite() : Component
    function set parentComposite( parentComposite : Component ) : void
}
```

Listing 9-14. `IComposite.as` (DisplayObjectContainer) interface

```
public interface IComposite
{
    function addChild( child : DisplayObject ) : DisplayObject;

    function addChildAt( child : DisplayObject , index : int ) : DisplayObject;

    function getChildAt( index : int ) : DisplayObject;

    function getChildByName( name : String ) : DisplayObject;

    function getChildIndex( child : DisplayObject ) : int;

    function removeChild( child : DisplayObject ) : DisplayObject;

    function removeChildAt( index : int ) : DisplayObject;

    function setChildIndex( child : DisplayObject , index : int ) : void;

    function swapChildren( child1 : DisplayObject , child2 : DisplayObject ) : void

    function swapChildrenAt( index1 : int , index2 : int ) : void;
}
```

Listing 9-15. `Leaf.as` (DisplayObject)

```
public class Leaf implements IComponent
{
}
```

17. What are the two most significant differences between the State pattern and the Strategy pattern?

   1. The Strategy pattern requires the client to change behaviors, whereas the State pattern conceals the behaviors from the client for uniformity. (The state changes itself; the strategy is changed by the client).

   2. The change in behaviors in the Strategy pattern reflects the needs of the client, whereas the change in behaviors in the State pattern reflects the change in the context's state.

18. Suppose a loader uses the following states: Closed, OpeningConnection, Loading, and Loaded. Given the interface of ILoader shown in **Listing 9-16**, assemble a loader using only the State pattern, ensuring that the loader can load a new request at any given point in time, as well as be destroyed, without using any conditional statements.

Listing 9-16. Loader interface

```
public interface ILoader
{
        function close();

        function load( request : URLRequest , context : LoaderContext = null ) : void;

        function loadBytes( bytes : ByteArray , context : LoaderContext = null ) : void;

        function get content() : DisplayObject;

        function get contentLoaderInfo() : LoaderInfo;

        function get ldr() : Loader;

        function dispose() : void;
}
```

Listing 9-17. AbstractLoadersContext.as

```
public class AbstractLoadersContext extends Sprite implements ILoader
{
        private var _ldr : Loader
        protected var _stateLoader : ALoaderStateObject

        public function AbstractLoadersContext()
        {
           addChild( _ldr = new Loader() );
            _stateLoader = createState( this )
        }
```

```
public function changeState( state : ALoaderStateObject ) : void
{
    _stateLoader.dispose();
    _stateLoader = state
}

public function close() : void
{
    _stateLoader.close()
}

public function get content() : DisplayObject
{
    return _stateLoader.content
}

public function get contentLoaderInfo() : LoaderInfo
{
    return _stateLoader.contentLoaderInfo
}

public function load( request:URLRequest, context:LoaderContext = null ) : void
{
    _stateLoader.load( request , context )
}

public function loadBytes( bytes:ByteArray, context:LoaderContext =null ) : void
{
    _stateLoader.loadBytes( bytes , context )
}

public function get ldr() : Loader
{
    return _ldr;
}

public function dispose() : void
```

```
        {
            _stateLoader.dispose();
        }

        protected function createState( abstractLoadersContext : AbstractLoadersContext)
                                                            ➡: ALoaderStateObject
        {
            throw new IllegalOperationError( 'createState must be overridden' )
            return null;
        }
}
```

Listing 9-18. LoadersContext.as

```
public class LoadersContext extends AbstractLoadersContext
{
        public function LoadersContext()
        {
            super();
        }

        override protected function createState( abstractLoadersContext :
                                        ➡AbstractLoadersContext ) : ALoaderStateObject
        {
            return EmptyLoaderStateObject( abstractLoadersContext );
        }
}
```

Explanation: LoadersContext uses a factory method, whereas the StateObjects don't, because LoadersContext declares the initial StateObject. This is subject to change more than the StateObjects because the individual states typically have a particular successor.

Listing 9-19. ALoaderStateObject.as extends Object

```
public class ALoaderStateObject extends Object
{
        protected var _ldrContext : LoadersContext
        protected var _ldr : Loader

        public function ALoaderStateObject( context : LoadersContext )
        {
```

```
        _ldrContext = context
        _ldr = context.ldr
    }

    public function close() : void
    {
    }

    public function get content() : DisplayObject
    {
        return null
    }

    public function get contentLoaderInfo() : LoaderInfo
    {
        return null
    }

    public function load( request:URLRequest , context:LoaderContext = null ) : void
    {
    }

    public function loadBytes( bytes:ByteArray, context:LoaderContext =null ) : void
    {
    }

    public function unload() : void
    {
    }

    public function unloadAndStop( gc : Boolean = true ) : void
    {
    }

    public function get ldr() : Loader
    {
        return _ldr;
```

```
        }

    public function set ldr( ldr : Loader ) : void
    {
        _ldr = ldr;
    }

    public function dispose() : void
    {
        throw new IllegalOperationError( 'dispose must be overridden' );
    }
}
```

Listing 9-20. EmptyLoaderStateObject.as **extends** ALoaderStateObject

```
public class EmptyLoaderStateObject extends ALoaderStateObject
{
    public function EmptyLoaderStateObject( context : LoadersContext )
    {
        super( context );
    }

    override public function get contentLoaderInfo() : LoaderInfo
    {
        return _ldr.loaderInfo;
    }

    override public function load( request:URLRequest,context:LoaderContext=null ):void
    {
        _ldr.load( request , context );
        _ldrContext.changeState( new OpeningConnectionStateObject( _ldrContext ) );
    }

    override public function loadBytes(bytes:ByteArray,context:LoaderContext=null):void
    {
        _ldr.loadBytes( bytes , context );
        _ldrContext.changeState( new OpeningConnectionStateObject( _ldrContext ) );
    }
```

```
override public function dispose() : void
{
    _ldr = null;
    _ldrContext = null;
}
}
```

Listing 9-21. OpeningConnectionStateObject.as extends ALoaderStateObject

```
public class OpeningConnectionStateObject extends ALoaderStateObject
{
    public function OpeningConnectionStateObject( context : LoadersContext )
    {
        super( context );
        _ldr.contentLoaderInfo.addEventListener( Event.OPEN , onConnectionOpen );
    }

    private function onConnectionOpen( event : Event ) : void
    {
        _ldrContext.changeState( new LoadingStateObject( _ldrContext ) );
    }

    override public function get contentLoaderInfo() : LoaderInfo
    {
        return ldr.loaderInfo
    }

    override public function dispose() : void
    {
        _ldr.contentLoaderInfo.removeEventListener( Event.OPEN , onConnectionOpen );
        _ldr = null;
        _ldrContext = null;
    }
}
```

Listing 9-22. LoadingStateObject.as extends ALoaderStateObject

```
public class LoadingStateObject extends ALoaderStateObject
{
    public function LoadingStateObject( context : LoadersContext )
    {
        super( context );
        _ldr.contentLoaderInfo.addEventListener( Event.COMPLETE , onComplete );
    }

    private function onComplete( event : Event ) : void
    {
        _ldrContext.changeState( new LoadedStateObject( _ldrContext ) );
    }

    override public function close() : void
    {
        _ldr.close();
    }

    override public function get contentLoaderInfo() : LoaderInfo
    {
        return _ldr.loaderInfo;
    }

    override public function load( request:URLRequest, context:LoaderContext ):void
    {
        close();

        _ldr.load( request , context );
        _ldrContext.changeState( new OpeningConnectionStateObject( _ldrContext ) );
    }

    override public function loadBytes( bytes:ByteArray,context:LoaderContext ):void
    {
        close();
        _ldr.loadBytes( bytes , context );
```

```
            _ldrContext.changeState( new OpeningConnectionStateObject( _ldrContext ) );
    }


    override public function dispose() : void
    {
        _ldr.contentLoaderInfo.removeEventListener( Event.COMPLETE , onComplete );
        _ldr = null;
        _ldrContext = null;

    }
}
```

Listing 9-23. LoadedStateObject.as extends ALoaderStateObject

```
public class LoadedStateObject extends ALoaderStateObject
{
    public function LoadedStateObject( context : LoadersContext )
    {
        super( context );
    }


    override public function close() : void
    {
        _ldr.unloadAndStop();
        _ldr.unload();
    }


    override public function get contentLoaderInfo() : LoaderInfo
    {
        return  _ldr.loaderInfo;
    }


    override public function load( request:URLRequest,context:LoaderContext=null ):void
    {
        close();
        _ldr.load( request , context );
        _ldrContext.changeState( new OpeningConnectionStateObject( _ldrContext ) );
    }
```

```
    override public function loadBytes(bytes:ByteArray,context:LoaderContext=null):void
    {
        close();
        _ldr.loadBytes( bytes , context );
        _ldrContext.changeState( new OpeningConnectionStateObject( _ldrContext ) );
    }


    override public function dispose() : void
    {
        _ldr = null;
        _ldrContext = null;
    }
}
```

19. Write an AbstractShape class and its subclasses, Square and Circle, so they can be drawn and cleared. Additionally, construct an AbstractCommand class that can execute and unexecute code. There are two possible solutions; write both.

Listing 9-24. IGraphics.as interface

```
public interface IGraphics
{
    function draw() : void
    function clear() : void
    function get parent() : DisplayObjectContainer
}
```

Listing 9-25. AbstractShape.as constants WIDE and TALL are both 20 pixels. FILL_COLOR is yellow.

```
public class AbstractShape extends Shape implements IGraphics
{
        protected const WIDE : int = 20;
        protected const TALL : int = 20;
        private const FILL_COLOR : uint = 0xfff000;


        final public function draw() : void
        {
            addColor();
            doDraw();
            endFill();
```

```
        }

    final public function clear() : void
    {
        this.graphics.clear();
    }

    protected function doDraw() : void
    {
        throw new IllegalOperationError( 'doDraw must be overridden' );
    }

    private function addColor() : void
    {
        this.graphics.beginFill( FILL_COLOR , 1 );
    }

    private function endFill() : void
    {
        this.graphics.endFill();
    }
}
```

Listing 9-26. CircleShape.as

```
public class CircleShape extends AbstractShape
{
    override protected function doDraw() : void
    {
        var radius : Number = Math.sqrt( WIDE * WIDE + TALL * TALL );
        this.graphics.drawCircle( 0 , 0 , radius );
    }
}
```

Listing 9-27. SquareShape.as

```
public class SquareShape extends AbstractShape
{
```

```
      override protected function doDraw() : void
      {
          this.graphics.drawRect(0,0,WIDE,TALL);
      }
  }
```

Listing 9-28. AbstractShapeCommand.as

```
public class AbstractShapeCommand
{
      protected var _receiver : IGraphics;

      public function AbstractShapeCommand( rcvr : IGraphics )
      {
          _receiver = rcvr;
      }

      final public function execute() : void
      {
          doExecute();
      }

      protected function doExecute() : void
      {
          throw new IllegalOperationError( 'doExecute must be overridden' );
      }
}
```

Listing 9-29. ShapeCommandDraw.as

```
public class ShapeCommandDraw extends AbstractShapeCommand
{
      override protected function doExecute() : void
      {
          _receiver.draw();
      }
}
```

Listing 9-30. ShapeCommandUndo.as

```
public class ShapeCommandUndo extends AbstractShapeCommand
{
        override protected function doExecute() : void
        {
            _receiver.clear();
            _receiver.parent.removeChild( DisplayObject( _receiver ) );
        }
}
```

Listing 9-31. AbstractShapeUndoCommand.as

```
public class AbstractShapeUndoCommand extends AbstractShapeCommand
{
        public function undo() : void
        {
            doUndo();
        }


        protected function doUndo() : void
        {
            throw new IllegalOperationError( 'doUndo must be overridden' );
        }
}
```

Listing 9-32. ShapeCommandWithUndo.as

```
public class ShapeCommandWithUndo extends AbstractShapeUndoCommand
{
        override protected function doExecute() : void
        {
            _receiver.draw();
        }


        override protected function doUndo() : void
        {
            _receiver.clear();
            _receiver.parent.removeChild( DisplayObject( _receiver ) );
```

```
        }
}
```

20.   The Execute method accompanies which design pattern?

The Command pattern

21.   Explain the advantage of the Abstract Factory pattern over the Factory Method pattern

Unlike a factory method, an abstract factory is an object that manufactures products. This allows the abstract factory to be parameterized among other objects to which the manufacturing request can be delegated.

22.   In ActionScript 3.0, what are the three design patterns used in the EventSystem to carry out events of DisplayObjects?

Composite pattern

Chain of Responsibility pattern

Observer pattern

23.   Three objects make up an image loader in an application: a loader, an image mask, and a description box. Using these three objects, the sequence must occur in the following order:

a.   An image loads.

b.   The mask transitions to reveal the image.

c.   Text appears, giving a description.

Demonstrate how the Chain of Responsibility pattern can properly compliment the output of the following client code in **Listing 9-33**.

Listing 9-33. DocumentClass using the Chain of Responsibility pattern to accomplish its sequence

```
public function DocumentClass()
{
    var img : AbstractView = new ImageView();

    var mask : AbstractView = new MaskView();
        img.addHandler( mask );

    var tf : AbstractView = new TextFieldView();
        mask.addHandler( tf );

    tf.addHandler( IHandler( new NullHandler() ) );
}
//... [object ImageView] target hit;
//... [object MaskView] target hit;
//... [object TextFieldView] target hit;
//... [object NullHandler] target hit: end of Chain;
```

Listing 9-34. IHandler interface

```
public interface IHandler
{
        function addHandler( successor : IHandler ) : void;

        function forward() : void;
}
```

Listing 9-35. AbstractView

```
public class AbstractView extends Sprite implements IHandler
{
        protected var _handler : IHandler;

        public function AbstractView()
        {
        }

        public function addHandler( successor : IHandler ) : void
        {
          _handler = successor;
        }

        final public function forward() : void
        {
          doForward();
          _handler.forward();
        }

        protected function doForward() : void
        {
          trace( this + ' target hit' );
        }
}
```

Listing 9-36. ImageView.as loads the following image: www.spilled-milk.com/000.jpg.

```
public class ImageView extends AbstractView
{
```

```
        protected var ldr : Loader

        public function ImageView()
        {
            super();
            ldr = new Loader();
            ldr.contentLoaderInfo.addEventListener( Event.COMPLETE , onImageLoad ) ;
            ldr.load( new URLRequest( "http://www.spilled-milk.com/000.jpg" ) );
            addChild( ldr )
        }

        public function onImageLoad( event : Event ) : void
        {
            forward();
        }
}
```

Listing 9-37. MaskView

```
public class MaskView extends AbstractView
{
        public function MaskView()
        {
            super();
        }
}
```

Listing 9-38. TextFieldView

```
public class TextFieldView extends AbstractView
{
        public function TextFieldView()
        {
            super();
        }
}
```

24. What pattern decouples multiple subsystems from client messaging by funneling those
     implementations into a simpler interface?   <u>The façade pattern</u>

25. Choose the appropriate associations:

Model — Composite pattern

View — Subject pattern

Controller — Observer pattern

Strategy pattern

Chapter 10

MVC: A Compound Pattern

I have tried to take few shortcuts with the demonstrations of patterns to help reinforce previous patterns even as I teach you new ones. While this absolutely bloated the code, and perhaps increased the difficulty, I refused to pull any punches. The justification as to why I did not rely on simple and unrealistic demos was so you could see how they are truly used in the real world. Also, I believe that simplification can often dilute a necessary impact. I wanted to demonstrate that patterns are often utilized with other patterns and are not always individual solutions.

I covered 15 of the 23 original Gang of Four design patterns, and these 15 were not chosen at random. They are the most utilized design patterns in the ActionScript 3.0 language by professionals within the interactive industry. This does not mean you should choose to stop at these 15. Design patterns are time-tested solutions to recurring programmatic dilemmas. The more you know, and, more importantly, the more you understand, the better.

OOP teaches four principles: encapsulation, data-hiding, polymorphism, and inheritance. While these are great guidelines to follow, it's often difficult to follow them to the letter, especially without having the proper tools to do so. OOP is a style of coding based on a thought process and nothing more.

Design patterns, on the other hand, are solutions that other object-oriented programmers have devised to fulfill aspects of object collaborations and object-oriented thought, thus further empowering OOP, which would otherwise cripple flexible code.

By making use of the tools you have just learned and by adding them to your programming repertoire, you can devise more separations among structures, adding to more reusable and more flexible code that may not have been possible before. One well-known pattern that illustrates this concept is the Model View Controller, or MVC.

OOP encourages the breakdown of complex problems into smaller, more manageable objects. This practice offers greater flexibility among objects utilized but also allows a problem to be solved incrementally. This can decrease an often overwhelming dilemma into smaller, more manageable hurdles to solve. Smaller issues are less cumbersome to get through as they often focus on fewer details.

In programming, the problem at hand is referred to as the problem domain (see **Figure 10-1**). The term *domain* refers to boundaries that encompass all details critical to the issue.

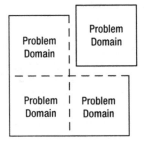

Figure 10-1. A localized problem that requires a solution.

Each attempt to break this problem down into smaller, more manageable issues represents a subdivision of the problem domain—in addition to being a problem domain within itself. While it may be unnecessary, the subdivisions can continuously be broken down into even smaller problems (see **Figure 10-2**).

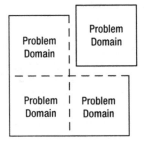

Figure 10-2. Deconstructing an overall problem domain into that of four smaller problem domains

As each subsection focuses on a particular aspect of a problem, each subdivision can be referred to as a problem domain, respectively (see **Figure 10-3**).

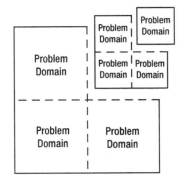

Figure 10-3. Any problem domain can continue to be made more granular.

It's often necessary to break down a larger issue into several smaller ones. This allows the mind to more easily comprehend the tasks necessary to solve such a problem. Of course, the more pieces of a puzzle, the more complicated it can become.

I have covered an extensive amount of solutions that you can now make use of to further the flexibility and communication between such granular objects.

As the Internet has expanded and computers have become much more powerful, the focus among applications has homed in on user experience and how the user interacts with the application. A means to incorporate the user and the application at one point in time was a problem to solve. Nowadays we can implement a design pattern that bridges the gap between the user and the application. This design pattern is known as the MVC.

The MVC: Model View Controller

Technical Overview

Intent: To provide users control over data as seen from multiple perspectives (see **Figure 10-4**).

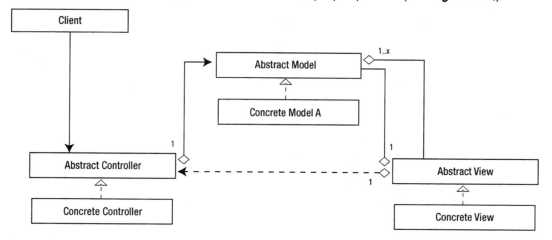

Figure 10-4. Class Diagram

Parts

- Model
- View
- Controller
- Client

Benefits

- Increases cohesion of each aspect.
- Localizes a logic domain that can be easily maintained.
- Enables the Model's independence from the UI.

Drawbacks

- The MVC is complex.
- Compounded drawbacks among the patterns that it contains.
- Changes among the interface of one component may affect another.

A Comprehensive Look

The Model View Controller, or MVC, is made up of three aspects, as the name suggests: the Model, the View, and the Controller. Trygve Reenskaug conceived its origins for the main purpose of allowing users to manipulate complex data sets via multiple presentations.

The first aspect of the MVC, being the Model, localizes the set of data, or states, and behaviors required in fulfilling the logic of the problem domain. This is referred to as the logic domain. The model, or logic domain, possesses the appropriate methods by which its data can be retrieved and mutated accordingly.

The participation of the Model can be that of either an active or passive role. As a passive participant, the model remains absent of any further duties, which pushes the onus of any change in state onto that of the Controller. As an active participant, the Model adopts the role of publisher/notifier, in which Views as well as Controllers can receive notifications of change in states via subscription, achieved with the Observer pattern (Chapter 8).

The View in the MVC represents a graphical representation of any number of particular aspects possessed by the Model. As one view may visually reflect only one chosen aspect of the model, there is no limit to the amount of views that can be used along with a Model.

As far as the role of the View, visual representation among the Model's internal representation is its only focus. The absence of logic necessary to a problem domain within a View is what allows all visuals to be interchangeable among other Views.

The Controller in the MVC is the mediator between the user's input and the logic domain. The role of the Controller is to provide the user the means to interact with the Model, as it possesses appropriate bindings among the Model's interface. To achieve flexibility, a controller is assigned to a View often by way of the Strategy pattern (Chapter 7).

If the Model is not an active participant, the Controller must provide notification to the view it pertains to, so that it can properly remain synchronized with the Model. A View should only be notified after all states are properly assigned to the Model.

The MVC is a challenging pattern to grasp, as there are many variations regarding the particulars among the three objects that make up the triad. One reason for this is that the MVC is a compound pattern. In short, this means the MVC makes use of multiple design patterns already discussed to enable the three aspects to make use of one another. The most important understanding among the MVC is the separation among the three aspects, which provides distinct boundaries among the three components. This separation aims to ensure that relevant behaviors, or logic pertinent to each domain, remain intact when substituting or layering aspects of the triad.

The three components are:

1. The presentation, known as the View.

2. The system's interface, logic, structure, or state,

3. (or all the above) known as the Model.

4. The interpreter among a user's input to the system, known as the Controller.

Typically, the MVC makes use of the Observer, Strategy, Composite, and Façade design patterns, and, at its most granular state, is made up of 1:1:1 ratio.

The AS3.0 Cast

Abstract Model – The Interface

Because a Model is totally independent from Views and Controllers, they can be interchanged among various Views and Controllers. Therefore, a proper interface is required so that the data can be retrieved accordingly.

Concrete Model – The Logic Domain

It localizes and maintains the logic, state, and structure within a scope. The amount of data varies for the particular problem domain.

Abstract View – The Views Abstract Class

The Abstract View separates the associations between the Model utilized from the visual representations. Additionally, and optionally, the Abstract View can be the manufacturer of the expected Controller that will be used along with the View.

Concrete View – Implements Specifics

The Concrete View contains the necessary logic to instantiate the appropriate Controller.

Abstract Controller – The Abstract Class of the Controller

The Abstract Controller can be used to devise a common interface to which all Concrete Controllers can extend, allowing each to be substituted via the Strategy pattern. The Abstract Controller can also retain references to the View and Model, which it will make use of and supply any default behaviors that may be necessary.

Concrete Controller – Implements Specifics

The Concrete Controller implements the necessary means to bridge a user and the application. This means handling the aspects of the user interactions and interpreting those into requests of the Model.

Client – The Messenger of the Model

The client is most often the Controller, as it is the catalyst for any updates among itself and views. These requests may be triggered by a user's actions directly or indirectly.

When It's Useful

When form and function are bound too greatly to one another and deter reusability.

Demonstration

Trygve would be displeased if I did not mention that the most important aspect of the MVC is the user. The MVC's purpose is to bridge the gap between the user's mind and the computer.

The Model mirrors the user's mental model, which is the user's understandings/expectations imparted on the system. Consider your computer: regardless of its operating software, while it reads and writes bytes, it allows you (the user) to impart your vision into the confines of the computer and control how it presents stored bytes back to you. This would be the big-picture problem domain. As this example would be a rather huge demonstration, I will minimize the scale to that of a simpler problem domain.

For this demonstration, I will show you how to use the MVC to mirror the mental model of a user and how they interact with the icons on their desktop. (specifically the icon position and the icon name). You will be creating a model that holds relevant information of a folder/file within your application, such as the name and coordinates. It's important to remember that the problem domain under the microscope is a particular magnification of the big-picture problem domain, and therefore must be constructed with that in mind.

I begin with the Model; for this demonstration it will be the simplest of the three aspects.

The Model

The Model for this demonstration must allow the user to bestow their interpretation of how they choose to interact with their data, in a way that appears as if the user is manipulating the actual data itself. In a sense, the Model must represent the decisions of the user as if it were an extension of their mind.

For the purpose of allowing a user to manipulate the position of an icon on their desktop, as well as the file name, the Model must properly possess the ability to retain the location as well as identification of an icon.

While your application will not be saving the user's information, it's not out of the realm of possibilities, just out of scope for this demonstration. What it will be doing instead is maintaining the data, which can be possibly broadcast to any object.

In order to provide a means of notification, you will make use of the Observer pattern. To separate the role of "subject" from the role of Model, you'll begin with an abstract class known as `AbstractModel`, which will possess knowledge of possible observers that it will inform upon updates. You can achieve this behavior with the use of the ISubject interface; see **Listings 10-1** and **10-2**.

Listing 10-1. ISubject Exposes Two Methods, which Allow Observers to Register and Unregister from Notifications

```
public interface ISubject
{

              function addObserver( observer : IObserve , aspect : Function ) : ➡
                                                                 Boolean
              function removeObserver( observer : IObserve ) : Boolean

}
```

Listing 10-2. AbstractModel Implements ISubject, which Allows the Addition and Removal of Observers

```
public class AbstractModel extends EventDispatcher implements ISubject
{
        protected var dict : Dictionary;
```

```
        public function AbstractModel( target : IEventDispatcher = null )
        {
                super( target );
                dict = new Dictionary( false );
        }

        public function addObserver( observer : IObserve , aspect : Function ) : ➥
                                                                Boolean
        {
                dict[observer] = aspect;
                return true;
        }

        public function removeObserver( observer : IObserve ) : Boolean
        {
                dict[observer] = null;
                delete dict[observer];
                return true;
        }

        protected function notify() : void
        {
                throw new IllegalOperationError( 'notify must be overridden' );
        }
}
```

By extending AbstractModel, you can layer data specifics and dictate how the notification process occurs. Knowing that the Model retains the identity of each folder and its location, you can add the appropriate properties. While folders and documents will both posses similar attributes, you create a Model that is generic for both, as shown in **Listing 10-3**.

Listing 10-3. ConfigModel Subclasses AbstractModel and Supplies Additional Properties for UI Elements

```
public class ConfigModel extends AbstractModel
{
        private var _name : String;
        private var _xPos : int;
        private var _yPos : int;

        public function ConfigModel(target:IEventDispatcher=null)
        {
                super(target);
        }

        public function get name() : String
        {
```

```
            return _name;
    }

    public function set name( name : String ) : void
    {
            _name = name;
    }

    public function get xPos() : int
    {
            return _xPos;
    }

    public function set xPos( xPos : int ) : void
    {
            _xPos = xPos;
    }

    public function get yPos() : int
    {
            return _yPos;
    }

    public function set yPos( yPos : int ) : void
    {
            _yPos = yPos;
    }
}
```

The View

Next, you will focus on the View. A View will retain a reference to both its Model and the Controller to which the View relies. When using any number of Controllers along with a particular View, the View can rely on the Strategy pattern as a way to supply and partition the logic. Very often, a View and Controller are built at the same time with each other in mind and therefore can be added to the View via the Factory method. This particular demonstration makes use of the latter of the choices.

There are many possible icons that a user can interact with on a computer. In an effort to generalize these icons and to standardize their uniformity, you'll devise an appropriate abstraction.

AbstractView is the abstract class, which retains both the Model of the problem domain. As you know, your views will be subscribing to the model as observers, so it will implement the IObserve interface; see **Listings 10-4** and **10-5**.

Listing 10-4. IObserve Exposes an Interface, which Enables a Subject to Pass In Notifications

```
public interface IObserve
{
        function notify(str:String):void
}
```

Listing 10-5. AbstractView Extends IObserve in Order to Remain in Synch with the State of the Model

```
public class AbstractView extends Sprite implements IObserve
{
            protected var _mdl : AbstractModel

            public function AbstractView( mdl : AbstractModel=null )
            {
                    if(mdl)
                    this.mdl = mdl;

            }

            public function notify( str : String ) : void
            {
            }

            public function get mdl() : AbstractModel
            {
                    return _mdl;
            }

            public function set mdl( mdl : AbstractModel ) : void
            {
                    _mdl = mdl;
                    _mdl.addObserver(this,null)
            }

}
```

Having devised an abstraction that concerns itself mainly with the subscribing and unsubscribing, you now must add the abstract layer that focuses on the roles of a view. The role of the view must retain a reference to the model and its controller. AbstractFileSystemView will extend AbstractView and declare the Factory method that manufactures the View's Controller. This will allow varied views to be more easily created and implemented; see **Listing 10-6**.

Listing 10-6. AbstractFileSystemView is the Superclass of each File View Component

```
public class AbstractFileSystemView extends AbstractView
{

        protected var _strategy : AbstractController;

                public function AbstractFileSystemView( mdl : ConfigModel )
                {
                        super( mdl );

                }

        protected function createDefaultController() : AbstractController
        {
                throw new IllegalOperationError( 'createDefaultController ➥
                                                        must be overridden' );
                return null;
        }
}
```

Two possible views a user can expect are a folder and a file. As you might think, a folder makes use of composition whereas a file remains a leaf component. With this in mind, your MVC could make perfect use of the Composite pattern. In order to accomplish this, your abstraction must be properly layered with aspects of a component from the Composite pattern. The component possesses the appropriate references (such as image icon, textfield, and the parenting composite) that both file and folder require. This allows them to be indistinguishable from one another. You'll devise yet another extension of AbstractFileSystemView, which will become your component (see **Listing 10-7**).

Listing 10-7. OSComponent Extends AbstractFileSystemView and Layers Added References

```
public class OSComponent extends AbstractFileSystemView
{
        protected var _fileName : String;
        protected var _field : DisplayField;
        protected var _representation : Bitmap;
        protected var _parentComposite : OSComponent;
        static protected const PADDING : int = 4;

        public function OSComponent( mdl : ConfigModel )
        {
                super( mdl );
        }

        protected function dispatch( event : MouseEvent ) : void
        {
```

```
                event.stopPropagation();
                dispatchEvent( event );
        }

        public function open() : void
        {
        }

        public function close() : void
        {
        }

        public function get field() : DisplayField
        {
                return _field;
        }
}
```

Lastly, you add one additional layer to the OSComponent class that will contain the specifics of a Leaf within your application (see **Listing 10-8**).

Listing 10-8. LeafView Extends OSComponent and Supplies the Concretes Among Each Factory Method

```
public class LeafView extends OSComponent
{
        [Embed(source="/Users/FeZEC/workspace/CreationalPatterns/➥
                                        bin/Tree_defaultLeafIcon.png")]
        private var embeddedClass : Class;

        public function LeafView( mdl : ConfigModel = null )
        {
                super( mdl );
                _representation = createIcon();
                _field = createDisplayField();
                addChild( _representation );
                _field.y = this.height + PADDING;
                _field.x = (this.width - _field.textWidth) * .5;
                _field.addEventListener( MouseEvent.MOUSE_DOWN , dispatch );
                _field.addEventListener( MouseEvent.MOUSE_UP , dispatch );
                addChild( _field );
                _strategy = createDefaultController();
        }

        protected function createDisplayField() : DisplayField
        {
```

```
                return new DisplayField();
        }

        protected function createIcon() : Bitmap
        {
                return new embeddedClass() as Bitmap;
        }

        override protected function createDefaultController() : AbstractController
        {
                return new ComponentRenamerController ( _mdl , this );
        }
}
```

DisplayField is a textfield that possesses two additional operations: rename and display. These two methods toggle between the dynamic and input type of the textfield to allow for file/folder renaming (see **Listing 10-9**).

Listing 10-9. DisplayField is Responsible for Displaying a File/Folder Name

```
public class DisplayField extends TextField
{
        public function DisplayField()
        {
                super();
                autoSize = TextFieldAutoSize.CENTER;
                height = 10;
                width = 1;
                embedFonts = false;
                display();
        }

        public function rename() : void
        {
                var end : int = this.text.indexOf( '.' );
                type = TextFieldType.INPUT;
                selectable = true;
                setSelection( -1 , (end > -1) ? end : text.length );
                border = true;
        }

        public function display() : void
        {
                type = TextFieldType.DYNAMIC;
```

```
            selectable = false;
            border = false;
    }
}
```

The Controller

The final aspect of the triad is the Controller. As a Controller may require interchangeability among a system, it requires a superclass from which all similar Controllers extend. Because the Controller receives the input of a user, the Controller is expected to make changes within the Model for the view, coordinate changes of a View, or both. This depends on how you choose to use each aspect to communicate. Either way, a Controller must retain references of View and Model; therefore you can supply a superclass known as AbstractController, which will retain these references (see **Listing 10-10**).

Listing 10-10. AbstractController is the Superclass of all Controllers

```
public class AbstractController extends Object
{
        protected var _mdl : AbstractModel;
        protected var _view : AbstractFileSystemView;

        public function AbstractController( mdl : AbstractModel=null , ➥
                                    view : AbstractFileSystemView =null )
        {
            _mdl = mdl;
            _view = view;
        }

        public function get mdl() : AbstractModel
        {
            return _mdl;
        }

        public function set mdl( mdl : AbstractModel ) : void
        {
            _mdl = mdl;
        }

        public function get view() : AbstractFileSystemView
        {
            return _view;
        }

        public function set view( view : AbstractFileSystemView) : void
        {
```

```
            _view = view;
    }
}
```

What makes the Controller necessary is how each Controller handles the user's input relative to a View/Model. To demonstrate how a Controller coordinates changes with the View as well as the Model, you will devise a ComponentRenamerController, which makes use of the DisplayField within each View. Much like that of PC/Mac, a folder/file can be renamed if a user double clicks on the field within a particular range of milliseconds. ComponentRenamerController reflects that behavior on each View (see **Listing 10-11**).

Listing 10-11. ComponentRenamerController Allows for the Renaming of Each View in Your Problem Domain

```
public class ComponentRenamerController extends AbstractController
{
        protected var _display : DisplayField;
        protected var _timer : int;
        protected const MAX_DURATION : int = 1000;

        public function ComponentRenamerController( mdl : AbstractModel , ➥
                                                            view : OSComponent )
        {
                super( mdl , view );
                _timer = 0;
                _display = view.field;
                _display.addEventListener( MouseEvent.CLICK , onMouseClick);
                _display.addEventListener( FocusEvent.FOCUS_OUT , onOut );
                _display.addEventListener( KeyboardEvent.KEY_DOWN , onPossibleEnter );
        }

        private function onPossibleEnter( event : KeyboardEvent ) : void
        {
                switch(event.keyCode)
                {
                        case Keyboard.ENTER:
                                commit();
                                break;
                }
        }

        protected function onOut( event : FocusEvent ) : void
        {
                commit();
        }
```

```
        protected function commit() : void
        {
                _display.display();
                ConfigModel( _mdl ).name = _display.text;

                Mouse.cursor = MouseCursor.ARROW;
        }

        private function onMouseClick( event : MouseEvent ) : void
        {
                var currentTimer : int = getTimer();
                if ((currentTimer - _timer) < MAX_DURATION)
                {
                        _display.rename();
                }
                _timer = currentTimer;
        }
}
```

With your currently implemented code, you can make use of the DocumentClass to test the functionality of your use case scenario. You'll use the DocumentClass to instantiate your Model, and to it you will supply defaults for each piece of data, which could represent the default settings. The Model of another problem domain will supply this data, but for now you can simply add the Data here to witness its effects (see **Listing 10-12**). Next, a View is instantiated and the Model is supplied as a parameter.

Listing 10-12. DocumentClass Supplies Data to a Model, then Associates the Model with a View

```
public class DocumentClass extends Sprite
{
        public function DocumentClass()
        {
                stage.scaleMode = StageScaleMode.EXACT_FIT;
                stage.align = StageAlign.TOP_LEFT;
                mouseEnabled = false;

                var cm : ConfigModel = new ConfigModel();
                cm.name = "Default_Text.txt";
                cm.xPos = Math.random() * this.stage.stageWidth;
                cm.yPos = Math.random() * this.stage.stageHeight;
                addChild( new LeafView( cm ) );
        }
}
```

Once the application is running, by clicking down on the mouse twice slowly within one second on the display field, the display field of the presentation will turn into an input field, allowing the user to change the given name of the component. As the user is able to manipulate the text within the field, the Model only requires updating the currently stored filename to that chosen by the user.

Since the Model is unaware of either View or Controller, the task of updating the Model falls on the Controller.

This demonstration should arouse specifics points regarding the Model/View/Controller Pattern.

The first noteworthy point is that this particular MVC demonstration has made no use of the Strategy pattern or, arguably, the Observer pattern. I say "arguably" because you did add the ability into the code. It did, on the other hand, make use of the `Template` method and the `Factory` method. As a Compound pattern, the MVC is most concerned with the boundaries of presentation and structure. What this should illustrate is that the utilized patterns are not what make the MVC, but rather the Model, View, and Controller objects itself. Don't feel limited to the patterns that must be utilized along with them.

The second point worthy of noting is the tight boundaries among the three aspects. Not one allowed its code to bleed into a domain to which it did not belong, which allows for easier interchanging among aspects.

During the implementation of a given aspect, you may be compelled to write View-specific logic within the Model, or vice versa. Keeping the boundaries tight allows you the ability to achieve multiple views between a Model, vary Controllers among a system, etc.

FAQ

- Q: If this was a 1:1:1 MVC; is it safe to say that any aspect may overwhelm other aspects?
- A: Absolutely. The 1:1:1 MVC is the simplest form of the MVC. Just because the name of the pattern suggests 1 Model, 1 View, and 1 Controller, remember that the name is focusing on the boundaries of these aspects and nothing more. Your application may make use of several Views, 1 Model and 12 Controllers. Another possibility is that 1 Controller may need to coordinate 13 views. You get the picture.

Chapter 11

Object-Oriented Design... A Revisit

In Chapter 4, I made use of object-oriented analysis to reveal some of the many objects that you will be working with to achieve a successful solution for the Outerlite micro site. If you recall, the chapter concluded without commencing the second phase of the inception process, known as object-oriented design. While you were able to properly analyze your system without any knowledge of design patterns, lacking such information is not practical when determining a proper design.

It was imperative to end that chapter without delving into specifics until you had a better understanding of how these objects can communicate. This can help you maximize your abilities to build an architecture that is well constructed. Only now, with more tools in your toolbox, are you ready to continue with the object-oriented design phase.

Recap

Object-oriented analysis makes use of understanding a problem domain to reveal various objects that are required to solve such a problem. By assessing user flow and client requirements, you are able to gain further insight into added objects and how they will be utilized within your system. The multiple passes of a system during analysis allows for a problem domain to be broken into many smaller problem domains, making it easier to grasp and work with.

Analysis does not always reveal all of the objects that will be used in an application. Many objects may be discarded and additional objects may be required to facilitate existing objects and their associations. What analysis does well is reveal aspects of the big picture in the form of smaller problem domains.

During the object-oriented design phase, your goal will be to finalize all required objects, evaluate their behaviors within their system, and, lastly, to determine their collaborations within the system. You'll begin with the initially devised list of found objects from the OOA phase of Chapter 4.

Initially Identified Objects

1. Shell
   a. Site Loader
2. Site
   a. Blurb
   b. Navigation
      1. Product
      2. Scenic
      3. Footer
   c. Scenario Image XML
   d. Scenic Gallery
      1. Scenario XML
      2. Image Pre-loader
      3. Photo
      4. Information Call out
         i. Info photo
            a. Information XML
            b. Progress Bar
            c. Scenic Description
   e. Product Image XML
   f. Product Gallery
      1. Product XML
      2. Interior Navigation
         i. Buy Now
         ii. Previous
         iii. Next
      3. Image Pre-loader
      4. Product Image

5. Specs

    i. Description

    ii. Available colors

    iii. Available sizes

    iv. Buttons

g. Footer

    1. Contact Us

    2. Store Locator

    3. Mailing List

    4. Privacy Policy

    5. Terms & Conditions

    6. Buttons

As the list shows, there are many objects required for each particular problem. While your thorough analysis revealed these objects, you may have duplicates that would be unnecessary in OOP. It's wise to note that not every duplicate will share a common name, and, likewise, not all objects that have a duplicate name will possess a similar behavior.

In order to properly reveal duplicates in your system, which would be irrelevant, you must properly establish appropriate names for each object that reflect their distinct behaviors in the system. Of course, as of this moment you have not documented any behaviors and therefore will need to do so as well.

Candidate Classes

While the list of objects you found from your object-oriented analysis is not incredibly extensive, this will not always be the case. Depending on the project, you may find yourself working with hundreds of objects. When working with such an extensive number of objects, it becomes difficult to envision so many theoretical objects. For this reason, it's very convenient to work with what is known as *class responsibility/collaborations cards* (CRC cards, for short). Unfortunately, CRC cards are not something you can purchase; you actually produce your own utilizing index cards.

The convenience of a CRC card is that you can work with something that is tangible and can be manipulated. Since the time required to create them is minimal, should an object no longer be required by your application, you can easily throw a card away.

Ultimately, a CRC card represents a class, and, as the name suggests, the CRC models the class's name, responsibility, and its collaborations with other objects. The standard outline of a typical CRC card can be seen in **Figure 11-1**.

Class name:
Responsibility:
Collaborators:

Figure 11-1. CRC card

For the moment, you're not as concerned with a class's collaborations as you are with its responsibilities and class name. Eventually, you'll come back to its collaborations. The boundaries of the card represent the class's encapsulation, where its attributes and behaviors safely reside. The reverse side of the card is available to write in any available interface to which its collaborations of the system can message.

Making use of the CRC card and the currently identified objects, you can elaborate on the responsibilities of each object. Spend a moment to conceive an appropriate name to reflect such behaviors. **Figures 11-2** through **11-17** show the CRC cards for your objects.

Class name: Shell
Responsibilities:
The application domain among necessary definitions required for loading and monitoring the site.

Figure 11-2. Shell object from the identified objects

Class name: SiteLoader
Responsibilities:
Graphically represents the loaded bytes of the total load to the user.

Figure 11-3. Loader object from the identified objects

Class name: Outerlite
Responsibilities:
The application domain for all necessary definitions pertinent to fulfilling the goals required of the micro-site.

Figure 11-4. Site object from the identified objects

Class name: Welcome
Responsibilities:
Presents the branding message to the audience.

Figure 11-5. Blurb object from the identified objects

Class name: Shell
Responsibilities:
Allows the user the abillity to select product within the product gallery.

Figure 11-6. Product object from the identified objects

Class name: Product Thumbnail
Responsibilities:
Visually represents an individual product within the product navigation.

Figure 11-7. Added object of the Product Navigation

Class name: ProductGallery
Responsibilities:
Displays product image, details, available colors, and a product sub-navigation.

Figure 11-8. Product Gallery object from the identified objects

Class name: ProductLoader
Responsibilities:
Graphically represents the loaded bytes of the loading product to the user.

Figure 11-9. Image Preloader object from the identified objects

Class name: ProductImage
Responsibilities:
A large view of a selected Product.

Figure 11-10. Product Image object from the identified objects

Class name: ProductDetail
Responsibilities:
Displays relevant information pertaining to the current product.

Figure 11-11. Description object from the identified objects

Class name: ColorPallette
Responsibilities:
Contains the various colors in which the current product is available.

Figure 11-12. Available Colors object from the identified objects

Class name: ProductSubNavigation
Responsibilities:
Allows the user the ability to view the previous or next product within the gallery or even decide to buy it now.

Figure 11-13. Interior Navigation object from the identified objects

Class name: ScenicNavigation
Responsibilities:
Allows the user the ability to select a scene for viewing within the ScenicGallery.

Figure 11-14. Scenic Navigation object from the identified objects

Class name: SceneThumbnail
Responsibilities:
Represents an individual scene within the scenic navigation.

Figure 11-15. Added object required by ScenicNavigation

Class name: ScenicInformationCallOut
Responsibilities:
Provides captions to each scenic image currently shown in the image gallery and offers a means to download the image at a given resolution.

Figure 11-16. Information Call Out object from the identified objects

Class name: Footer
Responsibilities:
Contains appropriate links pertaining to key content.

Figure 11-17 Footer object from the identified objects

These CRC cards represent the defined class names and responsibilities of each object, without regard to buttons such as "Contact Us" and "Store Locator" for brevity. Assigning appropriate names and behaviors assists in the realization that each object can act as its own problem domain, revealing new objects.

Elimination Phase

Chapter 4 made use of an iterative process to analyze your main problem. However, that is not the sole means of determining objects within a system. Various texts suggest writing a story about the entire user flow of the site, extracting all nouns as possible objects and all verbs as possible methods among the objects. Once all objects have been considered, the process of elimination begins. I'm not as much a fan of this process as I am of the Spiral Method, as I believe repetition is beneficial to the thought process.

Due to your due diligence in the analysis phase, you are fortunate that you don't have many immediate objects that should be eliminated. You do, however, possess on your list objects that will be required as data but not to be used as classes within your application. The objects up for elimination are the following: Scenario Image XML, Scenario XML, Product Image XML, and Product XML.

With the removal of these XML files, you are left with only candidate classes for which you will devise appropriate collaborations.

Collaborations

All classes are written to fulfill a responsibility. Occasionally, a class is capable of fulfilling such responsibility on its own. In more elaborate systems, classes are written to communicate with other classes and/or objects to fulfill a single responsibility required by a client. It can then be said that each class/object collaborates to fulfill a single responsibility and may require several classes or objects to do so.

Finding collaborations is rather simple, as you already know the responsibilities of each object. What is left is to conceive which objects, if any, are required to aid each other in fulfilling such responsibilities.

As an example, let's assign the appropriate collaborations, if any, to your Shell object, as shown in **Figure 11-18**.

Class name: Shell
Responsibilities: The application domain among necessary definitions required for loading and monitoring the Outerlite site.
Collaborators: SiteLoader, Outerlite

Figure 11-18. Scenic Navigation object from the identified objects

It is hard to dispute how SiteLoader will assist the responsibility of Shell, but it's more difficult at a glance to see how Outerlite does; yet the two do in fact collaborate. To better reveal appropriate collaborations, you can make use of class diagrams to demonstrate the associations among the collaborative objects. Making use of the collaborations aspect of the CRC card is yet another step in ensuring that all objects will fulfill a role within an application. If no objects collaborate with an object, and the same object requires no collaborators of its own, then the object does not belong within your system. See **Figures 11-19** through **11-28**.

Class name: SiteLoader
Responsibilities: Graphically represents the loaded bytes of the total load to the user.
Collaborators: Outerlite

Figure 11-19. Loader object from the identified objects

Class name: Outerlite
Responsibilities: The application domain for all necessary definitions pertinent to fulfilling the goals required of the micro-site.
Collaborators: Welcome, ProductNavigation, ScenicNavigation, Footer

Figure 11-20. Site object from the identified objects

Class name: Welcome
Responsibilities: Presents the branding message to the audience.
Collaborators: None

Figure 11-21. Blurb object from the identified objects

Class name: ProductNavigation
Responsibilities: Allows the user the ability to select a product within the product gallery.
Collaborators: ProductThumbnail, ProductGallery

Figure 11-22. Product object from the identified objects

Class name: ProductThumbnail
Responsibilities: Visually represents an individual product within the product navigation.
Collaborators: None

Figure 11-23. Added object of the Product Navigation

```
Class name: ProductGallery

Responsibilities:
Displays product image, details, available colors, and a product sub-navigation.

Collaborators: ProductImage, ProductLoader, ProductDetail, ColorPallette,
ProductSubNavigation
```

Figure 11-24. Product Gallery object from the identified objects

```
Class name: ProductLoader

Responsibilities:
Graphically represents the loaded bytes of the loading product to the user.

Collaborators: ProductImage
```

Figure 11-25. Image Preloader object from the identified objects

```
Class name: ProductImage

Responsibilities:
A large view of a selected product.

Collaborators: None
```

Figure 11-26. Product Image object from the identified objects

```
Class name: ProductDetail

Responsibilities:
Displays relevant information pertaining to the current product.

Collaborators: None
```

Figure 11-27. Description object from the identified objects

```
Class name: ColorPallette

Responsibilities:
Contains the various colors in which the current product is available.

Collaborators: ColorSample
```

Figure 11-28. Available Colors object from the identified objects

The ColorPallette's responsibility reveals the need for a new object, ColorSample. ColorSample will be responsible for representing a singe color to be presented by the ColorPallette. **Figure 11-29** makes note of ColorSample's responsibilities and collaborators. **Figures 11-30** through 11-34 show other relationships.

Class name: ColorSample
Responsibilities: A representation of a color.
Collaborators: None

Figure 11-29. Inclusion of a necessary object ColorSample

Class name: ProductSubNavigation
Responsibilities: Allows the user the ability to view the previous or next product within the gallery or even decide to buy it now.
Collaborators: Previous, Next, BuyNow, ProductGallery

Figure 11-30. Interior Navigation object from the identified objects

Class name: ScenicNavigation
Responsibilities: Allows the user the ability to select a scene for viewing within the scenic gallery.
Collaborators: Scene Thumbnail, ScenicInformationCallOut, ScenicGallery

Figure 11-31. Scenic Navigation object from the identified objects

Class name: SceneThumbnail
Responsibilities: Represents an individual scene within the scenic navigation.
Collaborators: None

Figure 11-32. Added object required by ScenicNavigation

Class name: ScenicInformationCallOut
Responsibilities: Provides captions to each scenic image currently shown in the image gallery and offers a means to download the image at a given resolution.
Collaborators: None

Figure 11-33. Information Call Out object from the identified objects

Class name: Scene Iterator
Responsibilities: Contains appropriate links pertaining to key content
Collaborators: Contact us, Store Locator, Mailing List, Privacy, Branding

Figure 11-34. Footer object from the identified objects

Understanding such collaborations and their associations will further your understanding of how objects connect within the system. There are five main associations: Is a part of, Has-a, Is-a, Knows of, and Depends upon. As you may recall from Chapter 4, I covered each association except for Depends upon, which is a concept you might remember from the Observer pattern (Chapter 8).

Diagramming

You can make use of the Unified Modeling Language (UML) to further elaborate on your collaborations. Remember that there are various diagrams that can assist in describing object collaborations, but this book is only concerned with class diagrams.

Figures 11-35 through **11-37** illustrate your associated objects with the use of UML. One thing to note is the addition of the AbstractView object to which all objects extend. Its purpose will provide default behavior and allow polymorphism among all views.

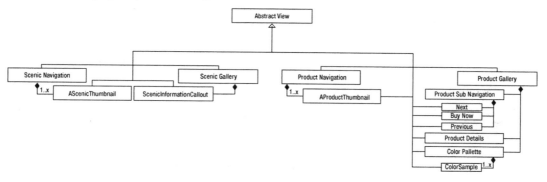

Figure 11-35. High-level diagram of your object collaborations

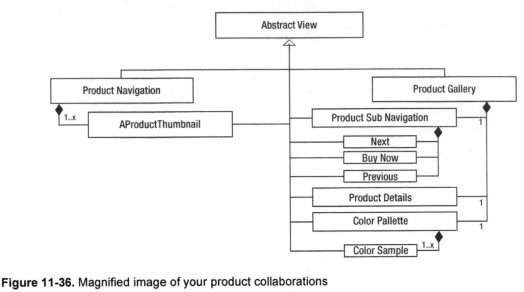

Figure 11-36. Magnified image of your product collaborations

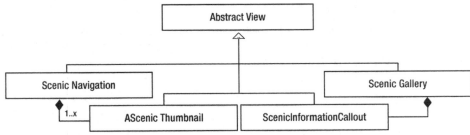

Figure 11-37. Magnified image of your scenic collaborations

These objects that you have devised are used as both visual representation of a user's actions, as well as visual elements with which a user can interact, making them a user interface. To bridge the gap between the user and the application, you know that you can utilize the MVC. Due to the dependencies of these objects and the actions of a user, you can funnel all requests into a localized model to which all subscribing views can respond accordingly. **Figure 11-38** represents the inclusion of the Model View Controller to your application.

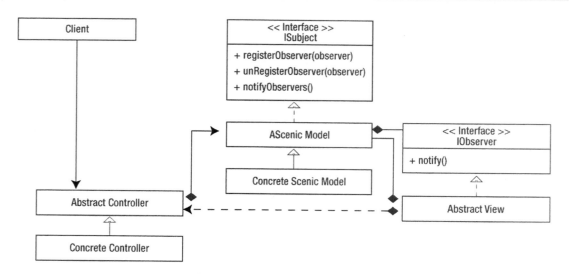

Figure 11-38. Collaborations managed with the MVC pattern

As discussed in Chapter 10, the Controller and the Views work together to maintain the synchronizations among the model. Each View will possess a Controller, which will be responsible for interpreting user interactions and translating them to meaningful input among the model, where state dependent views and controllers can remain synchronized upon notifications from the model. AbstractView, as the superclass to each visual element, allows a Model and Controller to be present.

One dependency that will not be able to be fulfilled by the Model will be the linear succession of the ProductSubNavigation. You know that ProductSubNavigation will allow users to continue to browse the Outerlite product line in a linear fashion with regards to the currently viewed product. It should be apparent that you need to maintain a chosen index by the user to continue to iterate successively either forwards or backwards within a collection, but such data is not a client requirement but rather a design requirement and therefore likely to change.

Therefore, the ProductSubNavigationController will be responsible for translating the index of a collection in a manner that reflects the appropriate direction as chosen by the View, as well as updating the Model with the updated index. You can use an iterator to make use of such functionality. As the user has two ways to navigate the collection, the index of the iterator must remain synchronized to the currently selected index. It will also be the role of the ProductSubNavigationController to ensure this.

The ProductNavigationController is responsible for populating the ProductThumbs from the ProductCollection. As a user may expect the order of their sequence to be the expected order of the ProductSubNavigation, it will be wise to make use of the same iterator to maintain consistency among the ProductCollection. Therefore, it will be the responsibility of the ProductNavigationController to populate the products with the assistance of an iterator (see **Figure 11-39**).

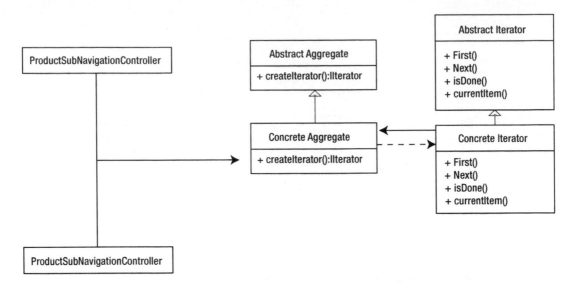

Figure 11-39. ProductSubNavigationController and ProductNavigationController instantiating an Iterator among the ProductCollection

It may also be useful to utilize an iterator to populate the scenic navigation. Of course, with an iterator you have to have a collection, which is something you don't currently have with your list of objects. Therefore, you have to take this into account, which also means you will need to devise a way to obtain these collections (see **Figures 11-40** through **11-43**).

Class name: ProductCollection
Responsibilities: Maintains a collection of products.
Collaborators: ProductIterator

Figure 11-40. ProductCollection added to your objects

Class name: ScenicCollection
Responsibilities: Maintains a collection of scenic images.
Collaborators: SceneIterator

Figure 11-41. ScenicCollection added to your objects

Class name: ProductIterator
Responsibilities: Traverses the index of the ProductCollection.
Collaborators: None

Figure 11-42. ProductIterator added to your objects

Class name: SceneIterator
Responsibilities: Traverses the index of the ScenicCollection.
Collaborators: None

Figure 11-43. ScenicCollection added to your objects

With any inclusion of a new object, it's best to devise their collaborations, if any. Likewise, if they are collaborators of any other objects within the system, such collaborations should be noted.

As you may recall, you had four XML files in the original list, which you removed from your objects, but they will still be utilized once you determine whether you load them in as one XML file or two. Your model will maintain these collections along with the current index where the appropriate data can be obtained.

The Creative Direction

At this moment the implementation phase is almost in sight. There is just one last thing that needs to be done: you need to know the design vision. You have, up to this point, constructed the framework of your application and separated the functionality from the form. Therefore, you are now ready to sprinkle in the details that are the most likely to change and close the chapter on object-oriented analysis and design until your next project.

Implementation

As you can witness from the class diagrams, your application is taking form right before your eyes. You can just about see the big picture of how everything will work together. However, an application does not run on schematics, but rather code. So where does all of this conceptualizing, diagramming, analyzing, and designing get you? It allows you to become familiar with the ins and outs of the application as if you'd been using it for years, even before the application has been constructed. This can only come from proper analysis and design. Having an understanding of the objects, structure, collaborations etc, allows you to truly have an intimate understanding of the code before a single line is written. This is the reason you can take charge as a team leader or be involved with any such changes that arise.

Before you can begin writing code, there's one last area that must be conceived. This area is the methods, which allow for such collaborations among your objects. What methods must an object possess? What are the return types that are utilized? Such signatures need to be considered.

At this point, you need to take your prior knowledge and all you have learned from this book and apply it here. It is from here that you need to travel on your own.

Chapter Summary

Object-oriented design, object-oriented analysis, and implementation are three entirely separate phases. You may often be tempted to condense all phases into one in haste, but as they say "haste makes waste." The goal of object-oriented design is to ensure that all objects during implementation are necessary, not redundant—and reusable as well. It also adds more structure in a team environment when each member needs to divide and conquer. Only proper design can come from proper analysis, and only proper implementation can come from proper design. Also, any changes during the phase of implementation can be better combated, as you have already determined the structure for the entire application.

Chapter 12

Getting Real

I've covered an immense amount of intense information, and if you've made it this far, I applaud you. If you've made it this far feeling more confident in your understandings of design patterns and how they tie into OOP, then I can say my job is *nearly* complete. I stress "nearly" because I would be doing you a disservice if I did not cover the aspects that make up real world scenarios, which can impair your programming decisions.

Writing this textbook offered me the ability to provide custom examples to exemplify a particular need for a specific pattern. These custom examples also enhance your ability to understand how and why a particular pattern could solve a particular dilemma you need to overcome. Not every problem you will face will be as simple; in fact, some problems will require a great involvement in OOA&D to reveal the appropriate collaborations. While this may seem legitimate and necessary to you, this will be viewed as a luxury to a company. This is not the half of it; there will be many other obstacles that stand in your OO path.

Object-Oriented Obstacles: O³

The industry of RIA is very cutthroat in more ways than one. Clients are unforgiving, projects are expensive, many project managers and designers have a technical disconnect, and development is often the last phase of a project. While many agencies believe they want developers who are object oriented, what they really want is for a project to be completed. For this and many reasons I will soon cover, practicing proper OO techniques can be quite a challenge for an aspiring developer.

Always a Student

Programming is not the simplest career, let's be honest. We may know our material but the subject area is always changing and evolving. There is always something to learn, and therefore we are always students. As developers, our learning may be initialized by our eagerness to know more, but often the origin of learning can arrive with a new project. The realm of what a client can for is seemingly endless. This is because they are looking for what hasn't been done—and what sells. A new task may involve motion, audio, data visualization, etc.

Business is Business

Agencies may be bidding against one another to acquire business and will find ways to trim areas to win that business. These areas are budget and time. Depending on company size and/or structure, the developer does not necessarily determine the deadlines, and they may not even get a say. The pressure of a deadline then starts to make an impact as time designated for OO/AD and object-oriented thoughts diminishes. Rapid prototypes, or step-by-steps, could be required of the developer, and these take away from the opportunity to utilize OOP and design patterns.

You may want to resort to a third party and be more lackadaisical with your code to beat the deadline. Unfortunately, the third party code may not be up to your standards, and your rushed code may not be anything that can be reused; but, at this point, getting the job done would be the most satisfying.

Now, taking precedence over OOP skill is business. OOP sounds great, but it doesn't sell.

Varied Priorities

Ideally, it would be great if all developers on a project shared the same vision. Working with five people building reusable code would create a large stockpile quickly. It would also make the utilization of OOP more feasible given time constraints. However, not all programmers share the same vision, and those that don't may be on your team.

Object-Oriented Solutions

Luckily, every cloud has a silver lining and knowing the pitfalls of OOP can provide insight to combat such obstacles.

Software

As mentioned in Chapter 3, an editor can greatly improve your coding abilities with its built-in features. The faster you are able to code or navigate between your folders/files, the more time you have to pause and think. Many editors provide the ease necessary to navigate OO code and therefore should be given due diligence when searching for a solution to purchase.

While paper is always the fastest way to devise object collaborations, it does decrease the amount of time you may have to physically implement code. Rather than delay the progressing of implementation on a tight deadline, kill two birds with one stone with such applications like UML4AS.

UML4AS is a unified modeling tool for the ActionScript 3.0 language that allows the modeling of UML while generating the ActionScript classes for you. The UML4AS is free and works along with the Eclipse IDE as a plug-in. This is great because Flash Builder/Flex and FDT both make use of the Eclipse platform. You can download the plug-in at www.uml4as.com/.

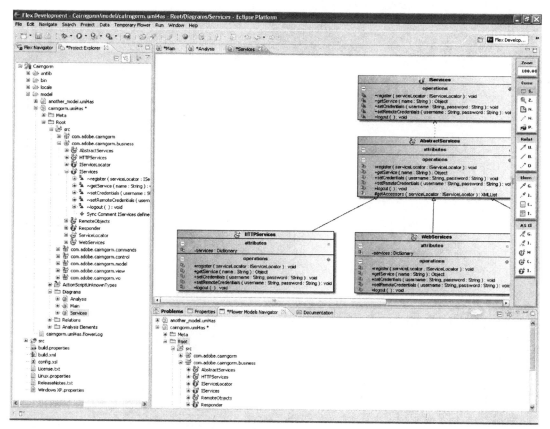

Figure 12-1. A screen grab of UML4AS in action

Dedication

Perseverance is the best advice I can give towards thwarting O^3. If you truly want to be better at anything, constant use is the best solution. Familiarity will ultimately reduce hesitancy and any reluctance towards injecting patterns into a project with a deadline. Utilization of OOP and design patterns will be the only solution for building a library for of reusable code.

Remember to stick with it. You can't expect to learn OOP and design patterns any other way. Consistently read books, practice, and experiment. Even while you're learning something new for a project, perhaps even a new language, you will still get to take knowledge of design patterns with you. The knowledge of design patterns can be brought to other object-oriented languages.

User Groups

When people in your environment do not have the same interests, it is difficult to find support and reinforcement. User groups are a great option to finding others with similar interests, common goals, and a system of support. You may also find someone from a local user group willing to speak to your company or agency. They may be able to provide an informative presentation or productive workshops for quick tips and tricks. It can also increase the possibility of welcoming new thinking.

Index

Q

CPSIA information can be obtained at www.ICGtesting.com
Printed in the USA
LVOW131418091011

249735LV00002B/1/P